ADOBE® PHOTOSHOP®

LIGHTROOM® CC

EDIT LIKE A PRO

1ST EDITION

LATE AUGUST 2018 RELEASE
COVERING VERSIONS:

Windows / Mac: 1.5

iOS: 3.4

Android: 3.6

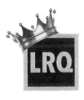

VICTORIA BAMPTON

Adobe Photoshop Lightroom CC—Edit Like a Pro (1st Edition)

Publication Date 21 August 2018
Updated 2018-08-29

ISBN 978-1-910381-07-6 (eBook Formats)
ISBN 978-1-910381-06-9 (Color Paperback)

TABLE OF CONTENTS

ACKNOWLEDGMENTS

A lot of people have contributed to this project, and although I'd love to thank everyone personally, the acknowledgments would fill up the entire book. There are some people who deserve a special mention though.

First and foremost, my heartfelt thanks go to Paul McFarlane, who has worked closely with me on this book, from the initial concept through to the finished product. Without his help, I'd still be working on it in a year's time!

I also have to thank the entire Lightroom CC team at Adobe, especially Tom Hogarty, Sharad Mangalick, Josh Haftel, Ben Warde, Jeff Tranberry, Thomas Knoll, Eric Chan, Max Wendt, Josh Bury, Simon Chen, Matt Johnson, Ben Zibble, Jeffrey Andrew, Julie Kmoch, Becky Sowada, Kelly Castro, Rikk Flohr and Rick Spaulding. Their vision for the future of Lightroom is exciting!

I'd like to thank David duChemin for challenging the way I think about photography, and sparking many of the ideas in this book. There's always more to learn!

Thanks are also due to the team of Lightroom Gurus, who are always happy to discuss, debate and share their experience, especially Jim Wilde, Sean McCormack, Laura Shoe, Jeff Schewe, Martin Evening, Andrew Rodney, Peter Krogh, Ian Lyons, John Beardsworth, George Jardine, Rob Sylvan, Jeffrey Friedl, Linwood Ferguson, Johan Elzenga, Kitty van Gemert, Linda Alschuler, Sam Cox, and the rest of the crew!

I'm also grateful to the members of the various Lightroom forums and my social media followers, who constantly challenge me with questions, problems to solve, and give me ideas for this book.

Special thanks have to go to my Dad. He's been a professional photographer for more than 40 years, and if it wasn't for him, I would never have become involved with photography.

And finally I have to thank you, the Reader. Over the years, you've honed my writing and teaching skills, and you continue to do so. The lovely emails you send me, and the reviews you post online, make all the late nights and early mornings worthwhile—so thank you.

Victoria Bampton—Southampton, UK, August 2018

IMPROVE THE BOOK!

Like Lightroom CC, this book is the 1st edition and it'll continue to develop and change over the coming years.

It's written in a new style, so I'd love to hear about what you like and what you think could be improved.

You can send me your feedback using the Contact form on the website at https://www.lightroomqueen.com/contact. I promise to read every email, even if I can't reply to them all personally.

CONNECT ON SOCIAL MEDIA

I'd love to connect with you on:

The Forum: https://www.lightroomqueen.com/community/

Facebook: https://www.facebook.com/lightroomqueen

Twitter: https://twitter.com/LightroomQueen

The Newsletter: https://www.lightroomqueen.com/newsletter/

INTRODUCTION

1

For many years, Lightroom has been the industry standard for photo editing. Ten years of development and new features, however, creates an ever-growing level of complexity. As a result, many photographers have found Lightroom increasingly difficult to learn and understand.

THE ALL-NEW LIGHTROOM CC

Lightroom has now been redesigned and rewritten for the needs of today's photographers. The new app retains the best of Lightroom's heritage, including the world-class non-destructive editing tools, but also adds cutting-edge image-analysis artificial intelligence, allowing you to find your photos by subject, even if you haven't manually added that information.

It's cloud-native, which means that the photos are stored safely in the cloud (on an Adobe server), and they're available on multiple devices, so you can work on your photos wherever you are.

Imagine you shoot some photos using your mobile phone, and during your coffee break, you edit them on your work laptop. Later, you're out with your tablet, and you stop to show someone the photos, complete with the edits you did earlier. Back home in the evening, you load the day's shoot from your DSLR onto your desktop, have dinner and view them on your Apple TV. It's your

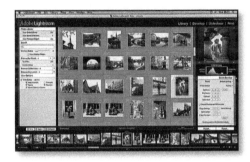

Lightroom Beta (released 2006)

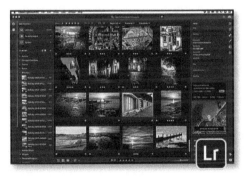

Lightroom CC (released 2017)

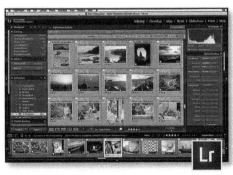

Lightroom Classic CC (released 2017)

choice.

At the time of writing this introduction, it's still only a few months old, so its feature set is limited, however it already has the majority of the tools amateur photographers need, and it will continue to grow over time.

LIGHTROOM CLASSIC CC

The traditional version of Lightroom, now rebranded as Lightroom Classic CC, isn't going away anytime soon. It continues to be supported and developed by a separate engineering team, for those who prefer a local folder-based digital asset manager.

Lightroom Classic CC is a distant cousin of the Lightroom CC ecosystem. Its communication with the cloud is limited as it's focused on single-desktop editing, so we won't demonstrate Lightroom Classic in this book, other than how to migrate to and from Lightroom Classic.

However, if you use Lightroom Classic as well as Lightroom CC, you'll be pleased to know that the same editing principles and thought processes explained in this book also apply to Lightroom Classic. The tools are simply arranged into slightly different panels. In the Lightroom CC Members Area, you'll find a bonus PDF showing where to find each slider in Lightroom Classic.

Lightroom Classic's organization tools are covered in detail in another of my books, *Adobe Lightroom Classic CC - The Missing FAQ*.

THE BOOK FORMAT & BONUS DOWNLOADS

This book is broken up into topic-based sections, each containing bite-sized lessons. It's written in a logical workflow order, with each lesson building on the previous lesson. You can skip around, but you'll get more out of the book if you read it in order.

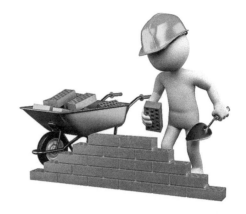

DIAGRAMS & CROSS REFERENCES

Wherever possible, I've used annotated illustrations and graphics rather than thousands of words, so you can grasp the information quickly.

Likewise, instead of constantly repeating the same information, page references link to related topics, and these are clickable links in the eBook formats.

At the end of the book, you'll find a glossary of unfamiliar terms (page 311) and a full index (page 315), so you can easily look up information again later.

MULTIPLE OPERATING SYSTEMS

Lightroom runs on multiple operating systems and devices. The same principles of use apply, but the user interface varies due to screen size, and some behavior varies depending on the operating system.

To keep things simple, if there are only minor differences, they'll be listed inline, for example, *action (Windows) / action (Mac) / action (mobile)*. If there are more significant differences, we'll discuss the desktop behavior first, and then the mobile apps. We'll come back to the web interface on page 285 and Apple TV app on page 291.

FOCUS ON EDITING

A large portion of the book is focused on editing photos, because that's why most of us are using the software. Unlike most books, we won't just discuss what the individual sliders do, but also how the sliders work together, and the way professional photographers *think* as they're editing their own photos.

NEW LESSONS & UPDATES

As Lightroom CC is subscription software, Adobe adds new features every couple of months. This means all printed books will be out of date within a few months of release— but don't worry, I've got you covered. I'm constantly updating the eBook formats for changes and new features, and these are available to download from the Lightroom CC Members Area.

A year's access to the Lightroom CC Members Area is included in your book purchase, and you can extend your access at a low cost, so you always have the most up to date information.

ACCESS TO THE MEMBERS AREA

If you purchased this book direct from my Lightroom Queen website, your Members Area access will have been set up automatically at the time of purchase, and login details sent to you by email.

If you purchased your book from Amazon, Barnes&Noble or another retailer, you'll need to register your copy of this book to gain access to the Members Area. For instructions, turn to page 314.

WORKFLOW

2

Before we start using the software itself, let's talk briefly about workflow. It's one of the most popular topics among photographers, but why? What does it actually mean?

WHAT IS WORKFLOW?

The term workflow simply describes a series of steps undertaken in the same order each time. For photographers, this workflow runs from the time of shooting (or even before), through adding your photos to Lightroom, sorting and selecting your favorites, editing and retouching them, and then outputting to various formats, whether on screen or in print.

WHY HAVE A CONSISTENT WORKFLOW?

If you do the same thing in the same order every time, you reduce the risk of mistakes. Photos won't get lost or accidentally deleted, metadata won't get missed, and you won't end up redoing work that you've already completed.

There's no perfect workflow for everyone, as everyone's needs and priorities are different. The following pages (starting on page 6) guide you through the workflow we'll follow through the pages of this book, and we'll come back to more detailed diagrams of specific stages, such as rating your photos (page 78) and editing your photos (page 116). As you gain experience, you can start to build your own ideal workflow.

Once you've settled on a good workflow, that isn't the end of the story. You'll likely find that you continue to tweak it, as you discover slightly more efficient ways of doing things. It'll continue to build with time and experience, as well as with the introduction of new Lightroom tools. The principles, however, remain the same.

IN THIS SECTION, WE'LL CONSIDER:

• The basic steps of a Lightroom CC workflow.

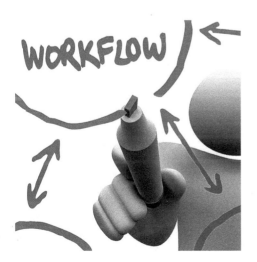

THE LIGHTROOM FAMILY WORKFLOW

Find your existing photos and video clips, wherever they're currently stored (page 24), and capture new photos using your mobile device (page 33) or camera (page 37).

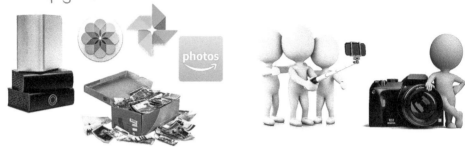

Add them all to Lightroom on your desktop (page 26) or mobile device (page 29).

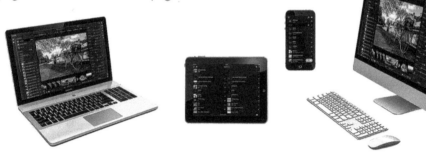

Sync with the cloud so you can access all of your photos from any device, whether you're at your desktop or laptop (page 44) or traveling with a mobile device (page 47), and store a copy locally so they're available even when you're offline.

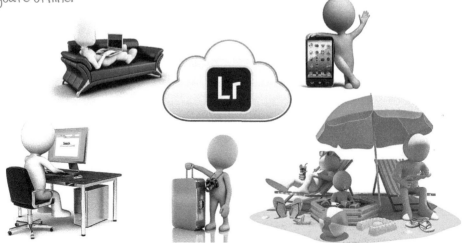

View the photos on a desktop as a grid of thumbnails (page 50) or full size photos (page 53) or on a mobile device (page 55).

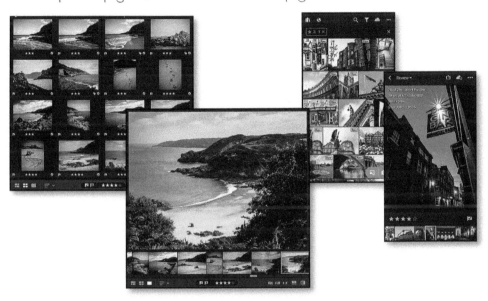

Now take that untidy bunch of photos, delete the bad ones (page 70) and organize the rest by date (page 61), and group them into albums (page 63) and stacks (page 68).

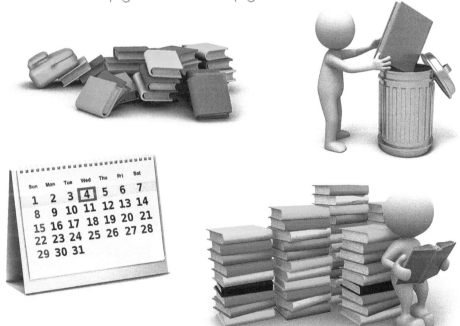

Add metadata to help you find photos again later, such as stars and flags (page 75), descriptive text (page 80), keywords (page 85), a map location (page 84) and dates (page 83).

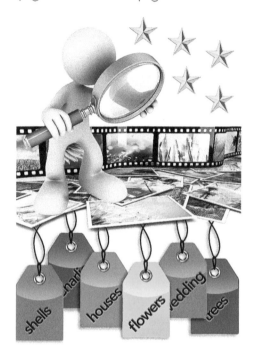

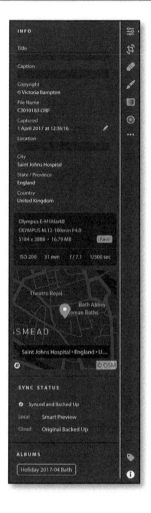

Display only your best photos by filtering using stars, flags, keywords and other metadata (page 90), or send Adobe's AI robot to search for you (page 88).

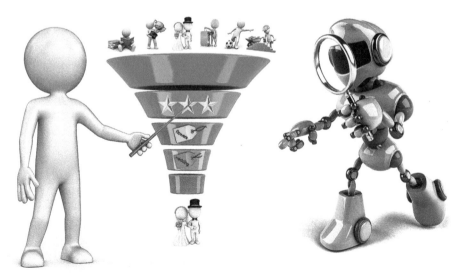

Then it's time to start editing, but you don't want to waste time going in circles, so first analyze the photo (page 99) and make a plan, just like the pros.

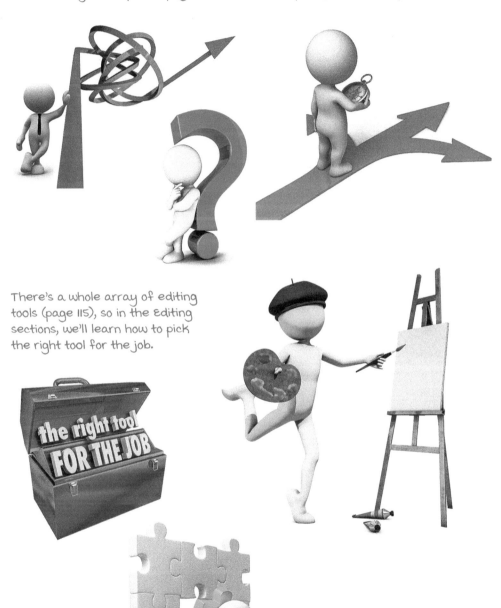

There's a whole array of editing tools (page 115), so in the Editing sections, we'll learn how to pick the right tool for the job.

the right tool FOR THE JOB

Once we have all the pieces of the puzzle, practice makes perfect, so we'll try a series of start-to-finish edits (page 249) to improve your editing skills.

Looking great? Now you'll want to share your photos with the world!

Save the edited photos to your hard drive (page 278) to email them to friends, or upload the photos to be printed at an online lab.

From your mobile device, email your editing photos or share them on social media (page 246) and other photo sharing websites.

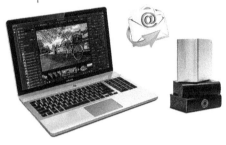

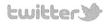

Log into the Apple TV app (page 291) to display a slideshow.

Or share entire albums as web galleries (page 285), so your friends, family and clients can view your photos, wherever they are in the world.

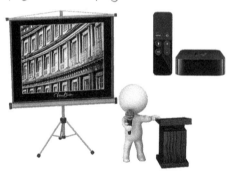

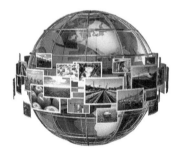

And don't worry, there's no need to get frustrated when your computer misbehaves, as we'll discuss standard troubleshooting steps too (page 295).

Ready to learn? Let's get started...

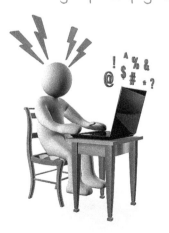

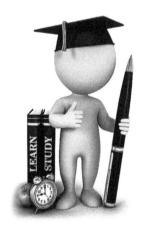

GETTING STARTED

3

I'm sure you're excited to get started, but you may also be a little apprehensive if you're not completely comfortable with computers. Even if you consider yourself computer literate, every program is different, and you won't want to risk losing any of your photos or create additional work for yourself.

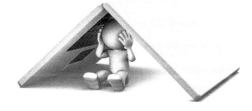

APPS RUN LOCALLY

Although Lightroom stores the photos in the cloud, the application itself installs and runs on your computer or mobile device. This means that you can still use Lightroom even if your internet connection goes down.

The apps automatically sync with the cloud, uploading new photos to your Lightroom library, so you have access to all of your photos everywhere.

In this section, we'll briefly run through the basics of installing Lightroom and finding your way around, before we move on to adding photos in the next section.

LIGHTROOM ON THE WEB

If you're using someone else's computer or device, there's no need to install the Lightroom app. You can access your photos using Lightroom Web, by navigating to https://lightroom.adobe.com in any modern

web browser and logging in with your Adobe ID. You can also share web gallery links with family, friends and clients, to allow them to view the photos. We'll come back to the web interface starting on page 285.

IN THIS SECTION, WE'LL CONSIDER:

• The computer/device specification you'll need.

• How to install Lightroom on all of your devices.

• How to find your way around the interface.

WHAT DO YOU NEED TO USE LIGHTROOM?

Ready to get started? You'll need...

• A trial or active subscription that includes Lightroom CC and cloud storage space.

• A computer or mobile device that meets (or preferably exceeds) the minimum specification.

• A reliable internet connection.

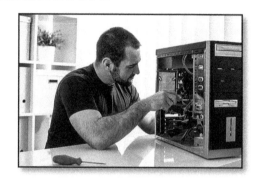

SUBSCRIPTION

There are multiple Adobe Creative Cloud subscriptions, each including different apps and amounts of cloud storage space.

The Lightroom CC photography bundle, which includes Lightroom CC (for Windows, macOS, iOS, tvOS, Android and Web) and 1TB cloud storage space, is ideal for many photographers. If you later run out of space, you can pay for additional cloud storage. As your skills progress, you can add Photoshop too.

If you don't already have a subscription, here's the link to sign up: https://www.Lrq.me/LRCC.

If you don't have a desktop or laptop computer, mobile-only subscriptions are available through the Apple App Store or Google Play Store as in-app purchases. They're about half the price of the photography bundle, however the storage space is much more limited (only 100GB), and these mobile-only subscriptions are locked to a single operating system (iOS or Android).

Whichever subscription you choose, you're not locked in. If you choose to cancel your subscription in the future, you'll have a

year to download all of your photos to your desktop computer before they're deleted from Adobe's servers.

DESKTOP SYSTEM REQUIREMENTS

Adobe publishes minimum system requirements (shown as bullets below), but these are a bare minimum to make Lightroom run. Higher specification hardware significantly improves performance. These minimum specifications are occasionally updated as new operating systems and features are released, so to check the latest system requirements, visit https://www.Lrq.me/cc-sysreq

If you've purchased your computer in the last 2-3 years, it's likely to be able to run Lightroom. However, if you're considering buying a new computer, it helps to have a basic understanding of what these specifications actually mean, so let's take a closer look...

Operating System

• *Required: Windows 10 (64-bit) Version 1511 or later, or macOS 10.11 (El Capitan) or later.*

If you're running an older operating system,

you'll need to upgrade to run Lightroom. Support for new operating systems is added when they're released to the public.

CPU / Processor

• *Required on Windows: Intel® or AMD processor with 64-bit support.*

• *Required on Mac: Multi-core Intel processor with 64-bit support. (That's any Mac that can run a supported operating system.)*

The CPU is the "brains" of the computer. It tells the other computer components what to do, depending on the instructions given by the software and the user.

CPU's come in different clock speeds (measured in GHz), which determines how quickly computations are made, so higher numbers are generally better.

CPU's are also available with different numbers of cores, which allow them to do lots of different things at once. Lightroom makes good use of multiple cores for image processing tasks such as editing and exporting photos, so a quad-core processor is a great choice if you're buying a new computer.

RAM / Memory

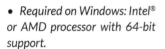

• *Required: At least 4GB of RAM, but ideally 8GB or more.*

RAM, or Random Access Memory, is short-term storage for the data the CPU's working on, allowing it to be quickly stored and retrieved as it's needed.

When your computer runs out of space in RAM, it has to write the data out to the hard disk, which is much slower.

I'd recommend 16GB if you're buying a new computer and your budget will stretch.

GPU / Graphics Card

• *Required: At least 1 GB of Video RAM (VRAM). 2 GB of dedicated VRAM is suggested for large, high-resolution monitors, such as 4K and 5K resolution monitors.*

• *Also required on Windows: OpenGL 3.3 and DirectX 10-capable video adapter for GPU-related functionality.*

• *Also required on Mac: OpenGL 3.3–capable video adapter for GPU-related functionality.*

The GPU, or graphics card, does more than just display the image on screen. It's designed to do thousands of calculations at once, but just for graphics-related tasks.

The GPU needs somewhere to temporarily store all of this information, and this is where the VRAM (or video memory) comes into play. The bigger the screen, the more information it needs to store in VRAM, so the more VRAM you need.

Lightroom uses the GPU to speed up certain tasks, such as rendering the preview of the photo on high resolution (4K/5K) screens, so if you have a high resolution monitor, you'll want a more powerful graphics card too.

Hard Drive Space

• *Required: At least 10GB of available hard drive space.*

• *Note, the Mac version can't install on a volume that uses a case-sensitive file system or on removable flash storage devices (such as USB sticks).*

The hard disk drive is long-term storage. This is where you store all of your files, including the computer's operating system, the program files and your photos.

Hard drives can be stored inside your computer (internal drives) or connected using a cable (external drives). SSD's are faster than traditional spinning disks, so they're a better choice for your computer's boot drive.

Lightroom requires a relatively small amount of disk space, as most of the photos are stored in the cloud and they're just downloaded as you need them. However, although the minimum specifications state only 10GB is required, more space may be needed on the boot drive if you have tens of thousands of photos.

It's worth keeping at least one local copy of all of your photos as a backup. To do so, you can simply buy and plug in an external drive, and tell Lightroom to store the original files there, and the rest happens automatically. We'll learn about this on page 45.

MOBILE SYSTEM REQUIREMENTS

The mobile apps also have minimum system requirements, and again, higher specification hardware significantly improves performance.

On iOS, you need to be running *iOS 10 or later* on a recent iPhone, iPad or iPod, including:

• *iPad Pro, iPad 4 and later, iPad Mini 2 and later.*

• *iPhone 5, iPhone 5s, iPhone 5c, iPhone 6, iPhone 6S, iPhone 6 Plus, iPhone 6S Plus, iPhone SE, iPhone 7, iPhone 7 Plus, iPhone 8, iPhone 8 Plus, iPhone X and later.*

• *iPod Touch 5th Generation.*

Android devices need to be running *Android OS 4.3.x or later* with this minimum specification:

• *Processor: Quad Core CPU with 1.5 GHz frequency and ARMv7 architecture (2.2 GHz or higher recommended).*

• *RAM: 1 GB (2 GB recommended).*

• *Internal storage: 8 GB.*

Some features are only available on high specification devices, for example, on iOS, only devices with a 12MP+ camera can capture in DNG format, and on Android, only a few phones can capture HDR (high dynamic range) images.

For Adobe's latest system requirements for mobile devices, check https://www.Lrq.me/ccmob-sysreq

INTERNET CONNECTION

• *Adobe says: Internet connection and registration are necessary for required software activation, validation of subscriptions, and access to online services.*

As Lightroom uploads all of your photos to the cloud, you do need a reasonably fast unmetered internet connection (or a lot of patience).

Lightroom continues to work when you go offline, whether your connection drops or you go on vacation. It asks you to connect briefly every so often (about every 30 days) to confirm your subscription status, but it will usually allow you to postpone this check for up to 99 days.

Some features don't work without an

internet connection, including:

• Photos/videos can't download from the cloud for viewing/editing if they're not already stored locally.

• New photos/videos and edits can't sync up to the cloud.

• New photos/videos added on other devices and edits made on other devices can't sync down from the cloud.

• Searching for photos/videos using the text search field won't work.

• The map in the Info panel and reverse geocoding (address lookup) won't work.

If you know you're going be offline, you can store smart previews or originals locally while you still have an internet connection, so the photos are available for viewing and editing offline. (See page 45 and page 48.)

PRIVACY CONCERNS

No one has access to your photos unless:

• They have access to your Adobe account.

• They have access to your computer/ mobile device.

• You choose to share them.

By default, Adobe does automatically collect some usage information to help the engineers improve the software. This includes your computer specifications and which tools you use in Lightroom, but not your photos or other personal information.

Adobe also utilizes machine learning, which means you can search the content of your photos in Lightroom without having to manually tag them.

If you want to learn more about how this information is used, or adjust your preferences, log into your account on Adobe's website, and go to *Manage Account > Security & Privacy > Privacy*.

INSTALLING & OPENING LIGHTROOM ON THE DESKTOP

You can activate Lightroom on two desktop computers at any one time (such as a desktop and laptop, or home and work), in addition to your mobile devices.

INSTALLING USING THE CC APP

The desktop app installation and updates are managed using the Creative Cloud app (often shortened to CC app), which is a small app that runs constantly in the system tray (Windows) or menu bar (Mac).

To install the CC app, follow Adobe's instructions at https://www.Lrq.me/ccinstall When the installation completes, sign in with your Adobe ID and password.

To install Lightroom, select the *Apps* tab in the CC app, find Lightroom CC (not Lightroom Classic CC) and click the *Install* button to start the installation.

After installation, Lightroom opens automatically. To open Lightroom again in future, click the *Open* button in the CC app, or go to *Start menu > Adobe Lightroom CC* (Windows) / *Applications folder > Adobe Lightroom CC > Adobe Lightroom CC.app* (Mac).

While Lightroom's open, let's set up a shortcut for easier access. On Windows, right-click on the icon in the Taskbar and select *Pin to Taskbar*. On macOS, right-click on the icon in the Dock and select *Options > Keep in Dock*.

THE CREATIVE CLOUD APP (WINDOWS/MAC)

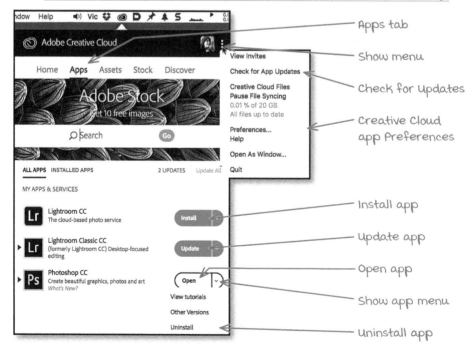

WELCOME SCREEN & TIPS

When Lightroom opens for the first time, it displays some welcome screens, followed by a series of tips to introduce you to the main features.

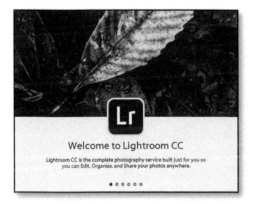

If you've already synced photos to the cloud, previews immediately start downloading.

If Lightroom Classic or an earlier version of Lightroom is installed on the computer, Lightroom may ask whether you wish to migrate your catalog. If so, say no for now, as we'll cover this process in detail on page 39, avoiding some potential problems.

DESKTOP WORKSPACE BASICS

Once the welcome screens are out of the way, you're looking at the Lightroom workspace. You might also hear it called the UI, or user interface.

In the center is the preview area, where your photos are displayed.

Down the left and right sides are panels, which are opened and closed using the buttons along the outside edges. The panels on the left are used for organizing photos, and the panels on the right contain the metadata and editing tools.

On the following two page spread, there's a quick reference guide to the workspace, so you can learn the names of the main elements. There's nothing more frustrating than looking for something in a book's index when you don't know its name! The page references link to pages where the different elements are discussed in more detail.

CHECKING FOR UPDATES

Lightroom is updated regularly, adding new camera support, new features and bug fixes. To check for updates within Lightroom, go to *Help menu > Updates*. This automatically opens the CC app, where you can click the *Update* button to start the update installation.

WINDOWS VS. MAC

The screenshots in this book were captured using a Mac, but Lightroom works the same way on Windows. Any exceptions, for example, file paths or keyboard shortcuts, are noted.

KEYBOARD SHORTCUTS

Throughout the book, we'll focus primarily on which buttons to click to accomplish a task, but many tools are also available as menu commands or keyboard shortcuts. As you become more familiar with Lightroom, the shortcuts will help to increase your efficiency. For your easy reference, I've added a Keyboard Shortcut list to your Members Area downloads.

THE LIGHTROOM WORKSPACE (WINDOWS/MAC)

menu bar   Progress bar   Search
(page 88)

Window buttons (on
the right on Windows,
left on mac)

Add Photos (page 23)

My Photos
navigate by date or
album (page 49)

Open/Close Panels
To open & close panels
on the left or right of
the screen, click the
buttons down the edges.
When you open a panel
on one side, the other
side closes. To change
this behavior, go to
Preferences > General >
Panel Tracks > manual

Preview Area
(page 53)

Filmstrip (page 50)

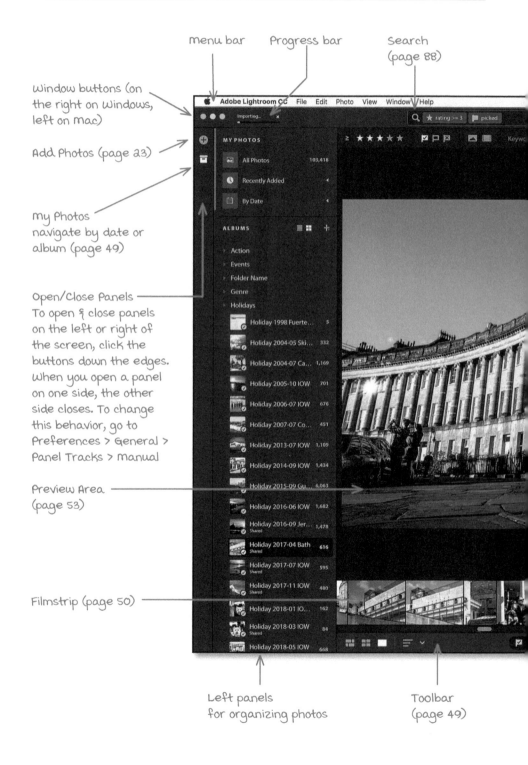

Left panels
for organizing photos

Toolbar
(page 49)

Refine View (page 90)

Share/Save a Copy
(page 277)

Sync Status
(page 44)

Sliders

Crop (page 129)

Healing Brush
(page 235)

Adjustment Brush
(page 208)

Linear Gradient
(page 215)

Radial Gradient
(page 215)

... menu
(page 115)

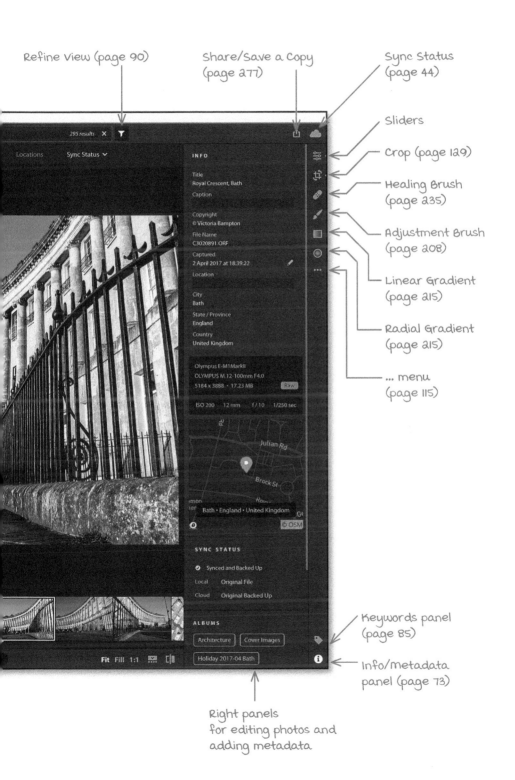

Keywords panel
(page 85)

Info/metadata
panel (page 73)

Right panels
for editing photos and
adding metadata

INSTALLING THE MOBILE APPS

The Lightroom CC mobile apps can be downloaded onto all of your mobile devices, to provide easy access to your photos wherever you are.

INSTALLING THE APPS

To install Lightroom on your phone or tablet, visit the Apple App Store (iOS) or Google Play Store (Android), as you would for any other app. Here are the direct links:

iOS: https://www.Lrq.me/ios

Android: https://www.Lrq.me/android

Once the installation completes, return to your Home screen and tap on the app icon to open Lightroom. You need to be connected to the internet while setting it up.

The first time you open Lightroom on mobile, it displays a series of welcome screens, highlighting the main features.

To sync your photos with the cloud, you'll need to sign in. (If you don't sign in, it remains in a limited "free" mode.) Tap the cloud icon in the top left corner and log in using your Adobe ID and password. If you've already synced photos to the cloud, previews immediately start downloading.

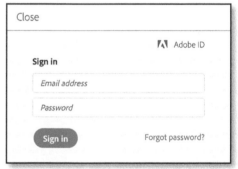

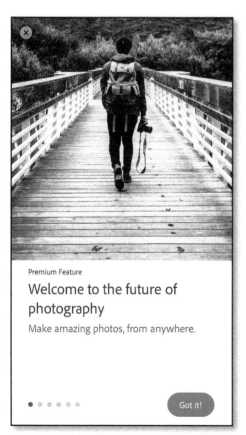

The first time Lightroom uses a device feature, such as the camera or notifications, it asks for permission. These permissions can be granted or revoked again later in *Settings app > Lightroom CC* (iOS) / *Settings app > Apps > Lightroom CC* (Android).

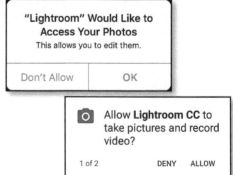

MOBILE WORKSPACE BASICS

The iOS and Android apps use a series of screens, due to their smaller screen size. There's a brief overview on page 22, and we'll explore the individual screens in more detail a little later in the book. The Organize view (page 66) is used for organizing photos into Albums. The Grid (page 57) and Detail (page 59) views allow you to browse and edit photos.

IOS VS. ANDROID

There are slight differences between the iOS and Android apps, due to operating-system-specific features, and also between phones and tablets due to their screen sizes. Different teams work on developing the apps in parallel, so some features are available on one operating system before the other. Where there are significant differences, these are noted.

One of the most notable differences is the Settings (Preferences). We'll come back to the individual settings on page 298 (iOS) / page 300 (Android). To find them on iOS, tap the cog icon if you're in Organize view, or ... *icon* > *Settings* in Grid or Detail view. On Android, tap the hamburger icon in the top left corner of the Organize view.

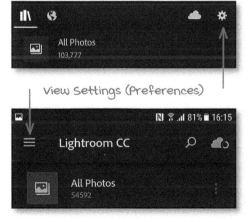

View Settings (Preferences)

KEYBOARD SHORTCUTS

If you're using an external keyboard with your phone or tablet, there are a few keyboard shortcuts you can use, for example, to assign a star rating to your photo. For your easy reference, I've added a Keyboard Shortcut list to your Members Area downloads.

THE LIGHTROOM WORKSPACE (IOS/ANDROID)

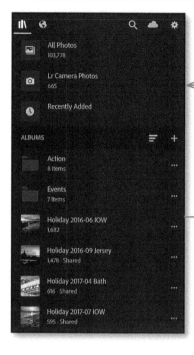

1. Lightroom opens to Organize view

2. Tap All Photos or an album to open it into Grid view

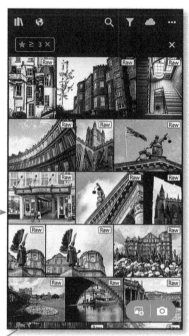

3. Tap a photo to open it in Detail view

5. Tap arrow to go back

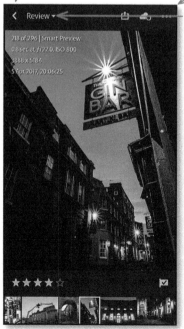

4. To switch between Detail views, tap the menu at the top on small devices, or the buttons down the side on tablet apps

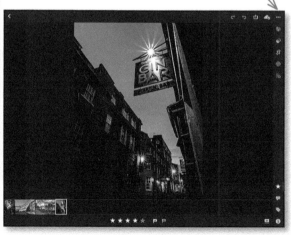

ADDING PHOTOS & VIDEOS

4

Before you can start organizing and editing your photos, you need to get them into Lightroom.

ALL OR NOTHING

It's worth adding all of your photos to Lightroom, wherever they're coming from, because:

• You'll be safe in the knowledge that you won't lose any photos, even if your computer crashes or your phone is lost or stolen.

• You'll have all of your photos in one place, so they'll be easy to browse.

• You'll be able to access them on any device, so you can share them with others.

• You can improve your photos using industry standard editing tools.

• You can become a better photographer by studying your previous photos.

• You can see how your photography skills are improving over time.

FILE FORMATS

Lightroom can manage a wide range of file formats. There's a full list at https://www.Lrq.me/file-formats

In addition to photos, many photographers also shoot short video clips on their mobile devices. Lightroom allows you to view and organize some video formats, but you can't edit them using Lightroom. For simplicity, we'll refer to adding photos, but the same principles apply to adding videos.

IN THIS SECTION, WE'LL CONSIDER:

• Where you might find your existing photos.

• How to add photos to Lightroom.

• How to capture photos on mobile devices.

• Camera settings that affect editing flexibility.

• How to migrate photos and edits from Lightroom Classic.

FINDING YOUR EXISTING PHOTOS

You likely already have a large number of photos stored on your computer's hard drive or in another company's cloud. Before you can add them to Lightroom, you need to find them.

WHERE ARE YOUR PHOTOS?

I can't tell you where you've stored your photos, but these are the most frequent places to check:

• Your phone or tablet.

• Your camera's memory card.

• The Pictures or Photos folder on your computer.

• Other internal or external hard drives.

• DVD's/CD's.

• Cloud services, such as Google Photos, Dropbox or iCloud.

• Organized using other software that stores the files in its own library, such as iPhoto, Aperture or Photos.app.

• In boxes, albums or slide trays of photos shot on film. (You might consider photographing or scanning them to create digital files.)

Importing from your phone/tablet, camera, memory card reader or hard drive is very straightforward using the instructions on page 26, but there are a few things to look out for when importing from other photo editing software...

IMPORTING FROM LIGHTROOM CLASSIC/1-6

If you're migrating from Lightroom Classic CC or earlier, turn to page 39 to use the migration tool. This retains most of the organization and edits done in Lightroom.

A word of warning before you start: the migration is a one-way process. Continuing to use and sync Lightroom Classic after migration is a recipe for disaster.

If you're unsure whether Lightroom CC offers all of the functionality you require, don't migrate until you're certain. Instead, use Lightroom Classic to sync smart previews to the cloud so you can view/edit them in Lightroom CC. This will allow you to fully test Lightroom CC before committing to switching over completely. See the Cloud

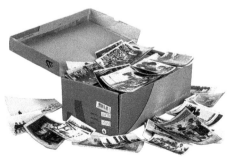

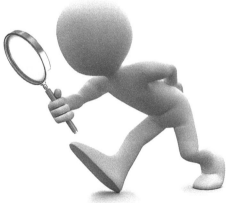

Sync chapter of my book, *Adobe Photoshop Lightroom Classic CC - The Missing FAQ* to avoid potential problems. I've also published a feature comparison at https://www.Lrq. me/lightroom-cc-vs-classic-features/

IMPORTING FROM CLOUD SERVICES

If your photos are on a cloud service, you'll need to download them to your computer to add them to Lightroom, as there are no direct transfer tools. These are a few frequent services:

Google Photos—Use Google Takeout to download the photos to your computer.

Dropbox—Use the Dropbox desktop app to download the photos to your computer.

iCloud Photos—Use iCloud for Windows app or Photos app for macOS to download the photos to your computer.

IMPORTING FROM APPLE PHOTO APPS

iPhoto, Aperture and Photos default to storing photos in a special kind of folder called a package file, which is not easily accessible using other software. To access the photos, use the app to export them to a standard folder. Select the *Original* format option where possible, to avoid degrading the quality, and check the *Export IPTC as XMP* checkbox to include the metadata where possible.

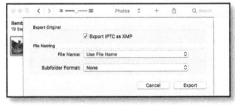

IMPORTING FROM OTHER SOFTWARE

If you've previously used other software to organize and edit your photos, you may want to preserve these edits, where possible.

Some editing software can write the metadata (that's things like titles, captions, keyword tags and star ratings) back to the files using a standardized format called XMP, which Lightroom can understand.

To check whether your software can write some or all of the metadata to the files, search the web for the name of your software and XMP, for example, *Picasa XMP*.

Some photo editing software stores the edits non-destructively, so these image adjustments are not applied to the originals. To retain these edits, save a copy of the photos as JPEG format and add these to Lightroom along with the unedited original.

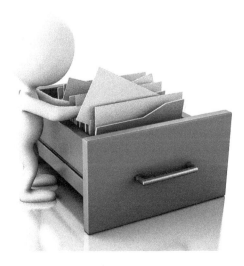

ADDING PHOTOS ON THE DESKTOP

Once you've found your photos, you're ready to start adding them to Lightroom. You're in control of which photos (or videos) you import, and the same principles apply whether you're adding existing photos from your hard drive or new photos from your camera.

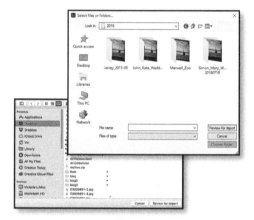

STEP-BY-STEP

1. If your photos are not currently stored on the computer, plug in the mobile phone, tablet, camera or memory card reader. (Card readers are generally more reliable than camera cables.)

2. Click the **+** symbol at the top of the left panel bar.

3. To add photos from a memory card or mobile device, select the device from the pop-up.

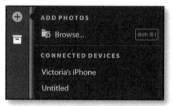

4. To add photos from your computer's hard drive, select **Browse...** from the pop-up to show the standard file browser for your operating system. (If no memory cards or mobile devices are connected, Lightroom skips the pop-up and immediately opens the file browser for you.)

Select a folder (such as the Pictures folder) or individual photos then click **Choose Folder** (Windows) / **Review for Import** (Mac) to move to the next window.

If your photos are currently organized into folders by topic, you may want to add one folder at a time (rather than selecting the parent folder) so you can create an album per folder, retaining your topic-based organization.

5. The thumbnails start to appear in a Grid view. There's a larger labeled diagram on page 28.

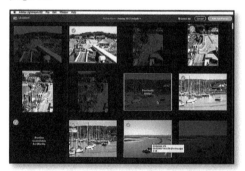

6. Select the photos you want to import by clicking the **checkmark** in the top left corner of each thumbnail. To select or deselect all of the photos at once, toggle the **Select All** checkbox.

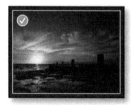

To check a series of consecutive photos, click on the first of the photos so it shows a white border. Hold down the Shift key and click the last photo in the series, so they're all surrounded by a white border, then click the checkbox on one of the selected photos to check them all.

7. If the selected photos are all from the same shoot or topic-based folder, you may want to group them into an album (page 63) to make them easy to find later.

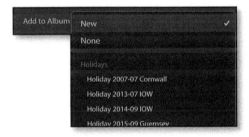

In the **Add to Album** pop-up, select *New* to create a new album, or select an existing album from the list. (A quick tip: as the number of albums grows, this list can become hard to scroll, but if you select the album in the Albums panel *before* opening the Add Photos dialog, the album is automatically selected in the *Add to Album* pop-up.)

8. Click **Add X Photos** to start importing the photos into Lightroom.

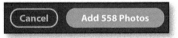

9. The dialog closes and a progress bar appears in the top left corner of Lightroom, showing the current status. Float over it to see the image count. If more than one task is in progress, click on it to see the individual tasks.

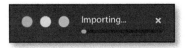

10. The photos appear in the preview area,

and you can start looking through them immediately (page 49). If you run into any problems adding photos or videos, turn to page 303.

CLEANING UP AFTER ADDING PHOTOS

Adding photos to Lightroom doesn't remove them from their previous location, so you may want to clean up after adding them to Lightroom.

If your photos were on a camera memory card, keep the photos on the memory card as a backup until they're safely uploaded to the cloud. Once they've finished uploading, reformat the memory card in the camera, rather than simply deleting the photos. This helps to avoid card corruption.

If the photos were stored on the hard drive, you may choose to delete the original folders once the photos/videos are safely in Lightroom, to free up space on your computer. Before you delete these folders, double-check all of the photos imported into Lightroom and the folders don't contain any non-photo/video files, for example, Word documents or other file formats that aren't supported by Lightroom.

THE ADD PHOTOS DIALOG (WINDOWS/MAC)

Show photo
sources to add ——→
new photos

Browse computer
hard drives

memory cards,
cameras,
phones, tablets

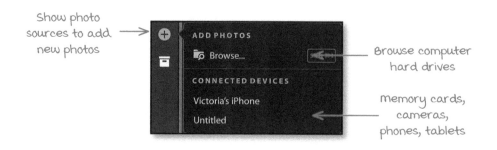

Return to
dialog to
change
source

Thumbnails
of photos
in selected
source

Add to
Album

Select all
thumbnails

Close dialog
without
adding photos

Add the
selected
photos to
Lightroom

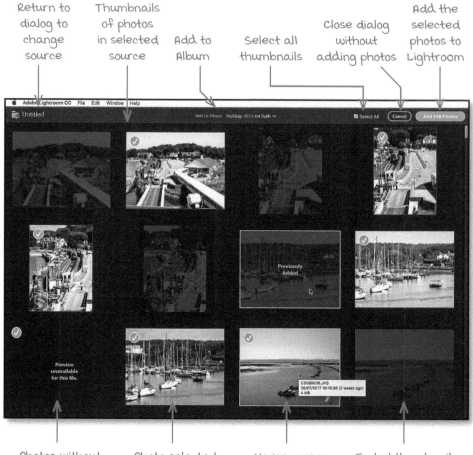

Photos without
previews may
still import ok
(page 303)

Photo selected
to be added
to Lightroom

Hover cursor
to show tooltip
containing
photo info

Faded thumbnails
are duplicates of
photos already
in Lightroom
(page 303)

ADDING PHOTOS ON IOS/ANDROID

Rather than having to plug your mobile device into your desktop computer, you can add photos directly into the Lightroom mobile apps. The photos can be added to your library automatically or you can add photos manually.

Adding photos automatically saves you having to remember to upload your photos. On iOS, you must open the Lightroom app occasionally to allow the photos to import, whereas on Android, the import happens in the background.

ADDING PHOTOS AUTOMATICALLY

To automatically add new photos captured using other camera apps, go to Lightroom's *Settings*.

On iOS, select *Import* and toggle the *Auto Add Photos* and *Auto Add Videos* switches to the right.

On Android, select *Preferences > Enable Auto Add* and toggle the *Auto Add New Photos* switch, along with the *JPGs/PNGs* and *Raws* switches. (Videos can't currently be imported on Android.)

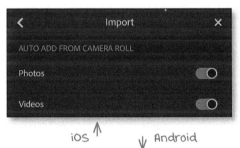

iOS ↑   ↓ Android

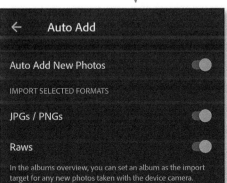

ADDING PHOTOS MANUALLY

Auto Add only adds new photos automatically, but you can add older photos using the *Add Photos* button. The process varies slightly by operating system:

iOS

1. Tap the blue *Add Photos* button at the bottom of the Organize or Grid view.

Add Photos ⟶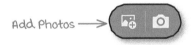

2. If you were viewing an album, Lightroom asks whether to add photos from the *Camera Roll*, *All Photos* or *Files*, so select *Camera Roll*. (Alternatively, selecting *Files* allows you to import photos from cloud storage such as iCloud or Dropbox or external storage units like Gnarbox or WD My Passport Wireless.)

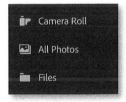

3. Lightroom displays the photos stored on your mobile device. At the top of the grid, select the album of your choice, for example, *Camera Roll*. Photos already imported into Lightroom have a LR icon in the corner.

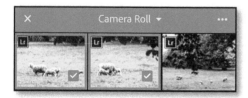

4. Drag your finger across the photos to select them (shown by a blue border), or tap the ... button to select all. (If you just tap on a photo, it opens into the Edit view, and doesn't import the photo until you tap the checkmark.)

5. When you've finished selecting the photos to import, tap the *Add X Photos* button at the bottom of the screen to confirm your selection.

4. Tap the photos individually, a segment at a time, or tap the ... button to select all. Selected photos have a blue border.

5. When you've finished selecting the photos to import, tap the *Add* button to confirm your selection.

Android

1. Tap the blue *Add Photos* button at the bottom of the Organize or Grid view.

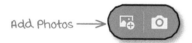

2. If you were viewing an album, Lightroom asks whether to add photos from the *Device*, *All Photos* or *Files*, so select *Device*. (Alternatively, selecting *Files* allows you to import photos from cloud storage such as GoogleDrive or Dropbox, or external storage units like Gnarbox or WD My Passport Wireless.)

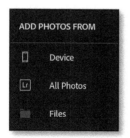

3. At the top of the grid, select the grouping of your choice, for example, *Time* or *Device Folders*.

ADDING DSLR/MIRRORLESS PHOTOS ON IOS/ANDROID

If you're shooting with a separate camera, for example, your DSLR or mirrorless camera, you can add the photos to Lightroom on your mobile device instead of the desktop. This is particularly useful when traveling without a laptop, allowing you to start viewing, editing and sharing them.

STEP-BY-STEP

Due to differences in the operating systems, the steps are slightly different:

iOS

You'll need a Lightning to USB adapter and a cable to connect your camera, or you'll need a Lightning to SD card reader.

1. Insert the memory card into the SD card reader, or connect the camera and turn it on.

2. Open Photos app, if it doesn't open automatically, and select *Import* at the bottom.

3. In the top right corner, tap *Import All*, or tap specific photos then tap *Import*. (Having to first import into Photos app is a limitation

of the operating system.)

4. When Photos app finishes importing the photos, you can choose to *Keep* the photos on the memory card or *Delete* them. I'd recommend keeping them on the card, at least until they're safely uploaded to the cloud, so that you have a backup. Also note that Photos app might not import photos or videos from all cameras, so it's worth double checking everything has copied before clearing the memory card.

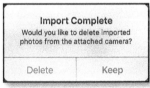

5. Once the photos have safely imported into Photos app, you can add them to Lightroom automatically (using Auto Add) or manually. Once they're safely in Lightroom, you can delete them from Photos app to free up space on your iPhone/iPad (but I'd still suggest keeping a copy on the memory cards as a backup).

Note that Lightroom only adds the raw file from raw+JPEG pairs. This is an iOS limitation.

Android

You'll need a supported OTG cable or adapter, and you may need a cable to connect to your camera.

1. Connect the camera to the mobile device using a supported OTG cable/adapter. Ensure the camera is turned on and is in PTP or MTP mode.

2. In the app picker, select Lightroom CC. If your device automatically opens another app, you'll need to check your device manufacturer's documentation to clear the default setting.

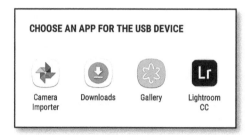

3. Tap specific photos to select them (shown by a blue border), or tap the ... icon to *Select All*, *Select None* or filter by file type. Once you've selected the photos, tap *Add*.

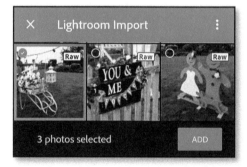

4. Lightroom asks whether to add the photos to *All Photos*, to a specific album or to create a new album. By default, *All Photos* is selected. Once you've made your choice, tap *Add* again.

5. Lightroom displays a progress dialog while it copies the photos to your Android device. When it's finished importing the photos, you can disconnect the camera. I'd recommend keeping the photos on the card, at least until they're safely uploaded to the cloud, so that you have a backup.

CAPTURING PHOTOS USING THE LIGHTROOM CAMERA

The iOS app and Android phone app include a built-in camera which has some specific advantages over other camera apps. (The camera isn't currently available on Android tablets.)

BENEFITS OF LIGHTROOM'S CAMERA

Manual camera controls—In addition to the standard Auto mode, there's a Pro mode offering manual controls such as shutter speed, ISO, white balance, and manual focus point.

Shoot-through presets—Unlike the default camera apps, the shoot-through presets are non-destructive. For example, if you want to preview the photo in B&W when shooting, and then later decide you'd prefer the photo in color, you can simply reset the edit settings.

Non-destructive crop for zoom—If you zoom in while composing the photo, it's stored as a non-destructive crop that can be changed later, when you realize you've cropped out something important.

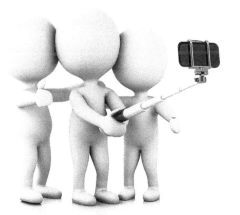

Raw capture—On iOS devices with a 12MP camera running iOS10 and above, and also on some Android phones, the raw data can be saved as DNG format for greater editing flexibility.

HDR capture—Small mobile device camera sensors have a much more limited dynamic range than many traditional cameras, so highlight or shadow detail can be clipped. On some devices, Lightroom can capture multiple exposures and automatically merge them to create an image with much greater dynamic range, while retaining the editing flexibility of raw data.

Long Exposure—Introduced as a technology preview on iPhones, and hopefully coming to Android in a future release, Lightroom can capture multiple sequential images and merge them into something that looks like a long exposure image, blurring any motion. Unlike a traditional long exposure image, it's smart enough to figure out which areas of the photo are really moving and which bits are blurred due to camera shake, so you can even capture 5 second exposures hand-held.

Depth Capture—Introduced as a technology preview on the iPhone 7+, 8+ and X, the Depth capture mode uses the dual cameras to create a depth map that can be used to darken or blur backgrounds using the selective editing tools, like Apple's Portrait mode.

(To enable technology previews, go to *Settings > Technology Previews* and enable the features you want to try.)

Auto Import—The photos are automatically added to Lightroom, and synced to the cloud, so you never need to worry about losing your photos.

On the following pages, there are diagrams demonstrating the location of each of these settings. Some of the settings are only available on more powerful devices due to the complexity of the image processing involved, or the limitations of the operating system.

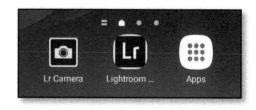

EASY ACCESS

To open Lightroom's camera, tap the blue camera icon in Organize/Grid view.

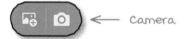

← Camera

On iOS, you can use the Lightroom camera widget for quicker access. To view the widgets, swipe right over the Home screen, Lock screen, or while you're looking at your notifications. To add the Lightroom widget, scroll down to the end of the widgets and tap *Edit*, then tap the + next to Lightroom CC and drag it into the order you prefer.

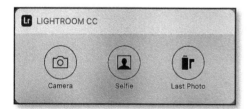

On iOS devices that support 3D Touch, you can also deep press on the Lightroom icon on the Home screen and select *Take Photo*.

On Android, the Lightroom Camera is available as a separate widget which can be added to the Home Screen for fast access. To do so, go to *Android's Settings app > Display > Home Screen > Widgets*. Search for Lightroom Camera and drag it into position on your Home Screen.

LIGHTROOM'S CAMERA (IOS)

Available options vary depending on the device used

Flash
On/Off/Auto

File Format (JPEG/
DNG, if available)

Front/Rear Camera

Back to Lightroom

Pro Capture
Settings... from
left to right:

... button to Show/
Hide menu. menu
options from left
to right are:

Exposure
Compensation (also
swipe left <> right)

Crop to Aspect Ratio
(non-destructive)

Shutter Speed

Self-Timer

ISO

Grid Overlay
and Level

White Balance

Auto / manual
Focus (tap on photo
to auto focus,
hold finger to lock
focus). manual
Focus shows green
focus peaking mask.

Highlight
Clipping Warning
(zebra lines)

Camera Settings
dialog (below)

Apply Preset
(non-destructive)

Reset (or double-
tap individual
settings)

Exposure Lock

Recent Captures

Lens (Wide/
Telephoto, if
available)

Shooting mode
Auto/Pro/HDR/Long Exposure/
Depth (if available)

Shutter (also use
volume keys)

Pinch/Spread to
Zoom in/out (non-
destructive crop)

Increase screen brightness
while using camera

Add GPS location data

When shooting HDR/
long exposure, save
unedited photo too

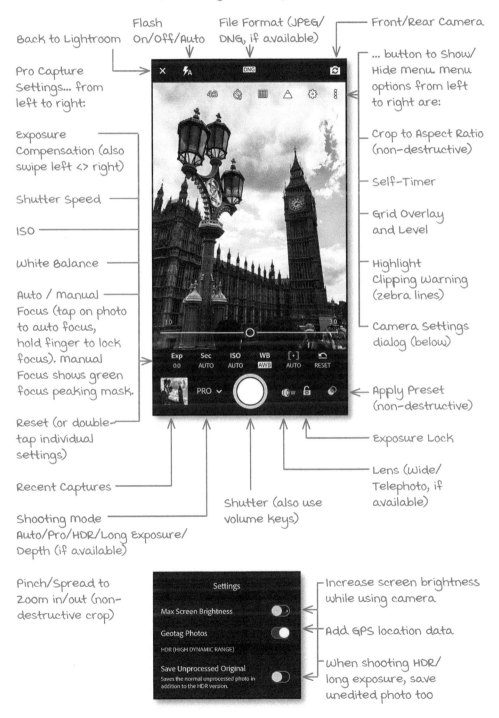

LIGHTROOM'S CAMERA (ANDROID)

Available options vary depending on the device used

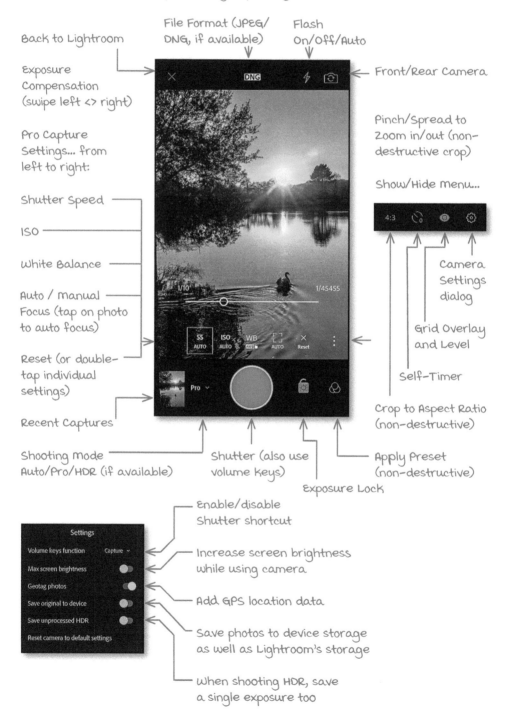

Back to Lightroom

File Format (JPEG/ DNG, if available)

Flash On/Off/Auto

Exposure Compensation (swipe left <> right)

Front/Rear Camera

Pinch/Spread to zoom in/out (non-destructive crop)

Pro Capture Settings... from left to right:

Show/Hide menu...

Shutter Speed

ISO

White Balance

Camera Settings dialog

Auto / manual Focus (tap on photo to auto focus)

Grid Overlay and Level

Reset (or double-tap individual settings)

Self-Timer

Recent Captures

Crop to Aspect Ratio (non-destructive)

Shooting mode Auto/Pro/HDR (if available)

Shutter (also use volume keys)

Apply Preset (non-destructive)

Exposure Lock

Enable/disable Shutter shortcut

Increase screen brightness while using camera

Add GPS location data

Save photos to device storage as well as Lightroom's storage

When shooting HDR, save a single exposure too

SET A GOOD FOUNDATION WITH YOUR CAMERA SETTINGS

Whether you're shooting with a mobile device or a separate camera, your settings will affect the ease of editing your photos as well as the quality of the end result. This isn't a camera manual, so we won't go into detail, but there are a few main settings to look out for...

RAW VS. JPEG—WHAT'S THE DIFFERENCE?

Arguably, the most important decision is your file format.

JPEGs are already processed by the camera in the way the camera manufacturer thought the photo should look. (The same applies to Apple's newer HEIF format.)

Raw files are the unprocessed sensor data, ready for you to process the way you prefer.

Raw vs. JPEG creates a bit of a religious war on the internet, and the decision is yours, but consider a few pros and cons...

WHY SHOOT JPEG/HEIF

Most photographers start out with JPEGs, and many phones and compact cameras only offer JPEG format. Newer Apple devices default to HEIF format. There are some advantages:

Space—JPEGs are much smaller than raw files, and HEIF files are smaller still. That means you can fit a lot more photos on your memory card or phone.

Speed—JPEGs and HEIF files come out of the camera ready to go, whereas raw files require editing. Speed shooters, such as sports photographers, often prefer JPEG for this reason.

Camera Settings Applied—The photos look exactly the same as they did on the back of the camera.

Compatibility—All image editing software understands JPEG format, whereas raw files must first be converted to standard image formats using software like Lightroom. HEIF files are not widely supported yet.

WHY SHOOT RAW

Raw files are bigger, and you do have to edit them, but there are some huge advantages:

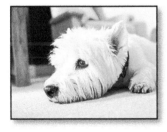

Image captured with incorrect white balance and overexposed

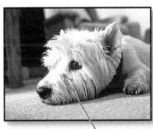

Edited JPEG. The clipped highlights couldn't be recovered and the color is unnatural

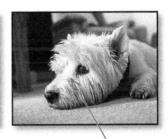

Edited raw file. Notice the detail recovered on the nose and head, and natural colors

Dynamic Range—Raw files have a much wider dynamic range than JPEGs. This means that clipped highlight or shadow detail can often still be recovered from a raw file, whereas in the JPEGs, that detail's gone forever. You can see the difference in the dog's face.

Mistake Recovery—We all make mistakes, and if you have to make significant exposure changes, there's far more data to work with in a raw file, resulting in a higher quality image.

White Balance—Raw files can have their white balance adjusted while editing (page 176), whereas it's already applied to the pixels of JPEGs. This gives much more flexibility when editing, as you can see in the photo of the dog.

IF YOU'RE SHOOTING RAW

If you're shooting raw, there are a few things to bear in mind:

Unprocessed Raw Data—When you shoot in your camera's raw file format, the data isn't fully processed by the camera. Each raw processing software (like Lightroom) interprets the raw data in a slightly different way. As a result, the photos won't look exactly the same in Lightroom as they did on the back of the camera. There isn't a right or wrong rendering—they're just different.

Camera Picture Styles—While many cameras offer picture styles such as Portrait, Landscape and Monochrome, these editing presets only apply to the JPEGs (and the preview you see on the back of the camera), not the raw data. When you add the raw photos to Lightroom, these effects disappear, ready for you to edit the photos in whatever style you like.

ETTR—Short for "expose to the right," consider setting the exposure to be as bright as possible without clipping the highlights to pure white in order to retain the largest amount of data. Search the web for ETTR for more information on this concept.

Low ISO—To minimize noise, use the lowest ISO possible, balanced against the shutter speed and aperture, and avoid underexposing the photos.

Turn Off Smart Camera Settings—Some camera settings apply shadow brightening to the JPEG preview and histogram on the back of the camera, but not to the raw data. This may fool you into accidentally underexposing the photo, so these settings are best left disabled when shooting raw. Every manufacturer uses a different name, such as Auto Lighting Optimizer (Canon), Active D-Lighting (Nikon), Dynamic Range Optimization (Sony), Shadow Adjustment Technology (Olympus) and Intelligent Exposure (Panasonic).

IF YOU'RE SHOOTING JPEG/HEIF

If you're shooting JPEG/HEIF, there's less flexibility when editing, so you need to get your photo as perfect in-camera as possible.

Set White Balance—Make sure the white balance is about right when capturing the photo, using a WB preset (sunny, cloudy, etc.) or custom white balance. If the white balance is completely wrong, it won't be possible to fix it.

Expose Accurately—Overexposure results in clipped highlights (white areas with no detail) and this can't be recovered later. Underexposure results in lots of noise and blocked shadows (black areas with no detail) that can't be recovered.

MIGRATING FROM LIGHTROOM CLASSIC

If you're migrating from Lightroom Classic CC or an earlier Lightroom version, the migration tool makes it easy to move your photos to the cloud without losing the organization and edits done in Lightroom.

ONE-TIME MIGRATION

A word of warning—the migration is a one-way process. Continuing to use and sync Lightroom Classic after migration is not recommended because it won't let you migrate the same catalog again, and not all data syncs, so you'll end up with new metadata or photos orphaned in the Lightroom Classic catalog. Be sure of your decision before migrating.

NOT EVERYTHING MIGRATES

Many Lightroom Classic features don't exist in Lightroom CC. Some of the data gets transferred but remains hidden, and some information simply doesn't transfer.

Data that doesn't transfer to the Lightroom CC catalog includes:

• Folders and folder hierarchy (but you can convert to collections before migrating, which become albums in Lightroom CC).

• Develop History States (but the current Develop settings do transfer).

• Snapshots (but you could manually convert to virtual copies before migrating).

• Custom metadata from plug-ins.

• Creations (books, slideshows, prints and web galleries).

• Map module saved locations (but the GPS data itself does transfer).

• Smart collections.

• Shared web galleries will need to be shared again after migration, so the URL's may change.

Some data gets converted to Lightroom CC's format.

• Color labels become keywords.

• Virtual copies become real copies.

• Collection sets become album folders.

• Collections become albums.

Other data (such as faces) is retained but remains hidden in the underlying catalog, so it's still available if/when the feature is added to Lightroom CC.

WHAT YOU'LL NEED

To run the migration, you'll need:

• Lightroom Classic CC, Lightroom CC 2015 or Lightroom 6. If you're migrating from an earlier Lightroom version (1.0-5.7.1), you must first install a trial of Lightroom Classic CC and allow it to upgrade a copy of your catalog to Lightroom Classic format before running migration.

• On your boot drive (e.g., C:\ or Macintosh HD), you need space for the catalog and smart previews, which can be as much as 20% of the size of your Lightroom Classic catalog and original files.

• The migration process creates a copy

of your images, so you'll need free space for all of the originals, either on the boot drive or on another internal/external hard drive or NAS (network accessible storage). You can set the location of the originals in *Preferences > Local Storage* before opening the migration tool (page 46). This extra space is only needed temporarily, as the local cache can be cleared once the files have safely uploaded.

• Enough cloud storage space to hold all of your photos, otherwise Lightroom won't be able to upload your photos. The Photography Plan includes 20GB or the Lightroom CC plan includes 1TB. If you have a larger library, you can add extra storage space on your account page on Adobe's website.

• You can only migrate each catalog once, so make sure everything's set up before moving forward.

PREPARING YOUR CATALOG IN LIGHTROOM CLASSIC CC

Before you start the migration, there's some prep work to do in Lightroom Classic.

1. Go to *File menu > Optimize Catalog*.

2. Go to *Library menu > Find Missing Photos* to check that all of the originals are available. If some photos are marked as missing, follow the instructions at https://www.Lrq.me/lightroom-photos-missing-fix/ to locate the missing originals.

3. Create a smart collection to search for metadata conflicts. (Criteria is *Other Metadata > Metadata Status > is > Conflict Detected*.)

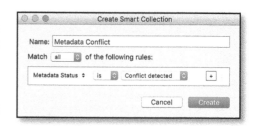

In the smart collection, click on the metadata icon in the corner of each thumbnail to fix the conflict. If you're happy that the catalog's metadata is correct (which is usually the case), click *Overwrite Settings*.

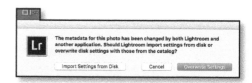

4. If you organize your photos into named folders in Lightroom Classic and wish to retain that organization, create collections/collection sets to replicate your folder structure (up to 4 deep). The quickest way to do this is to right-click on the parent folder and select *Create Collection Set "xxx"*. and repeat until all of your chosen folders have been replicated in the Collections panel.

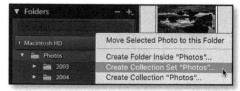

TRANSFERRING PRESETS

Develop presets designed for Lightroom 4 or later will also work in Lightroom CC, so you may want to import your profiles and presets.

1. Create a folder, perhaps on the desktop, to temporarily store the presets and profiles.

2. Copy any DCP format profiles, XMP format profiles and XMP format presets by:

On Windows, open the Start menu search box and type *%appdata%\Adobe\ CameraRaw*.

On macOS, go to *Finder > Go menu > Go to Finder* and paste *~/Library/Application Support/Adobe/CameraRaw*.

Copy the contents of the *CameraProfiles* and *Settings* folders to the folder you just created on the desktop.

3. If you're using Lightroom 6, Lightroom CC 2015, or Lightroom Classic 7.2 or earlier, also...

On Windows, open the Start menu search box and type *%appdata%\Adobe\Lightroom*.

On macOS, go to *Finder > Go menu > Go to Finder* and paste *~/Library/Application Support/Adobe/Lightroom*.

Copy the contents of the *Develop Presets* folder to the folder on the desktop.

4. Check if there's a *Lightroom Settings* folder next to your catalog, and if so, copy the contents of the *Develop Presets* and *Settings* folders to the temporary folder.

5. In Lightroom CC, go to *File menu > Import Profiles & Presets* and navigate to the folder on the desktop, then press *Import*. A progress bar displays at the top of the Preset and Profile Browser panels while they're importing.

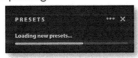

MIGRATING A CATALOG

Now it's time to start the migration itself...

1. Quit Lightroom Classic / Lightroom CC

2015 / Lightroom 6 and open Lightroom CC.

2. In Lightroom CC, select *File menu > Migrate Lightroom Catalog*.

3. In the information dialog that appears, click *Continue*.

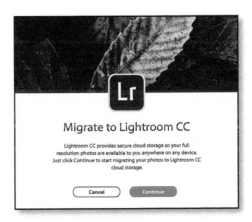

4. Review the information in the Before You Begin dialog and click *Continue*.

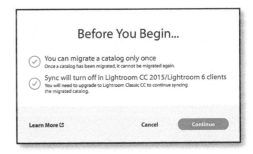

5. Select the catalog that you want to migrate, then click *Start Scan*.

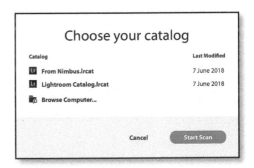

6. Lightroom scans the catalog and

launches the migration tool, displaying a progress bar for you to monitor. This step may take some time to complete, depending on the size of your catalog.

7. Review any exceptions that the migration tool reports, for example, if you don't have enough cloud or local storage space available. If you've prepared your catalog in advance, there may not be any exceptions. Stop and fix the problems, then click *Check Again*, or ignore the exceptions by clicking *Continue Anyway*.

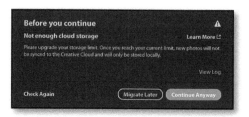

8. Review the information in the Catalog Ready for Migration dialog. If necessary, click *Open Log File* to check the details of any errors. Then click *Start Migration* to begin the migration process.

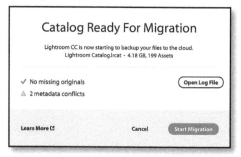

A progress bar is displayed during the migration process. Depending on the catalog size and your computer specifications, this step may take some time to complete (e.g., many hours, or even a few days if you have tens of thousands of photos), as it copies all of the photos into Lightroom CC's own storage space, ready for upload to the cloud.

9. When migration is complete, Lightroom CC displays a confirmation dialog. If there are exceptions, click *Open Log File* to review what went wrong. Otherwise, you're all done, and ready to start using Lightroom CC. Photos may take hours, days or weeks to sync to the cloud, depending on the speed of your internet connection and the number and size of the photos.

10. If you have more than one Lightroom Classic catalog, you can repeat the process. An album folder is created for each catalog, so you can identify the source of the photos.

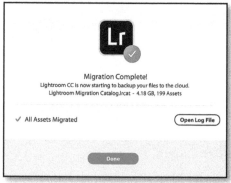

11. Once you're happy that everything's safely in Lightroom CC's storage space and you have a local backup of the originals (page 45), you may choose to delete the Lightroom Classic catalog and photos to free up hard drive space, or move them to a disconnected hard drive as an extra backup.

MIGRATION ERRORS

You may run into errors with the migration, since it's a relatively complex process. The most frequent issues and their solutions are listed at https://www.Lrq.me/migration-errors

SYNCING WITH THE CLOUD

5

Once you've added photos, Lightroom automatically uploads them to the cloud whenever you have an internet connection, and downloads changes made on other devices. The upload prioritizes photos that are flagged or starred, so your most important photos are backed up to the cloud as quickly as possible, and available on your other devices.

Lightroom's smart about minimizing the amount of space it uses on your computer's hard drive, so you don't need to worry too much about file management, but there are a few preferences that you may want to adjust, depending on your usage.

The sync and caching behavior is slightly different, depending on whether you're using a desktop (Windows/Mac) or mobile device (iOS/Android) so we'll look at each in turn.

IN THIS SECTION, WE'LL CONSIDER:

• How to control syncing on the desktop.

• How to control syncing on mobile.

• How to store photos locally for offline use.

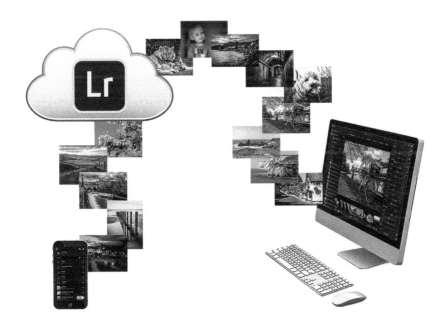

SYNCING ON THE DESKTOP & WORKING OFFLINE

Lightroom handles the syncing and file management, but the desktop apps give you a few options to tailor the sync and local cache to your own needs, depending on your internet connection, available hard drive space, performance priorities, etc.

CHECKING SYNC STATUS

You can check the **overall sync status** by clicking the cloud icon in the top right corner. **Synced and Backed Up** means the local database cache is in sync with the cloud. **Syncing X Photos** means originals and/or edits are currently being synced to/from the cloud.

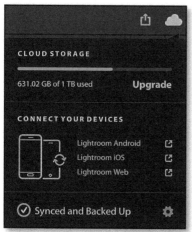

The **sync status of individual photos** displays in the lower right corner of their thumbnail in Square Grid view (page 50).

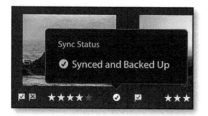

The badge style varies depending on the sync status:

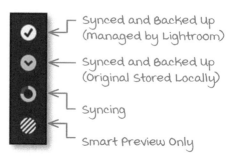

Synced and Backed Up (managed by Lightroom)

Synced and Backed Up (Original Stored Locally)

Syncing

Smart Preview Only

The Sync Status section of the Info panel (page 81) gives further information about the type of file that's stored in the cloud and currently downloaded to your computer.

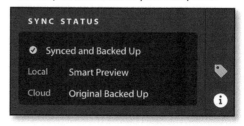

Original refers to the original file format. Lightroom CC uploads all originals to the cloud and downloads them when they're needed, for example, when zooming into 1:1 view or exporting full size files. The originals may also be cached locally, depending on your preference settings and range of behind-the-scenes criteria, such as how recently you've viewed the photo.

A **Smart Preview** is a smaller (2560px) proxy file that can be used in place of the original file for editing when the original isn't available.

If Lightroom says there's only a smart preview in the cloud, it's because you synced the photo using Lightroom Classic CC. In this case, you won't be able to access the full-size original until you add it to Lightroom (page 26).

PAUSING/RESUMING SYNC

If you're on a limited bandwidth connection, for example, on vacation or tethering a mobile phone, or you have a more urgent upload underway, you may want to temporarily pause sync.

To do so, click the cloud icon and float over the sync status line to display the **Pause Syncing** button. Later, return to the same location to resume syncing.

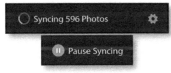

MANAGING THE LOCAL CACHE

Lightroom stores a local copy of the cloud database, along with small previews (and by default, some originals) at:

Windows—C: \ Users \ [your username] \ AppData \ Local \ Adobe \ Lightroom CC \ Data

Mac—Macintosh HD / Users / [username] / Pictures / Lightroom Library.lrlibrary

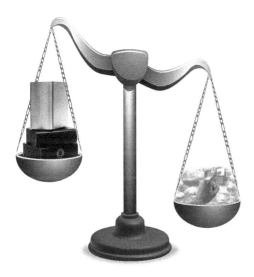

Lightroom automatically manages the amount of space it uses for its local cache, but it's a balancing act. Lightroom can use a larger amount of hard drive space to keep lots of previews and originals locally, or it can save local space by downloading files from the cloud as they're needed.

You can control the balance using the *Use photo cache size equal to X% of your remaining disk space* value in *Preferences > Local Storage.* This determines how much of the available disk space Lightroom can use on your main hard drive.

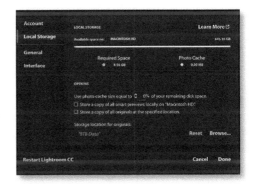

It's a target rather than a hard limit. For example, if you've added new photos that haven't uploaded to the cloud yet, Lightroom may need to use more space than you've specified, at least until it's finished uploading them.

STORING PHOTOS LOCALLY

Although Lightroom is smart about managing its local cache, it gives you some control over which originals are cached locally. There are a few reasons you may want to determine which files are stored locally, including:

Performance—It's usually faster to load a photo or video from a local hard drive than download it from the cloud.

Bandwidth—Working from a local cache means Lightroom doesn't need to download the files from the cloud, reducing your internet usage.

Work Offline—A local cache means you can continue working on your photos without an internet connection.

Backup—While extremely unlikely, something could go wrong with Adobe's servers, so it's worth having a local copy.

You may decide to only store specific albums locally, for example, the albums you're currently working on, or the albums containing your best photos. To mark an album for local storage, right-click on the album and select *Store Album Locally*. Unchecking it reverts to automatic management.

To keep a copy of all originals locally, check the *Store a copy of all originals at the specified location* checkbox in *Preferences > Local Storage*.

The *Store a copy of all smart previews locally on C:/ or Macintosh HD* checkbox retains a local copy of the smaller smart previews. This can be valuable for performance and offline work, especially if you don't have a local cache of all originals.

STORING ORIGINALS ON ANOTHER HARD DRIVE

By default, Lightroom stores any downloaded originals along with its database and preview files in its local cache.

Original photos can take a significant amount of disk space, but you can select another hard drive (e.g., an internal/external hard drive, or a network drive) to avoid filling up your main boot drive. The local database cache and previews still remain on the main hard drive. Only the originals move to your selected location.

To change the location of the original photos, click **Browse** in *Preferences > Local Storage* and navigate to another drive. Lightroom automatically moves any downloaded originals to the new location, so you don't have to do anything else. If you change your mind, the **Reset** button moves the photos back to the main hard drive.

When that location is unavailable (e.g., the external drive is disconnected), Lightroom obviously can't access the originals stored there, so it downloads them from the cloud as needed and stores them in the default location, along with any new photos you add to Lightroom. When you next restart Lightroom with the drive attached, Lightroom automatically moves any originals to your custom location.

BACKING UP THE LOCAL CACHE

If you delete a photo from Lightroom, it's deleted from the cloud and all connected devices. At the time of writing, there's no undo or trash facility to recover deleted photos. Therefore, I'd strongly recommend keeping an additional backup of your originals on another hard drive.

This isn't something that Lightroom handles for you, but standard backup software (such as Windows File History or Apple's Time Machine) can automatically keep a mirrored copy of your originals folder on another hard drive.

SYNCING ON MOBILE & WORKING OFFLINE

Like the desktop apps, Lightroom handles syncing and file management on iOS and Android devices, but there are a couple of preference settings to adapt Lightroom to your own workflow.

CHECKING SYNC STATUS

You can check the **overall sync status** by tapping the sync icon in the top right corner. Initially it tells you how many photos are still syncing, and when it's done, it changes to **Synced and Backed Up**.

PAUSING/RESUMING SYNC

If you're on a limited bandwidth connection, you can temporarily **pause sync**, tap the sync icon in the top right corner and then tap **Pause Syncing** button. Later, return to

the same location to resume syncing.

Syncing photos, especially full size originals, can quickly use up your cellular data allowance, so you may want to limit Lightroom to **WiFi only**. To do so, go to *Settings > Cloud Storage & Sync* (iOS) / *Settings > Preferences* (Android) and toggle **Use Cellular Data** to the left to disable it.

DOWNLOADING PREVIEWS

To minimize the amount of space needed on your mobile device, Lightroom is very selective about what it downloads.

Initially, Lightroom just downloads a local cache of its database, containing a list of your albums and photos.

When you start to view the photos in Grid

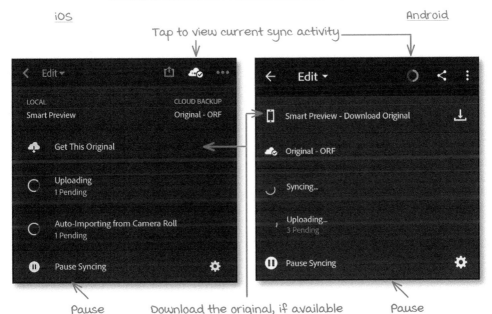

SYNC STATUS (IOS/ANDROID)

iOS

Android

Tap to view current sync activity

Pause

Download the original, if available

Pause

view, Lightroom downloads the thumbnails, and as you flip through the photos in Detail view, it then downloads the smart preview for those photos too.

Lightroom doesn't download the full size original from the cloud unless you do one of two things:

• In Detail view, tap on the sync icon and tap **Get This Original** (iOS) / **Download Original** (Android).

• You've disabled **Only Download Smart Previews** in *Settings > Cloud Storage & Sync* (iOS) / *Preferences > Settings* (Android) and you then view the photos in Detail view or store the album locally. (For screenshots of the various Settings screens, see page 298 for iOS or page 300 for Android.)

CACHING FILES TO WORK OFFLINE

If you're going to be offline, you can store albums locally, so you can still view and edit the photos without an internet connection by downloading them in advance.

Go to Organize view and tap the ... icon next to the album you wish to store locally, then select **Store Locally**. The photos download while you still have an internet connection, and the album cover photo is marked with a small blue arrow when the download is complete.

RECLAIMING SPACE

You can check how much space Lightroom's using on your device by going to *Settings > Local Storage* (iOS) / *Settings > Device Info & Storage* (Android).

On your Android device, you can make more space by moving the Lightroom data to your expansion storage (SD card). To do so, go to *Settings > Device Info & Storage > **Use SD Card***. (Unfortunately there isn't a similar option for iOS, due to operating system limitations.)

If you need to **clear some space** on your device, you can clear Lightroom's cache using the **Clear Cache** buttons. This only clears cached files that are already safely in the cloud, so you don't need to worry about originals that haven't uploaded yet.

It also retains any albums marked to store locally. To **clear the locally stored albums** on iOS, select the album's ... icon again and select *Disable Store Locally* and then *Clear Cache* from the same menu. On Android, select the album's ... icon and toggle *Store Locally* off. Then go to *Settings > Device Info & Storage > Manage Storage*, check the albums you want to clear and tap *Clear*.

VIEWING & ORGANIZING

6

Having added your photos to Lightroom, you naturally want to view them, and you probably want to start organizing them too.

On the desktop, click the *My Photos* button in the left panel bar or press the P key to show the My Photos panel. On mobile, select the Organize view, which is the first view you see when you open Lightroom.

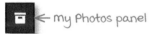 ← my Photos panel

Select **All Photos** to display all of your photos in the central preview area (desktop) / Grid view (mobile). *All Photos* is useful for scrolling through your photos or searching.

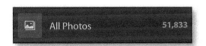

Your photos are automatically organized by the date they were captured. You can also choose to group specific photos into albums, album folders and stacks, so you can easily find them again later.

The Grid views allow you to view thumbnails of multiple photos, whereas the Detail view displays a much larger view of a photo, so you can take a closer look and zoom in to check it's perfectly in focus.

IN THIS SECTION, WE'LL CONSIDER:

• How to view your photos and videos in Grid and Detail views.

• How to change the sort order.

• How to select multiple photos.

• How to view photos grouped by date.

• How to group photos into albums.

• How to group similar photos into stacks.

• How to delete photos (carefully!)

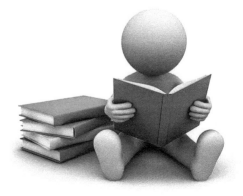

GRID VIEWS & SELECTIONS ON THE DESKTOP

The Grid views allow you to view and select multiple photos at once, so you can see them in context and quickly scroll through them, looking for specific photos.

GRID VIEW OPTIONS

There are two kinds of grid view—the Photo Grid and the Square Grid. To **switch between the Grid views**, use the buttons in the toolbar below the grid or press the G key.

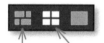

Photo Grid   Square Grid

The **Photo Grid** displays the photos in a mosaic pattern. It's a distraction-free view that doesn't waste any space, but vertical photos are smaller than horizontal photos, and panoramic photos can appear stretched.

The **Square Grid** view displays the photos in a grid of square cells with extra icons showing useful information, such as flags, stars, keywords and sync status.

The **size of the thumbnails** can be changed using the slider at the bottom of the grid.

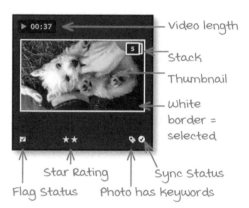

Video length
Stack
Thumbnail
White border = selected
Star Rating   Sync Status
Flag Status   Photo has Keywords

CHANGING THE SORT ORDER

You can change the order of the photos, for example, to see your vacation photos in the order that they were captured.

To **change the sort order**, click the sort order button in the toolbar below the grid. The options are:

Capture Date sorts the photos by capture date/time. If multiple photos were captured in the same second, the file name is used as a secondary sort to ensure they're in the right order.

Photo Grid   Square Grid

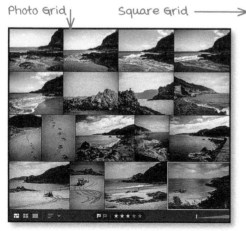

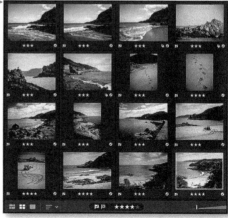

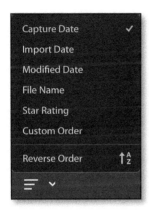

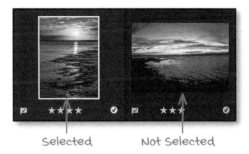

SELECTING PHOTOS

In the Grid views, you can select the photos you want to view, edit and share. Selected photos have a white border.

Selected   Not Selected

Import Date sorts the photos based on when you added them to Lightroom.

Modified Date sorts the photos based on whether you've changed their metadata or edited them.

File Name sorts the photos based on their file name.

Star Rating sorts the photos based on their star rating, from 0-5.

Custom Order displays the photos in a manual sort order for the album. At the time of writing, you can't drag and drop the photos into a custom sort order using the Windows/Mac apps, but you can do so using the iOS app, which then syncs back to the desktop.

To **reverse the sort order**, for example, from oldest to newest photos first, select **Reverse Order**.

If you select multiple photos in Grid view, your actions apply to all of the selected photos. For example, you can select 10 photos and add your copyright or star rating to them all in one go.

When you switch to the Detail view (page 53), most actions only affect the single photo you're viewing. (A few functions, such as saving edited photos to your hard drive, apply to all photos regardless of view mode.)

To **select one photo**, simply click on it, and the border becomes highlighted in white.

To **select a consecutive series of photos**, click on the first thumbnail, hold down the Shift key and click on last thumbnail in the series.

GRID VIEW TOOLBAR (WINDOWS/MAC)

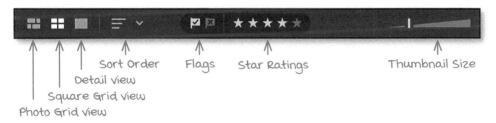

Photo Grid view
Square Grid view
Detail view
Sort Order   Flags   Star Ratings   Thumbnail Size

To **select multiple scattered photos**, click on the first thumbnail, hold down the Ctrl key (Windows) / Cmd key (Mac) and click on each of the other thumbnails, so they all have white borders.

To **select all** of the photos in the current view, go to *Edit menu > Select All* or use the keyboard shortcut Ctrl-A (Windows) / Cmd-A (Mac).

If the photos are already selected, you can deselect them, removing the white border.

To **deselect one or more photos**, hold down the Ctrl key (Windows) / Cmd key (Mac) and click on the thumbnails.

To **deselect all photos**, go to *Edit menu > Select None* or use the keyboard shortcut Ctrl-D (Windows) / Cmd-D (Mac).

DETAIL VIEW & ZOOMING ON THE DESKTOP

The Detail view displays a much larger view of the photo, so you can see every detail.

To **switch to Detail view**, click the button on the toolbar or press the D key. You can move between photos using the left/right arrow keys on your keyboard.

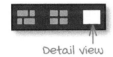

Detail view

FILMSTRIP

Below the main Detail preview is the Filmstrip, which displays thumbnails of your photos. This allows you to select a different photo without returning to the Grid view or using the keyboard.

To **show or hide the Filmstrip**, click the button in the toolbar or use the / shortcut.

Right-click on the Filmstrip to select *Filmstrip Style > Photo* or *Filmstrip Style >*

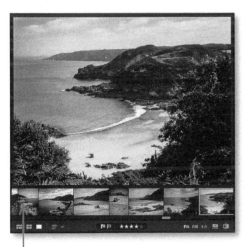

The Filmstrip has two styles:

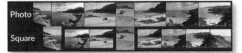

The Detail view toolbar is the same as Grid view, except the Thumbnail Size slider is replaced with these buttons:

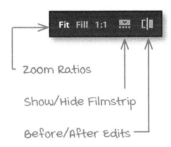

Zoom Ratios

Show/Hide Filmstrip

Before/After Edits

Square from the context-sensitive menu to **change the Filmstrip style**.

ZOOMING IN

To **zoom in** to see more detail, click the *1:1* button in the toolbar or press the Spacebar. Click *Fit* to zoom out again, or press the Spacebar again.

Fit view fits the whole photo in the preview area.

Fill fills the preview area, hiding parts of the photo.

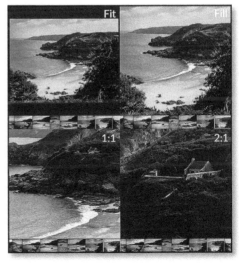

1:1 displays the individual pixels. This is called 100% zoom in some apps.

2:1 view can only be accessed using the keyboard shortcuts.

The Spacebar shortcut just toggles between the last two zoom ratios you clicked on, whereas the Ctrl = (Windows) / Cmd = (Mac) and Ctrl - (Windows) / Cmd - (Mac) shortcuts zoom in and out through all four zoom ratios.

When you're zoomed in, click and drag the photo to move it around to see hidden sections of the photo. If you're using an editing tool, such as the brush (page 208), hold down the Spacebar key while clicking and dragging.

PLAYING VIDEOS

Most photographers shoot short video clips on their mobile phones, even if they're not "into video."

While Lightroom is primarily designed for photographs, it is able to store and play many popular video formats.

The videos are identified using a small icon and timestamp at the top of the thumbnails.

When you open a video into Detail view, a play button appears in the center of the preview.

To **play the video**, click the triangular play button. Additional video controls appear below, allowing you to pause and scrub through the video timeline.

VIDEO PLAYBACK (WINDOWS/MAC)

Play/Pause

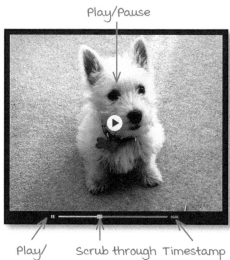

Timestamp on thumbnail

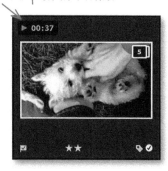

Play/Pause   Scrub through video   Timestamp

VIEWING PHOTOS ON A MOBILE DEVICE

Viewing photos in the iOS/Android apps follows the same principles, but because the interface is small, the panels are replaced with a series of screens, as demonstrated on page 22.

As you'll know the basics of your own phone/tablet operating system, we'll just cover a few less obvious features...

ORGANIZE VIEW

Like the Photos panel on the left of the Windows/Mac apps, the Organize view (illustrated on page 66 and page 67) allows you to organize your photos into albums and album folders. We'll come back to managing albums on page 63, but for now, tap on *All Photos* and we'll start viewing some of your photos.

GRID VIEW OPTIONS

Using the Grid view (illustrated on page 57 and page 58), you can view multiple photos, filter them and change the sort order.

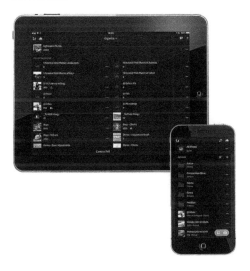

On iOS, you can change the **thumbnail size** by going to ... *menu > View Options > Small/Normal/Large Thumbnails.* If you two-finger tap on the thumbnails, you can cycle through a series of **metadata overlays**. (These features aren't currently available on Android.)

CHANGING THE SORT ORDER

To **change the sort order**, click the ... icon in Grid view to show the menu, then select *Sort by ....* In the following menu, you can select the sort order of your choice. To **reverse the sort order**, for example, from oldest to newest photos first, select *Reverse Order*.

On mobile, you can manually rearrange the photos into a **custom sort order**. Select *Custom* from the Sort menu, then tap *Edit* (iOS) / pencil icon (Android).

On iOS, tap photos to select them, then hold your finger on one of the selected photos and drag them to a new location between two photos. Tap *Done* when you're finished.

On Android, hold your finger on a photo and drag it to a new location between two photos, then release your finger. (You can only move one photo at a time on Android.) Press the X to return to Grid view.

DETAIL VIEW

The Detail views (illustrated on page 59 and page 60) are used for viewing and editing photos. It's split into 5 (iOS) / 3 (Android) view modes, each designed for different tasks.

Rate & Review mode is used for viewing photos and adding flags and star ratings (page 59).

Info view displays photo metadata and allows you to add a Title and Caption (page 82).

Keywords view on iOS allows you to view, add and delete keywords. On Android, keywords are found at the bottom of the Info view (page 82).

Edit view gives you access to all of the profiles, presets and sliders, as well as the crop and selective editing tools (page 121).

Activity view is only available on iOS. It shows likes and comments from shared web galleries (page 289).

To **view a photo in Detail view**, tap on it in the grid. To **zoom in or out**, double-tap on the photo, or use a spread/pinch gesture.

On tablets, there's a filmstrip at the bottom of the Detail views, to allow you to view and select nearby photos without returning to the Grid view. You can **show/hide the filmstrip** using the Filmstrip button.

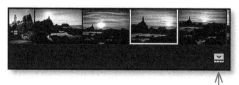

Show/Hide Filmstrip

The Filmstrip is also available in Rate & Review mode on iPhones, and you can show/hide it by going to ... *menu > Show/Hide Filmstrip*.

The iOS app can **play videos** imported from the device or downloaded from the cloud. Tap the play button in the center of the screen, or scrub along the timeline at the bottom of the screen. (This feature is not currently available on Android.)

SELECTING PHOTOS

On mobile, you can't select multiple photos to apply the same action to all of them at once, for example, to add the same keyword to multiple photos. However, there are a few things you can do to multiple photos, including:

• copy or move photos between albums

• remove photos from albums

• delete photos from the cloud

• share or save photos

Hold your finger on a photo in Grid view to **activate selection mode** (or go to ... *menu > Select*). Tap the photos to select them, or hold a finger down on a photo and then swipe across other photos to select multiple, and then tap an icon at the bottom (iOS) / top (Android) of the screen to share, remove, delete, or add/copy them to other albums.

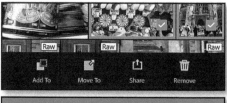

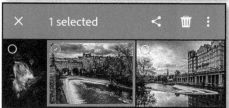

GRID VIEW (IOS)

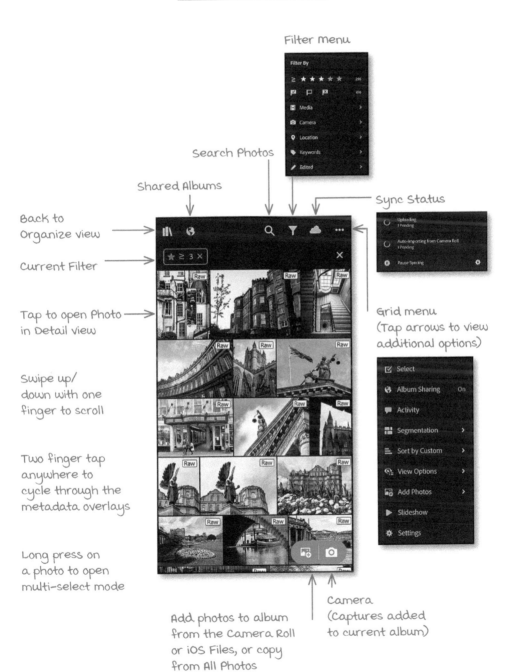

Filter menu

Search Photos

Shared Albums

Sync Status

Back to
Organize view

Current Filter

Tap to open Photo
in Detail view

Grid menu
(Tap arrows to view
additional options)

Swipe up/
down with one
finger to scroll

Two finger tap
anywhere to
cycle through the
metadata overlays

Long press on
a photo to open
multi-select mode

Camera
(Captures added
to current album)

Add photos to album
from the Camera Roll
or iOS Files, or copy
from All Photos

GRID VIEW (ANDROID)

Filter menu

Search Photos

Back to
Organize view

Album Name

Grid menu
(Tap arrows to view
additional options)

Tap to open Photo
in Detail view

Swipe up/
down with one
finger to scroll

Long press on
a photo to open
multi-select mode

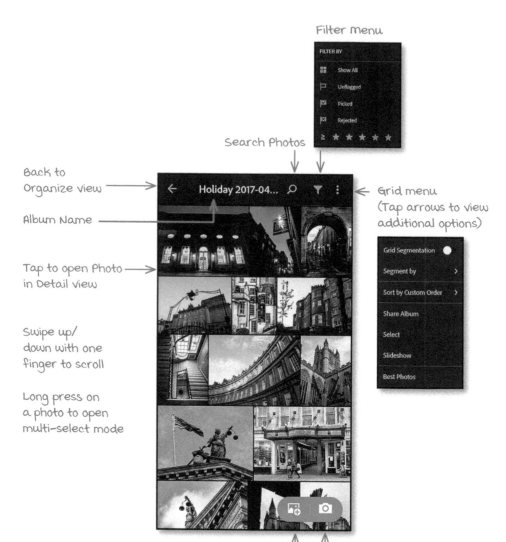

Camera
(Captures added
to current album)

Add photos to album
from the Device or
copy from All Photos

DETAIL VIEW (IOS)

Share menu

Sync Status

Tap to switch between Edit, Info, Keywords, Rate & Review and Activity views

Back to Grid view →

Two finger tap anywhere to cycle through metadata overlay & histogram, metadata only, histogram only or neither

One finger tap on metadata cycles metadata views

Swipe left <> right on the photo with one finger to view the next/ previous photo

Double-tap anywhere or pinch/spread to zoom in and out

Tap on the photo to hide controls

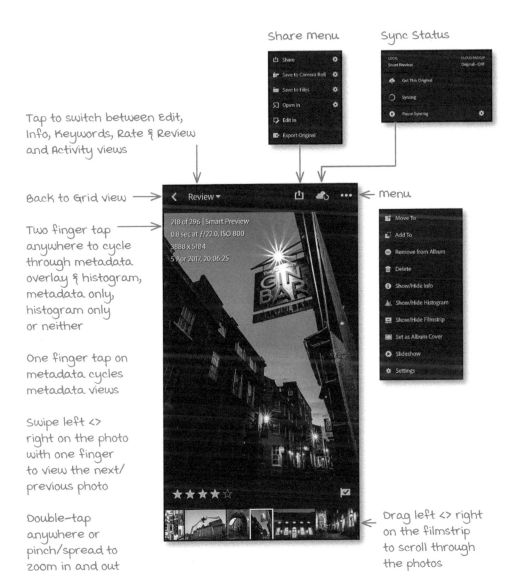

← menu

Drag left <> right on the filmstrip to scroll through the photos

DETAIL VIEW (ANDROID)

Sync Status

Share menu

Tap to switch between Edit, Info and Rate & Review views

Back to Grid view →

Enable metadata or histogram in the menu

One finger tap on metadata cycles metadata views

Swipe left <> right on the photo with one finger to view the next/ previous photo

Double-tap anywhere or pinch/spread to zoom in and out

Tap on the photo to hide controls

← menu

Drag left <> right on the filmstrip to scroll through the photos

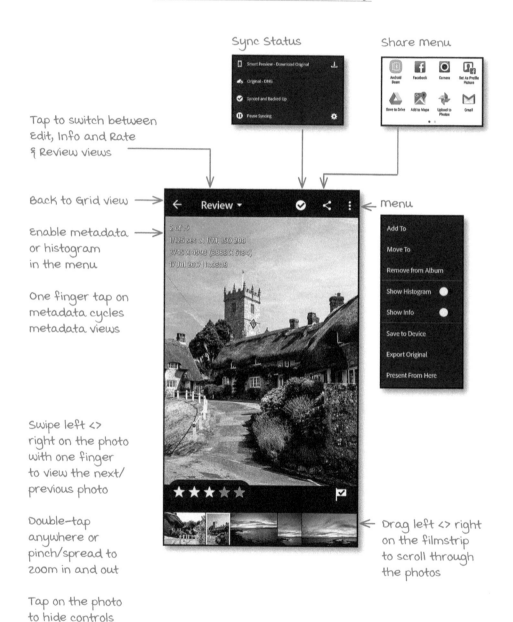

VIEWING PHOTOS GROUPED BY DATE

If you remember the date, month or even just the year that a photo was taken, you can use that information to narrow down the photos in the current view, rather than having to scroll through everything.

DATE VIEWS ON THE DESKTOP

On the desktop, beneath the *All Photos* view, Lightroom automatically groups the photos by date.

Recently Added displays the photos added during your five most recent imports. This is useful when you've just added photos shot on multiple dates.

By Date groups your photos by the date they were captured. You can display the entire year, month, or narrow it down to a specific day. This is particularly useful when you remember when you shot a photo, for example, the date of your wedding or vacation.

Click on the text or number to **display the photos captured in that year** or month, or click on the arrow to collapse/expand sub-dates.

To **display photos from multiple dates** at once, for example, multiple vacation days, click on one date and then either hold down Ctrl (Windows) / Cmd (Mac) and click on each of the other dates, or hold down the Shift key and click on the first and last dates in the series.

If you're already viewing a photo, and want to see other photos captured on the same date, right-click on the photo and select *Show Photos from Same Date*.

SEGMENTED VIEW ON MOBILE

On mobile, if you go to the *All Photos* collection, you can **segment the grid by date** (or other metadata).

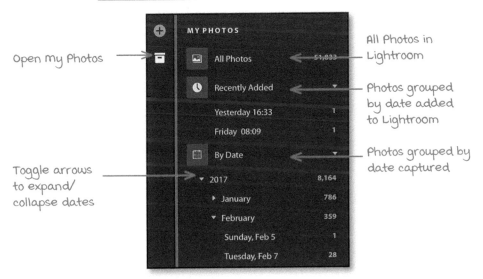

VIEW BY DATE (WINDOWS/MAC)

Open my Photos

Toggle arrows
to expand/
collapse dates

All Photos in
Lightroom

Photos grouped
by date added
to Lightroom

Photos grouped by
date captured

On iOS, tap the ... menu icon, select *Segmentation* and then select *Auto, Years, Months, Days, Hours, Flags, Star Ratings or File Types.*

On Android, tap the ... menu and toggle *Grid Segmentation,* then go to *Segment by...* to select the time period.

Tap the arrow on the right to collapse or expand individual segments.

VIEW BY DATE (IOS/ANDROID)

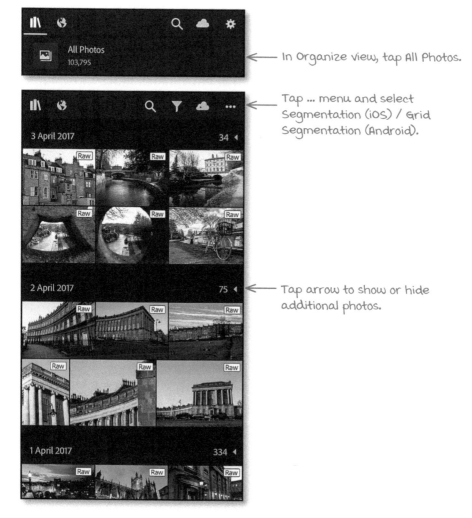

In Organize view, tap All Photos.

Tap ... menu and select Segmentation (iOS) / Grid Segmentation (Android).

Tap arrow to show or hide additional photos.

GROUPING PHOTOS IN ALBUMS

In the left panel group on the desktop, or in Organize view on mobile, are your albums. Albums allow you to group photos for a specific purpose, for example:

- Your best photos as a portfolio.

- Photos to share with someone, perhaps as an online gallery.

- Photos of an event, such as a vacation.

- Photos of specific genre.

- Photos you've published on social media.

- Photos for output as a slideshow, prints, or a photobook.

The same photo can appear in lots of different albums. Even if a photo is not in an album, it's still available in the *All Photos* and *By Date* views.

CREATING ALBUMS

To **create an album**, click/tap the **+** button at the top of the panel, select *Create Album*, then give the album a name.

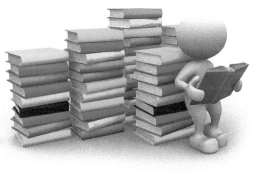

If you have a folder selected, you can place the album inside that folder by checking the *Inside folder* checkbox (desktop only). On mobile, the new album is automatically added to the selected folder. Folders are a way of grouping related albums, for example, family vacations. We'll come back to folders later in the lesson.

While creating an album on the desktop, you can also choose to include any photos that are currently selected.

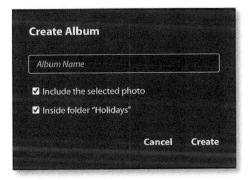

Create Album

Album Name

☑ Include the selected photo
☑ Inside folder "Holidays"

Cancel   Create

To **add photos to an existing album** on the desktop, select the photos in Grid view (or in the Filmstrip) and drag them to the album in the Albums panel.

On mobile, hold your finger on a photo in Grid view to activate selection mode (or go to ... *menu > Select*). Tap the photos to select them, or hold a finger on a photo and then swipe across other photos to select multiple photos. On iOS, tap the *Add To* button, or on Android, tap the ... menu and select *Add To*. Finally, select the target album, and tap *Add*.

If you're viewing an album on iOS/Android, there's an additional *Move To* option that removes the photos from the current album while adding them to a different album, which can be handy if you have an album of photos you need to sort into topic-based albums.

MANAGING ALBUMS

Your photo groupings are likely to change over time, so you'll need to know how to remove photos and manage the albums.

If you're viewing a photo on the desktop, check the Info panel to see **which albums contain that photo.** Click on an album name to view the rest of the album.

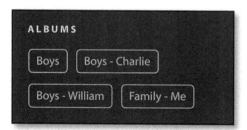

To **remove photos from an album** on the desktop, select the photos in the Grid view, then right-click and choose *Remove Photos* or press the Delete key.

On mobile, hold your finger on a photo in Grid view to activate selection mode, select the photos and then tap the trashcan icon and select *Remove from Album.*

Remove from Album just removes the photos from the selected album, but the photo remains available in the *All Photos* and *Date* views, as well as in any other albums that contained the photo. *Delete*, on the other hand, actually deletes the photos everywhere (page 70), so be careful to select the right option!

All of these *Remove from Album* options are also available in Detail view, but only apply to single photos.

To **delete an album**, right-click on the album (desktop) / tap the album's ... menu (mobile) and select *Delete*. This deletes the album, but not the photos inside the album.

To **rename an album**, right-click on the album (desktop) / tap the album's ... menu (mobile) and select *Rename*, then type the new name.

If the album name is too long to display in the Albums panel (desktop) / Organize view (mobile), float the mouse cursor over the album name to show the full name in a tooltip on the desktop, or rotate your mobile device to horizontal view.

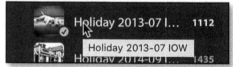

To **change the cover photo** on the desktop, click on the album, then right-click on a photo in Grid view and choose *Set as Album Cover*. On iOS, select the photo in a Detail view (e.g., Rate & Review), tap the ... menu and select *Set as Album Cover*. On Android, hold your finger on the photo in Grid view to select it, then tap the ... menu and choose *Set as Cover*.

The cover photos always show on mobile, but to **show/hide the cover photos** on the desktop (in order to minimize the vertical height required), click the view buttons at the top of the Albums panel.

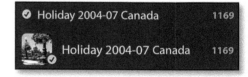

Album Names vs. Names & Cover Photos

GROUPING ALBUMS IN FOLDERS

As your list of albums grows, it can be hard to find specific albums. Like folders on your computer's hard drive, you can group the related albums into folders. For example, you may want to group all of your vacation albums together in a folder, and perhaps create another folder for albums related to your photography projects.

To **create a folder**, click the **+** button, select *Create Folder*, then give the folder a name.

To **move an album into a folder** on the desktop, or to nest folders inside of other folders (up to 5 deep), select it and drag it onto the folder, which turns blue, and release the mouse.

On mobile, tap on the album/folder's ... menu, then select *Move to Folder*. Select the folder to place it inside, then tap *Move*. (You can also create a new folder by clicking the + button, and then select it.)

To **move an album/subfolder out of folders**, and back up to the top of the list, drag the album/subfolder to the left, until a blue bar appears, and then release the mouse.

ALBUMS (WINDOWS/MAC)

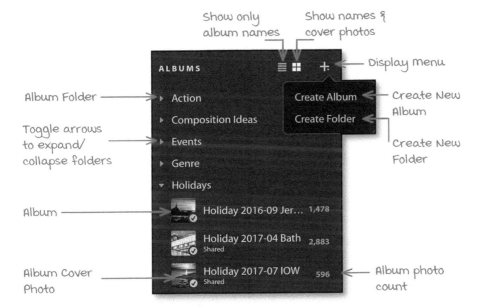

Show only album names

Show names & cover photos

Display menu

Album Folder

Toggle arrows to expand/ collapse folders

Album

Album Cover Photo

Create New Album

Create New Folder

Album photo count

Right-click on folder or album to rename/delete

Right-click on Album to share using Lightroom web

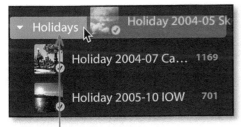

Drop the album/folder on a folder to nest them

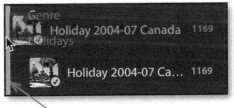

Drag an album/folder to the left to show the blue bar to un-nest them

On mobile, tap on the album/folder's ... menu, then select *Move to Folder*. This time, don't select a folder before tapping *Move*.

To **open/close a folder** to see the albums inside, toggle the arrow to the left of its name (desktop) / tap the folder (mobile).

To **view all of the photos** contained in all of the albums inside a folder, click on the folder name (desktop only).

To **delete a folder**, right-click on the folder (desktop) / tap the folder's ... menu (mobile) and select *Delete*. The folder and any albums inside the folder are deleted, but the photos themselves are not.

ORGANIZE VIEW (IOS)

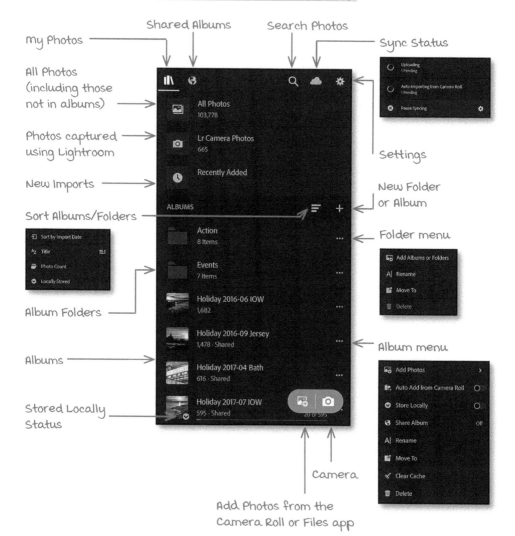

Shared Albums

Search Photos

My Photos

Sync Status

All Photos (including those not in albums)

Photos captured using Lightroom

Settings

New Imports

New Folder or Album

Sort Albums/Folders

Folder menu

Album Folders

Albums

Album menu

Stored Locally Status

Camera

Add Photos from the Camera Roll or Files app

ORGANIZE VIEW (ANDROID)

Settings

Search Photos

Sync Status

All Photos
(including those
not in albums)

Sort Albums/Folders

New Folder
or Album

Folder menu

Album Folders

Albums

Album menu

Stored Locally
Status

Camera

Add Photos from
the Device

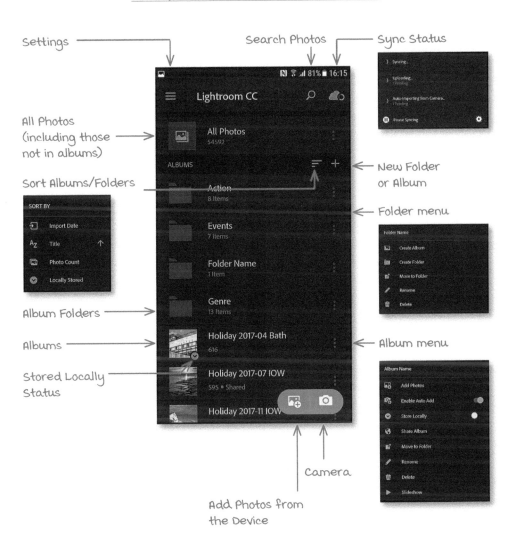

GROUPING PHOTOS USING STACKS

Sometimes you might shoot a series of similar photos, for example:

- A high speed burst to capture action.

- A series of photos to merge into a panorama.

- Bracketed exposures for HDR.

- Raw+JPEG pairs of photos, because you like the in-camera picture style.

- An original photo plus the TIFF you edited in Photoshop.

You may not want to delete the similar photos, but these groups of photos can clutter the grid view, making it hard to see the wood for the trees.

Stacking allows you to group similar photos and display them as a single photo in the Grid view. It's currently only available on the Windows/Mac apps.

MANAGING STACKS

To **stack photos**, select the photos in the Grid, right-click and select *Group into Stack*.

To **view the photos in a stack**, click on

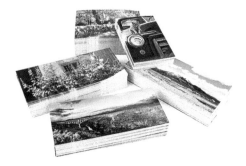

the stack icon. The thumbnails appear in a special Filmstrip at the bottom of the preview area.

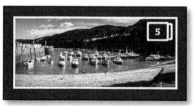

To **view the hidden photos in Detail view**, first open the stack by clicking on the stack icon, then switch to Detail view. The Filmstrip at the bottom of the preview area displays the stacked photos until you collapse the stack.

To **collapse the stack**, click the X button in the Filmstrip, or click the stack icon in the Grid again.

To **ungroup the stack** of photos, changing them back into separate photos, right-click on the collapsed stack and select *Ungroup*.

To **remove one or more photos** from a stack without ungrouping the whole stack, select the photos you want to remove, right-click and select *Remove Photo(s) from Stack* or select the photos and press the Delete key.

To **change the stack cover photo**, which is the one that shows in the main Grid view, right-click on your chosen photo and select *Set as Stack Cover* or drag the thumbnail onto the small square to the left of the stack.

STACKS ARE ALBUM-SPECIFIC

Stacks are album-specific, so stacking photos in one album does not stack them in another.

If you create a stack in *All Photos*, and then

add the stack to an album, it's stacked in the new album too, however the photos aren't automatically stacked in other existing albums.

If you create a stack in an album, it's displayed as a stack in *All Photos*, but not in other albums.

EDITING STACKS

In some situations, your actions affect all of the photos in a stack, whereas other actions only affect the cover photo.

The principle is that organizing tasks (such as adding or removing a stack from an album) apply to the whole stack, whereas editing tasks (metadata edits or slider adjustments) apply only to the cover photo.

To apply metadata to all of the photos inside a stack, you must expand the stack and select the photos and then apply your keyword or other metadata edits.

STACKS (WINDOWS/MAC)

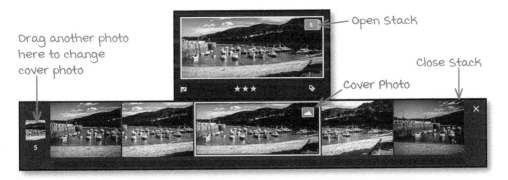

Drag another photo here to change cover photo

Open Stack

Close Stack

Cover Photo

DELETING PHOTOS

Whether your finger slipped, the camera settings were incorrect, or you just missed the moment, some photos simply aren't worth keeping.

While you could mark bad photos as rejects and hide them, completely deleting the really bad photos frees up space on your hard drive and in the cloud.

REMOVE VS. DELETE

In an earlier lesson, we discussed how to remove photos from an album (page 63), and in the last lesson (page 68), how to remove photos from a stack.

It's worth noting the difference in terminology between removing photos and completely deleting them.

Remove just removes the photos from the selected album or stack, but the photo remains available in the *All Photos* and date views.

Delete deletes the photos from the computer and from the cloud, so they're gone forever.

DELETING PHOTOS

On the desktop, to **delete photos completely**, select them, right-click and choose **Delete Photos**, go to *Edit menu > Delete Photos* or use the shortcut Alt-Delete (Windows) / Opt-Delete (Mac), then confirm your choice.

On mobile, hold your finger on a photo to activate multi-select mode (or go to ... *menu > Select*). Tap the photos to select them, or hold a finger down on a photo and then swipe across other photos to select multiple photos, then tap the trashcan icon and select *Delete*.

If you're viewing a single photo in a Detail view on iOS, tap the ... menu and select *Delete*. On Android, tap the Detail view's ... menu, select *Remove from Album* and then choose *Delete*.

The confirmation dialog on desktop, or the bar at the top of the screen on mobile, confirms the number of photos you're deleting. Always double-check this number!

GONE FOREVER!

This is so important, I'm going to repeat myself: The *Delete* command deletes the selected photos from the cloud and all synced devices—everywhere that Lightroom CC controls—and undo won't bring them back. Always double-check you're deleting the right photos, because they'll be gone forever.

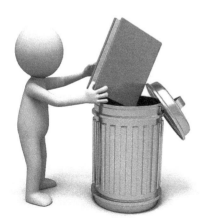

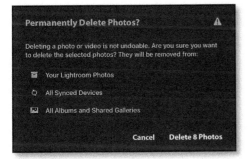

SAFELY DELETING PHOTOS

When you're sorting through photos, don't try to delete one photo at a time. It's inefficient, because you have to keep confirming your decision, and it's easy to make a mistake. Instead, mark them with a reject flag (instructions coming up on page 75), then use Refine View to show only the rejected photos (instructions to follow on page 88), select them all, double-check you definitely want to delete them, then go ahead and delete.

ADDING METADATA & SEARCHING

7

Using the Info and Keyword panels, you can view and add metadata.

To show the Info and Keyword panels on the desktop, click the button in the right panel bar, or press the I key for Info or the K key for Keywords.

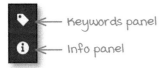

Keywords panel

Info panel

On a mobile device, tap on a photo to open into Detail view, then select the Info or Keywords view from the pop-up at the top of the screen on a phone, or the icons down the sidebar on a tablet.

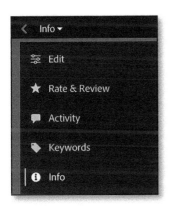

WHAT IS METADATA?

Metadata is often defined as 'data describing data.'

As far as photos are concerned, There are two main types of metadata:

EXIF data is technical information added by the camera at the time of capture. It includes camera and lens information such as the make and model, and image information such as the capture date/time, shutter speed, aperture, ISO, and pixel dimensions.

IPTC data is added by the photographer to describe the photo, for example, title, caption, keywords and the photographer's

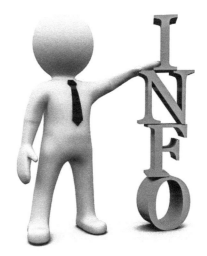

name and copyright.

Lightroom also stores all of your edits as metadata, which means that it records your changes as a set of text instructions (e.g., *Exposure +0.33, Highlights −30, Shadows +25,* etc.) instead of applying them directly to the image data. This means you can edit the photo again later without degrading the image quality.

WHY VIEW & ADD METADATA?

Metadata can help you find photos again later and examining the camera settings can also help you learn to become a better photographer. For example, if you find blur caused by movement in a photo, your shutter speed was too slow, or if the photo is too noisy (grainy), check the ISO value.

IMAGE ANALYSIS

In addition to the metadata you add manually, Adobe's computers scan your images looking for recognizable content. Like any artificial intelligence, it's not perfect, but it allows you to search for photos even if you haven't manually added metadata to describe the content.

IN THIS SECTION, WE'LL CONSIDER:

• How to flag and star rate photos.

• How to view metadata added by the camera.

• How to add titles, captions and copyright.

• How to view and add location metadata.

• How to add keywords.

• How to use Lightroom's image-analysis to search for specific subjects, without having to manually add metadata to the photos.

• How to refine the current view based on your flags or star ratings, keywords, camera models, locations and more.

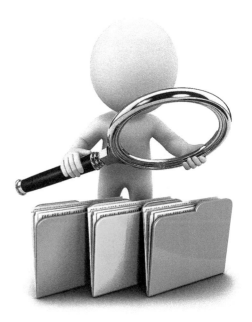

FLAGGING OR STAR RATING PHOTOS

Marking the best photos with flags or star ratings makes them easy to find again later.

WHICH PHOTOS ARE WORTH KEEPING?

How you decide which photos are deserving of a specific ranking is a personal decision, but there are a few questions that may help:

- Does the photo immediately grab you?

- Does the photo trigger a strong emotion or a memory?

- Does the photo tell a story or capture a special moment?

- Do you have a similar photo that's better?

- Is the subject (person/animal) making eye contact? Does it capture their personality?

- Are there significant technical issues, for example, is it in focus?

Move fast and don't agonize over decisions. Your gut instinct is often right.

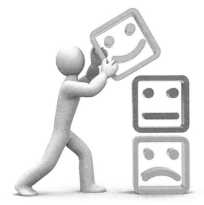

FLAGS VS. STARS

Lightroom offers two different ways of ranking your photos:

Flags have three different states—flagged (picked), unflagged and rejected. Most people use flags to mean:

- ○ Flagged—photos worth keeping

- ○ Unflagged—not sorted yet

- ○ Rejected—to be deleted

Star Ratings are used by photographers worldwide. Most use 5 stars for their very best portfolio images and 0 stars for unsorted photos.

APPLYING FLAGS OR STARS ON THE DESKTOP

There are multiple ways of applying a flag or star rating. On the desktop, these include:

- Click the icons in the toolbar beneath the photo in Grid or Detail view.

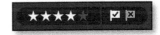

- Click the icons on the thumbnail border in Square Grid view. The icons appear as you float the mouse cursor over the border.

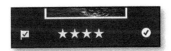

- Use the keyboard shortcuts: Z to flag, U to unflag, X to reject. 0-5 for 0-5 stars.

APPLYING FLAGS OR STARS ON MOBILE

On mobile, tap on a photo to open into a Detail view, then select the Rate & Review view from the pop-up at the top of the screen on mobile phones, or the star icon in the sidebar on tablets. You can then:

• Tap the icons in the toolbar beneath the photo in Grid or Detail view.

• Swipe up/down on the left of the screen for stars or on the right for flags.

• If you have an external keyboard connected, you can use the keyboard shortcuts: P to flag, U to unflag, X to reject and 0-5 for 0-5 stars.

BEST PHOTOS

If you're using an Android device (or the web interface), you can also try out a technology preview called Best Photos. This Adobe Sensei-based artificial intelligence analyzes your photos and tries to figure out which it thinks are your best photos.

It's not enabled by default, so go to *Settings > Technology Previews* and enable *Best Photos*.

To **see Lightroom's recommendations**, go to an album's Grid view and select ... *menu > Best Photos*. Lightroom analyzes the photos and then displays a grid of thumbnails. At the bottom is a slider to increase or decrease the number of photos it finds.

BEST PHOTOS (ANDROID)

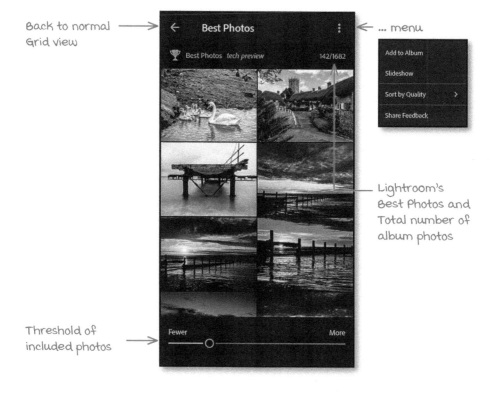

Back to normal Grid view

... menu

Lightroom's Best Photos and Total number of album photos

Threshold of included photos

If you agree with Lightroom's selection of photos, tap the ... *menu* and select *Add to Album* to create an album of these photos. Alternatively, you can tap on a photo to open it into Detail view to assign a star rating.

Flexibility is a wonderful thing, but so much choice can be confusing, so I've included my tried and tested desktop rating workflow on the following pages to help you get started.

RATING WORKFLOW

Everyone has a different system. Some photographers use Grid view and others prefer Detail view. Some like to rate their photos in a single pass, and others like multiple passes. Some like flags and some prefer stars. Whatever you pick, just be consistent.

MY RATINGS MEAN...

	meaning	What's Next...
⚑	Really bad photo worthy of deletion	Nothing (deleted)
★	Should be deleted really, but I'm a packrat	Nothing (ignored)
★★	Triggers a memory, but not great as a photo. The hotel room, a meal out with friends, etc.	A fast edit and a few keywords. They might end up in a photo book or slide show, but they'll never be great photos in their own right
★★★	A decent photo I'd be willing to show someone	
★★★★	Good photo, might end up on the wall or social media	A careful edit, possibly some Photoshop work, titles/captions and more extensive keywords. These are the photos that will end up on the wall or on social media
★★★★★	Best photos I've ever taken. Rare!	

MY DESKTOP RATING WORKFLOW

STEP I—FIND THE BEST AND WORST PHOTOS

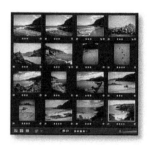

Start off in Grid view with large thumbnails.
It's easier to make decisions when you're
not bogged down in the details

Just flag or reject the ones you really like
or don't like. Leave the rest unflagged

  z Z Z₂.

"Yeah, keep that!"   "Boring..."   "Ooops!"

STEP 2—DELETE THE REALLY BAD ONES

Click the Refine View button
to show the filters   ◀— Refine view

Click the Rejected button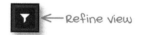

Select all (Ctrl-A / Cmd-A)

Go to Edit menu > Delete Photos to delete them
from your computer and the cloud (page 70)

STEP 3—HIDE THE PHOTOS THAT DON'T EXCITE YOU

Click the Reset button to clear the previous filter   **Reset**

Click the Unflagged button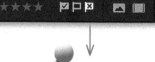

Select all (Ctrl-A / Cmd-A)

Press the number I key to give them I star,
meaning that you'll keep them for now,   ⭐
but not waste further time on them

STEP 4—GO BACK THROUGH THE GOOD ONES

Click the Reset button to
clear the previous filter

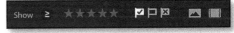

Click the flagged button to
show only flagged photos

Go back through the Flagged photos
again, occasionally switching to
Detail view to check focus

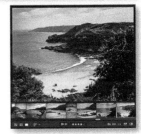

Press the number 2, 3 or 4 keys to
give them 2, 3 or 4 stars, depending
on how much you love the photo

"It's a bad photo but
it sparks a memory
or tells the story."

⭐⭐

"I like that!"

⭐⭐⭐

"I LOVE that! I'd hang
that on my wall!"

⭐⭐⭐⭐

STEP 5—ALLOW TIME TO PASS

Some months later, go back through
the 3 and 4 star photos and see if any
need to be upgraded or downgraded

It's easier to make an objective
decision when time has passed

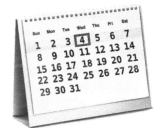

ADDING TITLES, CAPTIONS & COPYRIGHT

Some photographers like to add descriptive text to the photos to remind them of the story behind the photo.

The **Title** and **Caption** fields do have official IPTC definitions (http://www.iptc.org/), but many photographers simply use *Title* for a short image title (e.g., "Blue Eyes") and *Caption* for a more descriptive paragraph (e.g., "Kanika, the Amur Leopard cub, has piercing blue eyes").

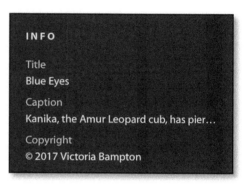

APPLYING METADATA

To **open the Info panel**, click the i button in the right panel bar (desktop/tablet), press the I key (desktop) or select **Info** from the pop-up at the top of a Detail view (phone).

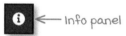 Info panel

To **add metadata** to a single photo, simply type in the Info panel and press Enter to confirm.

To **add the same metadata to multiple photos**, first select the photos in Grid view (desktop only), and then type the metadata in the Info panel.

Some cameras automatically add text into a metadata field, for example, Olympus cameras add *OLYMPUS DIGITAL CAMERA* as the caption. To **delete the metadata from multiple photos**, select them in Grid view (desktop only), click in the *Caption* field and delete the text.

ADDING COPYRIGHT

It's important to add your copyright to your photos. While it doesn't prevent theft, it does make it easy to identify you as the photographer, especially if you post the photos online.

In many countries, the **Copyright** notice requires the copyright symbol ©, the year of first publication and then the name of the copyright owner, for example, © *2018 Victoria Bampton*. Copyright laws vary by country, so please check your local laws for exact specifications.

You can have your copyright automatically applied to photos as you add them to Lightroom, so you don't forget. On the desktop, check *Preferences > General > Add copyright to imported images*. It's smart enough to only add copyright to new photos that don't have an existing copyright entry. For the equivalent setting on iOS, go to *Settings > General > Add Copyright*, or on Android, go to *Settings > Preferences > Photo Import Options > Add Copyright*.

But how do you type that © symbol? On the desktop, it's automatically entered for you. If you accidentally delete it, type Ctrl-Alt-C (Windows) / Opt-G (Mac). On iOS, you can type (c) followed by a space, and it's automatically converted. On Android, the copyright symbol may be found with the emojis or symbols on some third-party keyboards, or you can simply do a web search for *copyright symbol* and copy/paste from a web page.

PHOTO INFO/METADATA (WINDOWS/MAC)

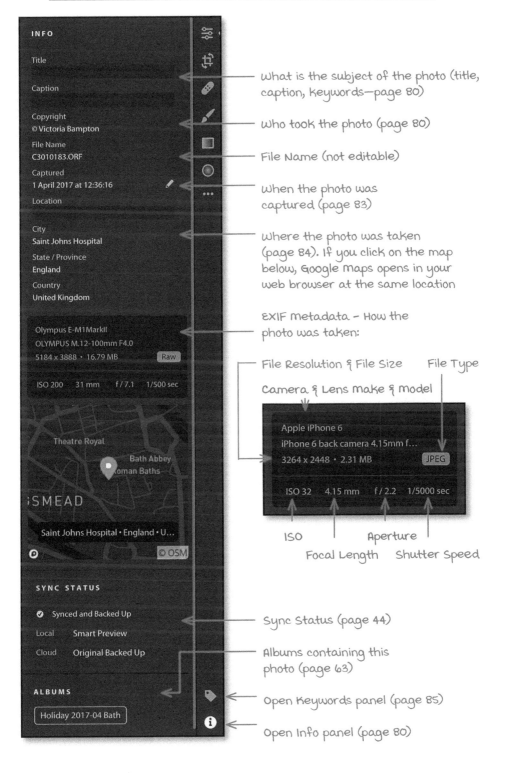

What is the subject of the photo (title, caption, keywords—page 80)

Who took the photo (page 80)

File Name (not editable)

When the photo was captured (page 83)

Where the photo was taken (page 84). If you click on the map below, Google Maps opens in your web browser at the same location

EXIF metadata – How the photo was taken:

File Resolution & File Size   File Type

Camera & Lens make & model

ISO

Aperture

Focal Length   Shutter Speed

Sync Status (page 44)

Albums containing this photo (page 63)

Open Keywords panel (page 85)

Open Info panel (page 80)

PHOTO INFO/METADATA (IOS/ANDROID)

iOS

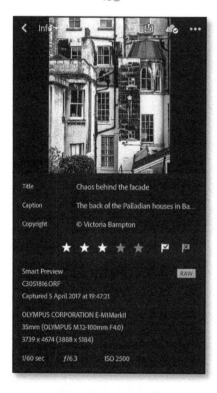

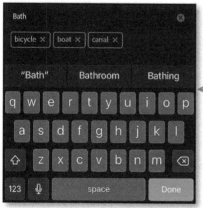

Android

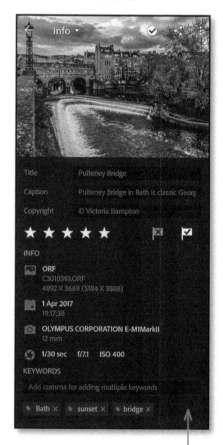

On iOS, keywords are in a separate view mode

On Android, keywords are at the bottom of the Info view

FIXING THE CAPTURE DATE & TIME

We've all done it... you go on vacation abroad, or Daylight Savings Time starts, and you forget to change the time stamp on the camera. It's not a problem though, as Lightroom on the desktop makes it easy to correct the time stamp. (This isn't currently available on mobile.)

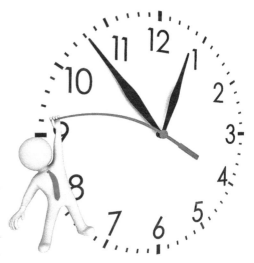

STEP-BY-STEP

1. Select the photos in the Photo Grid or Square Grid.

2. Go to *Photo menu > Edit Date & Time* or click the pencil icon next to the date field in the Info panel.

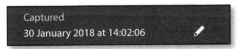

Captured
30 January 2018 at 14:02:06

3. In the Shift Date Range dialog, enter the correct date and time for the most recent photo in the selection. Other selected photos automatically shift by the same increment, rather than all being set to the same time.

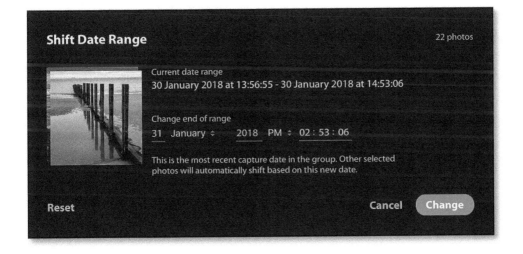

Shift Date Range   22 photos

Current date range
30 January 2018 at 13:56:55 - 30 January 2018 at 14:53:06

Change end of range
31 January ⇕   2018 PM ⇕ 02 : 53 : 06

This is the most recent capture date in the group. Other selected photos will automatically shift based on this new date.

Reset   Cancel   Change

VIEWING & EDITING THE PHOTO LOCATION

Location information on a photo can be useful for:

• Searching for photos by location, for example, vacation destinations.

• Knowing exactly where a photo was taken, so you can replicate it, perhaps at a different time of day or a different season.

This is currently only available on the desktop apps, and there isn't a way to copy a location to another photo.

AUTOMATIC GPS DATA

If your phone or camera embeds GPS metadata into the photos, the **City**, **State/Province** and **Country** fields are automatically populated, and the map appears below. This reverse geocoding is done on the server and then synced to your computer, so there may be a delay before the fields are populated.

MANUALLY ADDING A LOCATION

If your camera doesn't record the location, you can enter an approximate location manually. If you type the postal code / zip code into the **Location** field and the country into the **Country** field, Lightroom automatically looks up the rest of the address and displays the map.

MAP STYLES

If you right-click on the map, you can choose between *Road Map*, *Satellite*, *Hybrid* and *Terrain* map views. The *Hybrid* option is shown in this screenshot.

VIEWING IN GOOGLE MAPS

The small map is useful to see the approximate location, but sometimes you need more detail. If you click on the map, Lightroom opens your default web browser to the same location in Google Maps.

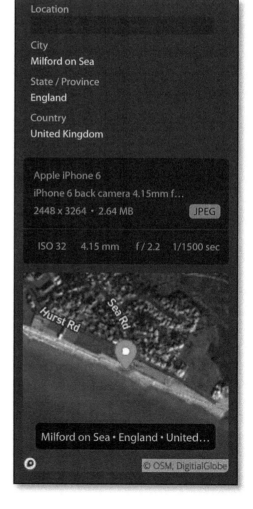

ADDING KEYWORDS

Keyword tags are text metadata used to describe the content of a photo.

Lightroom's image analysis technology is already able to identify many subjects, reducing the need for keywords. However, it's likely to be some time before software can correctly name your friends and family without some input from you, or tell the difference between a lesser spotted and great spotted woodpecker, so some keywords are still important.

Focus your efforts on your best photos, as they're the ones you're likely to want to find again in future.

TYPES OF KEYWORDS

If you've never keyworded photos before, you may be wondering where to start. There are no hard and fast rules for keywording unless you're shooting for Stock Photography.

Assuming you're shooting primarily for yourself, the main rule is simple—use keywords which will help you find the photos again later! For example, they can include:

Who is in the photo (people).

What is in the photo (other subjects or objects).

Where the photo was taken (names of locations).

Why the photo was taken (what's happening).

When the photo was taken (sunrise/sunset, season, event).

How the photo was taken (HDR, tilt-shift, panoramic).

CONSISTENCY

For keywords to be really helpful, you need to be consistent, for example:

Capitalization—stick to lower case for everything except names of people and places.

Quantity—either use singular or plural, but avoid mixing them. Either have "bird, cat, dog" or "birds, cats, dogs."

Verbs—stick to a single form, for example, "running, playing, jumping" rather than "run, play, jumping."

Name formats—consider how you'll handle nicknames, or last names for married women. Many use the married name followed by the maiden name (e.g., Mary Married née Maiden).

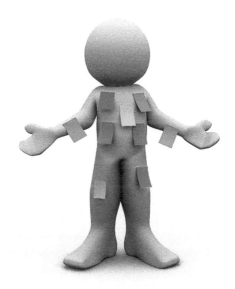

APPLYING KEYWORDS ON THE DESKTOP

To **open the Keywords panel** and activate the Add Keyword field, click the tag icon in the bottom right corner, or press the K key.

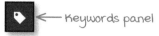 ←— Keywords panel

To **add a keyword**, type directly in the *Add Keyword* field, then press Enter. You can add multiple keywords by separating them using commas.

To **delete a keyword** from a photo, hover over it in the tag cloud so it turns red, then click.

To add to, or delete keywords from, **multiple photos** at once, you must be in Grid view with the photos selected. When you're in Detail view, your actions only affect the single visible photo.

APPLYING KEYWORDS ON MOBILE

To **open the Keywords view** on a mobile device, switch to Detail view and select Keywords view (iOS) / Info view (Android) using the pop-up (mobile) / icons in the sidebar (tablet).

To **add a keyword**, type directly in the text field. You can add multiple keywords by separating them using commas.

To **delete a keyword** from a photo on mobile, tap on the keyword tag.

Unlike the desktop, you can't select multiple photos at once, but on iOS, you can copy keywords from one photo to another, which is useful when you're adding a whole series of keywords. To do so, tap the ... menu, then select **Copy Keywords**. Move to the next photo, return to the ... menu and select **Paste Keywords**. (This isn't currently available on Android.)

There is one more advantage of keywording on a mobile device: voice recognition. By selecting the microphone on your device's keyboard, you can dictate your keywords.

KEYWORDS (WINDOWS/MAC)

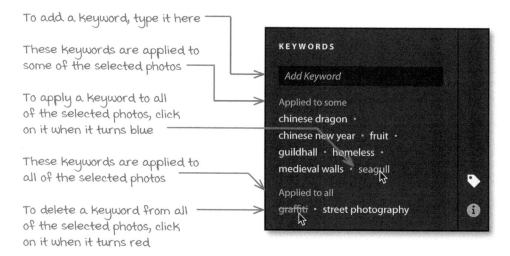

To add a keyword, type it here

These keywords are applied to some of the selected photos

To apply a keyword to all of the selected photos, click on it when it turns blue

These keywords are applied to all of the selected photos

To delete a keyword from all of the selected photos, click on it when it turns red

KEYWORDS

Add Keyword

Applied to some
chinese dragon ·
chinese new year · fruit ·
guildhall · homeless ·
medieval walls · seagull

Applied to all
graffiti · street photography

KEYWORDS (IOS/ANDROID)

Switch to Keywords view (iOS) or Info view (Android) →

← (iOS only) Tap ... and select Copy Keywords or Paste Keywords. First copy the keywords to the clipboard, then switch photos and paste to save typing them all over again

To add keywords, → type them here, separated by commas →

To delete a keyword, tap on it

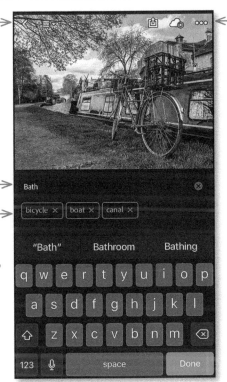

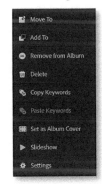

SEARCHING FOR PHOTOS

One of the main benefits of having all of your photos in one place is they're easy to search.

ENTERING SEARCH CRITERIA

The text Search field is always found at the top of the Lightroom desktop window, and the shortcut Ctrl-F (Windows) / Cmd-F (Mac) moves the cursor to the Search field. To **access the search field** on mobile, tap the magnifying glass icon at the top of Organize/Grid view.

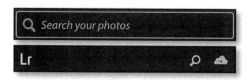

To **search your photos**, simply type the search terms in the search field and press the Enter key.

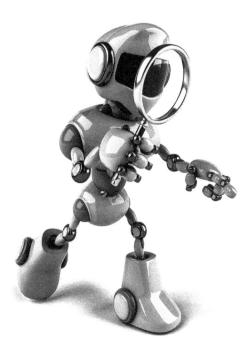

Lightroom searches the photos in the current view. To **search all of your photos,** select *All Photos* at the top of the My Photos panel (desktop) / Organize view (mobile).

To **delete a search term**, click on its token.

To **cancel the text search**, click the X at the end of the search field.

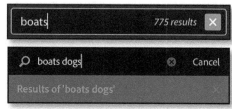

SEARCHING CONTENT

If your photos are synced to the cloud, Adobe's artificial intelligence machine learning tool, called Adobe Sensei, can search your photos and take a guess at their content.

This image-analysis allows you to find your photos, even if you never got around to adding keyword tags manually.

This automated tagging is done in Adobe's cloud, so there is a slight delay before they're searchable, and it does rely on you being connected to the internet.

You can search for all sorts of terms, for example:

• **Subjects**, such as *boats*, *cats*, *dogs*, *trees* or *water*, whether they're identified automatically or you've added them as keywords.

• **Colors**, such as *red* or *blue*.

- **Locations**, such as *London* or *UK*.

- **Cameras**, such as *Canon EOS 6D Mark II, Sony A6500*, or *iPhone X*.

- **Lenses**, such as *75-300mm*.

- **Dates**, such as *October 2017, or 21 August 2018*.

- **Filenames**, such as *IMG_2948*.

- **File Extensions**, such as *.jpg*

- **Other words** in the *Title* or *Caption* fields.

If you search for *boats sunset* it searches for photos that it thinks have both boats and a sunset. Once you add 4 or more words, it switches to probability (e.g., the photo matches 3 out of 4 words).

Try using AND, OR or NOT to narrow your search down further, for example, *boats AND sunset* finds the photos that it thinks have both boats and a sunset, but *boats NOT sunset* finds photos of boats shot in the daytime.

It's still early days for this type of search, so it will continue to improve over time. In the meantime, some of the suggestions will provide a few laughs. ☺

SEARCHING METADATA

You can also specify which metadata field to search by adding "facets." Type the facet followed by a colon (:) and a list of options pops up.

The available facets in English are:

camera: and **lens:** search the camera and lens models.
f: searches aperture (f-stop).

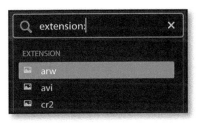

ss: searches shutter speed.
iso: checks the ISO rating.
flash: checks whether the flash fired.

rating: searches the star rating, from 0 to 5.
flag: searches the flagged/unflagged/reject status.
location: searches the GPS fields.
keyword: searches keywords you've manually added to the Keyword panel.
person: searches for people tagged using facial recognition in Lightroom Classic and then added to Lightroom CC using the migration tool. (Facial recognition is not currently available in Lightroom CC.)

type: separates photos and videos.
extension: searches by file extension, such as jpg or cr2.
orientation: searches for photos that are vertical, horizontal, panoramic or square.
edited: looks for photos that have been edited since importing into Lightroom CC.

These facets can be combined, for example, you might search for *rating:equal to 5 extension:cr2 camera:Canon EOS 5D Mk III*

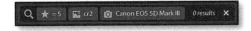

SEARCH LANGUAGE

Lightroom searches based on the language selected in *Preferences > Interface* on the desktop, or based the operating system language on mobile. If you need to search in Spanish, for example, you'll need the Lightroom interface in Spanish too.

REFINING THE CURRENT VIEW

The Refine toolbar filters the current view based on specific criteria, for example, to show all of your photos marked with 4 stars that were shot using your iPhone.

To **show the Refine toolbar** on the desktop, click the Refine button to the right of the Search bar. On mobile, tap the Refine button at the top of the Grid view.

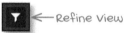
← Refine View

If you're viewing photos from a specific date or album, it only searches those photos. To **search all of your photos**, select *All Photos* at the top of the My Photos panel (desktop) / Organize view (mobile).

FILTERING BY STAR RATING

The star filters allow you to show/hide photos and/or videos based on their star rating. For example, to **show only photos with 3 or more stars**, click/tap on the third star.

The **symbol** to the left of the stars allow greater control, so you can filter based on:

≥ rating is greater than or equal to.

≤ rating is less than or equal to.

= rating is equal to.

For example, to display only photos with 0 stars, click/tap on the symbol to the left of the stars, select the = icon, and leave the stars themselves deselected.

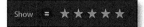

FILTERING BY FLAGS

The flag filters allow you to show/hide photos and/or videos based on their flag status.

To **show only flagged photos**, click/tap on the flag so it's highlighted.

Flagged only ⟶

To **show both flagged and unflagged photos** (hiding the rejected photos), click/tap on both the flagged and unflagged icons, so they're both highlighted.

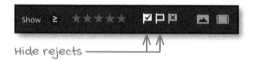
Hide rejects ⟶

To **show only rejected photos**, ready to delete them, click only the rejected flag so it's highlighted.

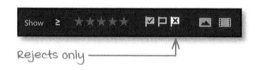
Rejects only ⟶

FILTERING BY MEDIA TYPE

The media type filters allow you to show only photos or videos. (Not currently available on Android, as videos don't sync to/from Android.)

Photos ⟶ 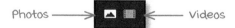 ← Videos

REFINING THE VIEW (WINDOWS/MAC)

Search for photos using text   Cancel text search   Show Refine View toolbar

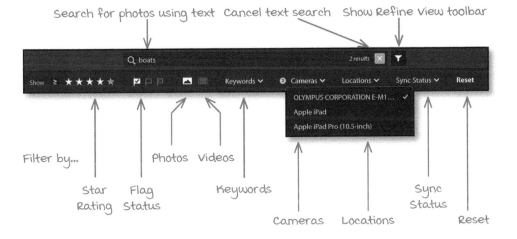

Filter by...

Star Rating   Flag Status   Photos   Videos   Keywords   Cameras   Locations   Sync Status   Reset

REFINING THE VIEW (IOS/ANDROID)

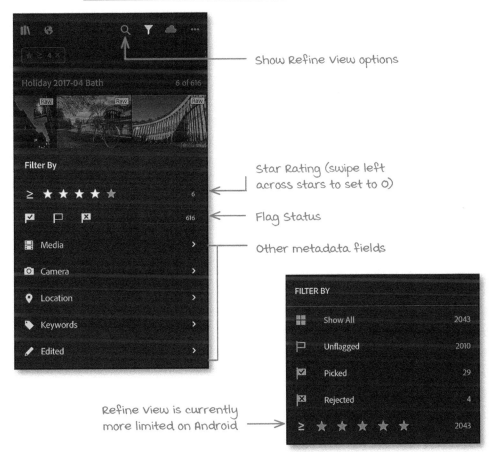

Show Refine View options

Star Rating (swipe left across stars to set to 0)

Flag Status

Other metadata fields

Refine View is currently more limited on Android

FILTERING BY KEYWORD, CAMERA, LOCATION OR SYNC STATUS ON THE DESKTOP

The **Keywords**, **Cameras**, **Locations** and **Sync Status** pop-ups (not currently available on Android) allow you to refine the view based on additional metadata. This metadata is searchable using the text search field (page 88), however the Refine pop-ups work even if you're offline.

The *Sync Status* criteria is particularly useful if you're having sync issues, as it shows which photos are yet to upload. It's also useful if you previously uploaded photos using Lightroom Classic, as it shows which photos only have smart previews available in the cloud.

As they all work the same way, let's use the *Cameras* pop-up to illustrate. Click on the pop-up to **show the list** of cameras. They're sorted by frequency, with the most-used camera first.

Click on one of the lines to select it, such as the Olympus E-M1 in the screenshot. Any photos shot with other cameras are hidden from view. You can click to select multiple lines to display photos from more than one camera.

To **remove a camera** from the selection, click on the line again. To cancel the camera filter and show photos from all cameras, click on the circular number icon on the pop-up.

CLEARING FILTERS

To reset the Refine filters to show all photos, click the **Reset** button (desktop), click the *Refine* button again (desktop) or select **No Filter** (mobile).

Click to show list of keywords, cameras or locations

Click number to clear all selected cameras

Click one or more white lines to show photos from selected camera

Click blue lines to uncheck cameras

INTRODUCTION TO EDITING

8

Most photographers want to get on to the fun bit—editing their photos! Editing photos is not about making them look fake or photoshopped, nor is it a new phenomenon. Photographers were editing their photos in the darkroom long before computers existed. Even the Masters, such as Ansel Adams, edited their photos, not to fix mistakes, but because a print can't match the dynamic range of the human eye.

WHY ARE YOU EDITING YOUR PHOTOS?

Before you starting editing, ask yourself why you're editing your photos. Are you editing...

• To fix mistakes? (Yes, even pros make mistakes!)

• To compensate for intentional overexposure (ETTR), done to retain the largest amount of data?

• To adjust the dynamic range of the photo to match the scene you remember?

• To draw the eye to specific areas of the photo?

• To match your artistic vision for the photo?

• For consistency, perhaps across your portfolio or in an album or on the wall?

• To crop in closer, because you didn't have a long enough lens?

The reason you're editing the photos will

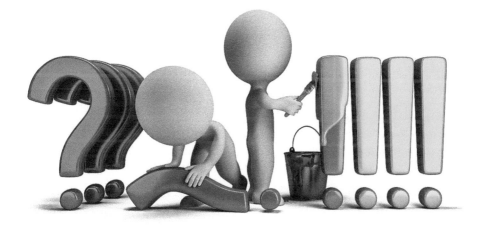

affect the editing choices you make, for example:

• If you're figuring out the kind of style you like, you might experiment with lots of different presets.

• If you're aiming for consistency, you'll view the images as a group rather than just individually.

• If you're editing an image to put on the wall, you'll probably spend more time on it than a photo to put on social media.

WHICH PHOTOS SHOULD YOU EDIT?

If you spend hours editing every photo you capture, you'll soon get frustrated. Consider these time-saving tips:

• Don't try to edit everything. Editing won't fix bad photos. They can be improved, but you can't make a silk purse from a sow's ear. Flag/star the photos first, and just edit the best ones.

• Just do a "quick" edit on most of the photos you decide to keep, and focus most of your editing time on the photos you'll be proud to share with the world.

HOW DO YOU USE LIGHTROOM TO EDIT YOUR PHOTOS?

You can get the gist of how Lightroom's sliders work simply through experimentation. It doesn't take a rocket scientist to work out that the *Exposure* slider brightens or darkens the photos.

However, many of Lightroom's sliders do all sorts of clever calculations behind the scenes. Understanding how the sliders work—and how they work together—means

you can get the best result.

We're going to focus on analyzing the photos before you start editing, and how to figure out what you need to adjust to fix or enhance them. For example:

• How do you know where to crop a photo?

• How do you know how bright or dark to make the photo?

• How do you decide on the color?

• How much sharpening should you apply?

• How do you know which photos will look better in B&W without testing it on every single one?

In the following sections, we'll answer these questions, and more besides.

IN THIS SECTION, WE'LL CONSIDER:

• Why it's worth learning photo editing skills instead of always relying on presets.

• How to avoid looking like a new photographer.

• The importance of calibrating your monitor.

WHY LEARN TO EDIT PHOTOS USING SLIDERS?

Most new photographers edit photos using profiles, presets and filters. So why bother learning to use the sliders?

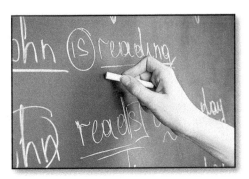

PHOTO EDITING IS LIKE A LANGUAGE

Photo editing is a skill, just like any other. If you're trying to learn a language, repeating phrases from a phrase book is only going to get you so far. To become fluent in a language, you have to learn its structure and vocabulary, so you can start to build your own sentences that can apply in any situation.

Editing photos is the same. Profiles and presets are like those pre-built phrases. They'll work okay in some situations, but they'll never be a perfect fit.

Skilled editing can enhance photos in a way that presets simply can't match. Learning which sliders to tweak is also much faster than hunting through hundreds of presets trying to find one that works.

PROFILES & PRESETS HAVE THEIR PLACE

Don't misunderstand me... profiles and presets have their place. Benefits include:

• Selecting a base profile can be a good starting point for your editing.

• Profiles and presets (especially those you've created yourself) can help to ensure consistency over a group of photos, or over your entire portfolio.

• Presets can be really helpful in learning the kind of styles of editing you prefer, and looking at which sliders are adjusted by presets is a great way of learning how to create a specific look.

IT TAKES TIME

Any new skill takes time to develop, and you'll improve with practice. When you first start trying to edit photos with sliders, rather than relying on presets, you won't always be happy with the result initially. But that's ok! That's the benefit of non-destructive editing—you can go back and change them later, as your skills continue to develop. If you've saved a "classic" edit (as opposed to a fashionable look), your future changes will be tweaks, not a complete overhaul.

LEARNING THE LANGUAGE OF EDITING

We'll start by introducing the sliders and tools, like adding new words to your vocabulary.

Then, we'll learn how to combine related sliders to get a specific result, like combining words to make a sentence.

Finally, we'll start combining different sets of sliders into full photo edits, like turning these sentences into whole conversations.

WHAT NOT TO DO WHEN EDITING

There are some weird and wonderful photo effects that are popular with new photographers. Play with them and get them out of your system. But then, if you want to be respected as a photographer, your photos should usually look like photos.

There are a few red flags that make it easy to identify new photographers, and of course, you don't want to look like a newbie, so here are a few things to avoid:

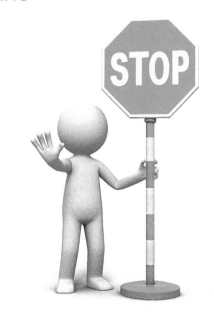

• You don't need to use every single slider on each photo, just as you don't need to use every word in the dictionary in each conversation.

• Less is more. Unless you're intentionally aiming for a surreal look, keep it natural. Sliders rarely need pushing to the ends.

• Be especially careful with photos of people. Glowing eyes, bright white teeth and plastic skin rarely look good.

• Watch your white and black clipping. Most photos benefit from a few pure white and pure black pixels, but you don't usually want large areas of white or black without detail.

• Reduce digital noise, but don't make it so smooth it looks like plastic.

• Avoid using too many different presets, because your photos won't look like "yours".

• Don't crop too far, as you'll cause visible pixelation (obvious square pixels).

• Watch out for halos either side of edges in the photo, whether they're wide halos caused by overzealous use of the *Highlights*, *Shadows* or *Clarity* sliders, or narrow halos caused by too much sharpening or chromatic aberration (a lens defect).

• Limit your use of the latest fad and fake film presets that go out of fashion again just as quickly as they arrived. Likewise, limit your use of special effects such as selective color (B&W photos with one element in color), as these effects date quickly.

• Don't go out and buy every software program on the market. Master the ones you already have first. "The grass is always greener on the other side of the fence" doesn't always hold true. Often you just need to learn which slider to adjust to make it greener on this side!

• Finally, don't spend hours on every photo. If you get stuck, consider printing it, sticking it on the wall and "living with it" for a while. This makes it easier to see what needs changing.

Don't worry, as you continue through this book, I'll show you how to avoid all of these issues and skillfully edit your photos.

THE IMPORTANCE OF CALIBRATING YOUR MONITOR

When you walk into a TV store and look around, you'll notice that all of the screens are slightly different. Some are a little brighter, some are a little darker, some are more contrasty, others have less contrast, some are more colorful, some are warm, some are cool... the differences go on.

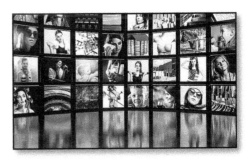

If you display the same image on all of these screens, they'll all look slightly different. The same applies to computer monitors and mobile devices. The same photo will look different, depending on the screen you're using.

THE AIM OF CALIBRATION

The aim of monitor calibration is to adjust all of these different screens to a standard, so the photo looks similar regardless of the screen you're viewing at the time.

When you put your photos out into the world, you can't control exactly how they'll look, because most people don't calibrate their monitors. However, editing your photos on a standardized system gives you the best shot at getting your prints to match the screen, and saves you having to re-edit your photos every time you switch to a different device.

HOW TO CALIBRATE YOUR DESKTOP MONITOR

Monitor calibration on the desktop isn't complicated. You simply need a monitor calibration tool and the software that comes with it. The main players are X-Rite's ColorMunki and i1 Display Pro devices, and Datacolor's range of Spyder devices. The software will differ slightly, but the principles remain the same.

STEP-BY-STEP

Let's use the i1 Display Pro to illustrate:

1. Install the software and drivers that come with the calibration device.

2. Follow the instructions in the software. Most ask you to make a few decisions:

Monitor Technology—Newer monitors are probably *White LED*, while older ones are mainly *CCFL*. The software often selects the right one automatically.

White Point—select *D65* or *6500*.

Luminance—select *120 cd/m2* as a starting point. (You may increase/decrease it later, if your prints are a little darker/lighter than you see on screen.)

Contrast Ratio—select *Native.*

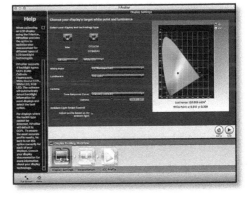

3. Place the calibration device on the screen, ensuring that it's flat against the screen with no ambient light creeping in the sides, and start measuring.

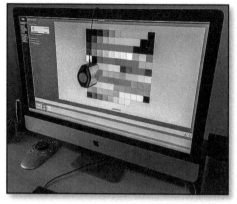

4. The software measures the brightness of the screen, and tells you how bright it is currently. Use the monitor buttons (or *System Preferences > Display* on a Mac with a built-in screen) to increase or decrease the monitor brightness until the line is in the green 'optimum' area. Most monitors are way too bright, so don't be surprised if you have to make a big adjustment.

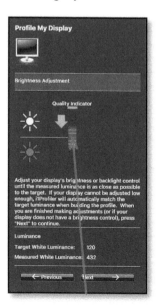

Adjust the monitor brightness until the line is in the center of the green area

Some high-end monitors make these adjustments automatically. Other monitors may also ask you to adjust contrast or RGB values to match the target values.

5. The calibration software then flashes a series of colors on the screen, measuring each in turn, so it can build a profile.

6. When the calibration finishes, give the profile a sensible name and click the *Save* button, then close the software.

CONTROLLING YOUR SURROUNDINGS

Your surroundings also influence your perception of brightness and color. Ideally, it's best edit your photos in dim light, with the light source no brighter than the screen. This may be as simple as closing the curtains and turning on a small desk lamp holding a daylight bulb.

ADJUSTING MOBILE DEVICES

Mobile devices can't be calibrated at an operating system level using hardware calibration tools. Apple devices display fairly accurate color out-of-the-box, but Android devices can be a bit more variable. In either case, screen brightness is usually too bright and needs reducing to match your calibrated desktop screen. There may also be automatic adjustment settings to consider, such as Auto Brightness or Apple's True Tone color adjustment.

ANALYZING THE IMAGE

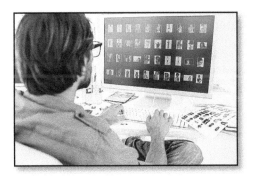

When you watch a professional photo editor editing a series of photos, it looks like they "just know" what to change. They don't start randomly moving sliders, hoping to hit on the right combination of adjustments. Instead, they first analyze the photo.

Due to years of experience, that analysis may only take a few seconds, and may be a subconscious process, but it happens every time. Without necessarily realizing they're doing so, they're essentially running through a series of questions in their head—and you can ask yourself the same questions. This process of analysis is the focus of this section.

PLAN YOUR JOURNEY

Starting to edit a photo without first taking the time to analyze it is like setting off on a road trip without first looking at a map. You'll end up somewhere, and the trip might still be fun, but you're unlikely to get to the best destination.

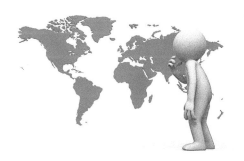

You don't have to plan every detail, but having a rough idea of where you want to end up means you can make good decisions along the way, and avoid going in circles.

We're going to break the analysis down into two categories:

- Technical Faults (page 103)

- Artistic Intent (page 110)

ANALYZING YOUR OWN PHOTOS

I've included a checklist and worksheet to help guide you through the process. Printable copies are available for download in the Members Area (page 314), and we'll use these worksheets again later in the book, when we edit some photos from start to finish (page 249).

Analyzing your photos may look like a lot of work, but once you understand what you're looking for, you'll be able to analyze your photo in a matter of seconds, like you do when shooting a photo.

You don't have to complete a written worksheet every time you sit down to edit a photo, but your editing will improve if you run through the process a few times on paper before switching to doing it in your head. As you gain experience, it'll become second nature.

IN THIS SECTION, WE'LL CONSIDER:

• How to analyze the image, looking for technical faults.

• How to analyze the image from artistic point of view.

• How to start to develop your own consistent editing style.

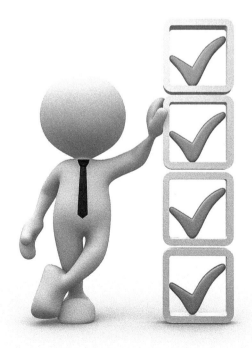

PHOTO ANALYSIS CHECKLIST

Technical

Light & Contrast
- [ ] Is the overall exposure about right?
- [ ] Is there enough detail in the highlights and shadows?
- [ ] Does the photo fill the entire dynamic range?
- [ ] Are the highlights and/ or shadows clipping?

Color
- [ ] Is there a color cast?
- [ ] Do the memory colors look natural?

Detail
- [ ] Is it sharp?
- [ ] Is there noise?
- [ ] Is there moiré patterning?

Optical Distortion
- [ ] Is there vignetting?
- [ ] Is there barrel/pincushion distortion?
- [ ] Is there chromatic aberration or other fringing?

Geometric Distortion
- [ ] Is the horizon straight?
- [ ] Are the vertical lines straight, or do they converge?

Sensor Dust
- [ ] Are there any sensor dust spots?

Output
- [ ] Does the photo need to fit a specific aspect ratio, for example, a frame?
- [ ] Does it need to match the color of another photo?
- [ ] How big is the photo going to be?

Artistic Intent

Purpose
- [ ] Why did I capture the photo?
- [ ] What's important in the photo?
- [ ] What did I want to show the viewer?

Story
- [ ] What's the story I'm trying to tell?
- [ ] How can I use light, contrast, color and saturation to help tell the story?

Mood/Emotion
- [ ] How do I want the viewer to feel?
- [ ] How can I use light, contrast, color and saturation to influence the viewer's response?

Simplify
- [ ] Are there any distractions I can exclude from the scene by cropping, darkening, blurring, etc?

Draw the Eye
- [ ] Can I guide the viewer's eye around the photo by highlighting or diminishing:
  - People
  - Contrasts in Size
  - Contrasts in Brightness
  - Contrasts in Color & Saturation
  - Contrasts in Sharpness
  - Lines
  - Something else?

PHOTO ANALYSIS WORKSHEET EXAMPLE

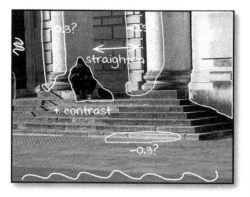

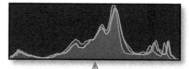

Good dynamic range, no notable clipping

TECHNICAL

Exposure
Needs a little more detail in his clothes. No pure white expected in the photo.

Color
Color doesn't add to the photo. The strong lines and stone texture would work well in B&W.

Detail
Shot at low ISO in good light, so no notable noise. Texture of stone can take some crunchy sharpening.

Optical & Geometric Distortion
Horizon needs straightening (use bricks in background).

Sensor Dust
None found.

Output
Nothing specific planned.

ARTISTIC INTENT

Purpose
The guy looked small and insignificant against the huge pillars of the government building.

Story
Is he homeless? Or just waiting for a friend? He looks cold and lonely.

Mood/Emotion
Very cold day (hat). Feeling lonely? High contrast B&W with lots of local contrast for a gritty urban look?

Simplify the Scene & Draw the Eye
Notes scribbled on photo.

Remove the sign from the door on the left.

Even up lighting on the pillars, front step and bricks in the background to reduce background contrast.

Increase contrast on face/clothing of man to draw the eye in that direction even more.

ANALYZING THE IMAGE—TECHNICAL FAULTS

One of the aims of the editing process is to get the best possible result from whatever data you captured, so there are some technical issues to look out for. You may not be familiar with all of the terminology, so we'll explain a few new terms as we go along.

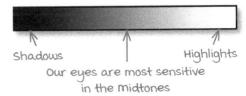

Shadows   Highlights

Our eyes are most sensitive in the midtones

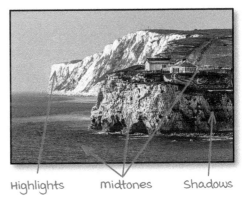

Highlights   midtones   Shadows

LIGHT

In the real world, our eyes don't care whether something is light or dark, as they automatically adjust to see detail in both the highlights and shadows, even in high contrast situations such as midday sun.

A photo (and especially a print) is unable to hold that wide a range of tones while still looking natural. Something has to give. Editing photos is a balancing act, determining which range of tones is most important and where you're willing to sacrifice detail.

Is the overall exposure about right? Is there enough detail in the highlights and shadows?

There is no such thing as "correct" exposure, but the human visual system (the combination of our eyes and brain) expects to see an image in a specific way. This means there's room for creative expression, but there's a narrow band of exposure most people prefer.

Our eyes are most comfortable when the main focus of interest is around middle gray (called the midtones). Therefore, the optimum exposure setting may lighten or darken the highlights or shadows to move the most important tones towards the midtones.

What does the histogram tell you?

A Histogram is a bar graph showing the distribution of tonal values. To show the histogram, click the ... button in the right panel bar and select **Show Histogram** or use the shortcut Ctrl-0 (Windows) / Cmd-0 (Mac).

The brightness of each pixel is measured from 0% (black) to 100% (white), so a histogram runs from the blackest shadow on the left to the brightest highlight on the right. Vertically it shows the number of pixels with that specific tonal value. A color photo is made up of three channels—red, green and blue—so the histogram has a line for each channel.

There's no such thing as a 'correct' histogram. When analyzing your photo, a histogram can provide some really useful information on the exposure values of your photo, but don't get too hung up on it. We're trying to make great photos, not great histograms! However there are a few useful things we can learn from the histogram...

Does the photo fill the entire dynamic range?

The difference between the brightest and darkest tones in the photo is called the dynamic range.

The histogram of a scene that has a much wider dynamic range than the camera could capture shows spikes at both ends. These are pixels that are currently pure white or pure black, but if it's a raw file, there may be detail that can be recovered with careful editing. This is called a **high dynamic range**, and these photos usually have too much contrast.

A histogram stuck in the middle of the range, without reaching the ends is a narrow or **low dynamic range**. In most cases, these photos benefit from stretching to create a real white and black point because they lack contrast. However some photos, such as those shot in thick fog, may not have any true white or black details.

READING THE HISTOGRAM

Number of pixels with that brightness value

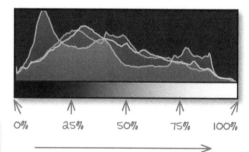

0%   25%   50%   75%   100%

Pixel brightness, from pure black (0%) to pure white (100%)

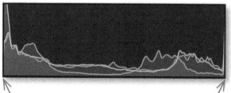

Spikes at the ends = dynamic range too wide, so detail is clipped

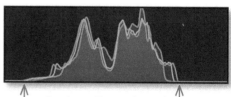

Data doesn't reach ends = low dynamic range

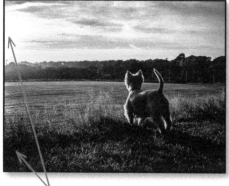

missing detail in the highlights and shadows

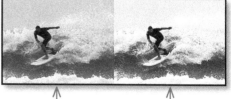

Low dynamic range   Stretched to full dynamic range

WATCH FOR CLIPPING

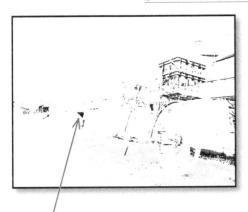

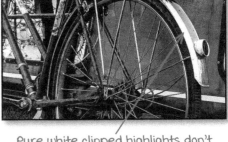

Pure white clipped highlights don't look out of place on shiny objects

Clipped blacks show as black on a white background. Pixels only clipped in one or two channels show in color

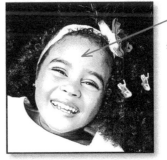

Avoid clipping skin tones

Are the highlights and/or shadows clipping?

If the last pixel on the left or the right of the histogram spikes, it means that a significant number of pixels in your photo are solid white or black without any detail. These are called clipped highlights or shadows, or you may hear them referred to as blown highlights and blocked shadows. Clipping can be a fault or it can be intentional.

To check whether the clipped pixels are in areas of important image detail, hold down the Alt key (Windows) / Opt key (Mac) while dragging the *Exposure*, *Highlights*, *Shadows*, *Whites* or *Blacks* sliders to view the clipping warnings.

In some areas of the photo, such as bright spots on shiny objects, clipping is expected. Small areas of clipping on a light source, such as a light bulb or the sun, can also look fine, but ideally you don't want large clipped areas, such as a window with no detail. Clipping on skin looks unnatural and is worth avoiding at all costs.

Some studio or product photographers like to clip their backgrounds to pure white or black, and intentionally compressing the shadow detail can be a creative choice. It's not always bad, as long as there's a smooth transition to image detail.

We'll use the tools in the Light and Effects panel to make these adjustments (page 151).

COLOR

Unless you're doing reproduction work, the main aim is visually pleasing color, which may not be the same as perfectly accurate color, due to the way the camera captures the scene. While you can make artistic choices, there are a couple of things to look out for...

KEEP COLORS NATURAL

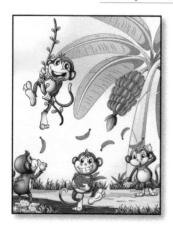

What's wrong with this image?
memory colors need to be accurate!

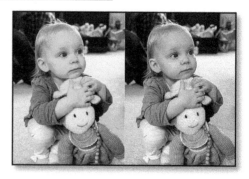

A color cast makes the
photo look muddy

Is there a color cast?

A color cast is an unwanted tint in the image, often caused by an incorrect White Balance setting. It makes the photo look muddy and hazy, like you're viewing it through a colored film. We're most sensitive to color casts in lighter tones. If you remove the tint, the other colors usually fall into place.

Do the memory colors look natural?

Some colors are burned forever into our memory. Think about skin tones. We recognize when someone looks jaundiced or ashen, or when they've applied fake tan, because the color of their skin doesn't match the color we expect to see. In the same way, we expect the sky to be blue, grass to be green, and bananas to be yellow.

As long as the memory colors remain natural, you can take liberties with other colors for artistic effect, without the photo looking "wrong".

We'll use the tools in the Color panel to make these adjustments (page 175).

DETAIL

If we have 20/20 vision, everything we look at is perfectly sharp, and our eyes automatically adjust to see detail in the shadows without any noise. Cameras have come on leaps and bounds over the last few years, but they're no match. Whether it's softness caused by imperfect optics or focusing, or noise caused by low light hitting tiny digital sensors, there's room for improvement in the detail of our photos.

Is it sharp?

We all grab photos that aren't perfectly in focus and most will be removed when ranking the photos, but occasionally there's just "something" about them that's worth keeping. You can't fix out of focus photos in Lightroom, but you can certainly improve them.

Is there noise?

If you shot in low light, used a high ISO, your camera has a very small sensor, or you need to significantly brighten the photo, then there's likely to be noise in the photo, making it look very grainy. This can be reduced in Lightroom.

CHECK THE DETAIL

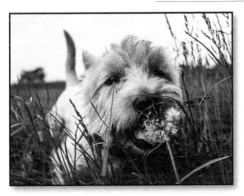

This was a grab shot, and the camera focused on the grass instead of his eyes, so it's not perfectly sharp but it sums up Charlie too well to throw away

High noise levels are usually found on high ISO photos

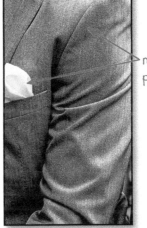

moiré pattern

Is there moiré patterning?

Moiré (pronounced mwa-ray) is a rainbow-like pattern which is often seen when photographing fabrics. It's caused by two patterns combining—in this case, the weave in fabric and the grid of the camera sensor—which creates a new pattern.

Sharpening and noise reduction can be optimized using the tools in the Detail panel (page 201) and moiré can be removed using the Brush tool (page 223).

OPTICAL DISTORTIONS

The way the light passes through the camera's lens can result in distortions that can distract from the content of the photo, so it's worth taking a moment to correct them.

Is there vignetting?

Vignetting is a darkening around the edges of the photo, especially in the corners.

Is there barrel/pincushion distortion?

Pincushion distortion causes straight lines to curve inward, while barrel distortion causes straight lines to curve outward. It's particularly noticeable when there are straight lines in the photo.

Is there chromatic aberration or other fringing?

Lateral chromatic aberration (often shortened to CA) is the little fringes of color that can appear along high contrast edges, where the red, green and blue light

OPTICAL & GEOMETRIC DISTORTIONS

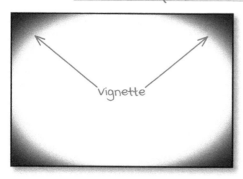

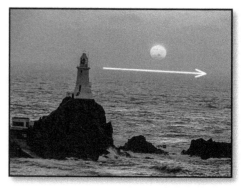

Horizons should be horizontal!

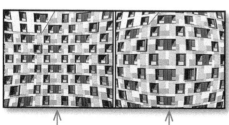

Pincushion distortion curves inward

Barrel distortion curves outward

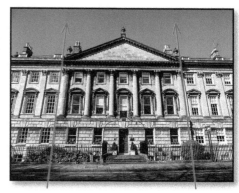

Due to the camera angle, the building appears to be leaning backwards

Compact and mirrorless cameras often fix these issues automatically, but where these distortions are still visible, we'll use the tools in the Optics panel to make these corrections (page 225).

GEOMETRIC DISTORTIONS

When you look around in real life, horizontal lines look horizontal and vertical lines look vertical, and even if you tilt your head, your brain compensates. However, if your camera sensor isn't perfectly aligned with those horizontal and vertical lines, the resulting

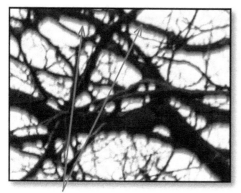

Halos of opposing colors (green and magenta here) are caused by chromatic aberration

wavelengths are unable to focus at the same point. It's most noticeable around the corners of photos taken with a lower quality wide angle lens, and doesn't appear in the center of the image.

photo looks wonky.

Is the horizon straight?

Most of us have trouble getting horizons perfectly straight at the time of shooting, and since the edge of the photo acts as a point of comparison, they stand out like a sore thumb.

Are the vertical lines straight, or do they converge?

If you're shooting buildings, have you noticed that they sometimes seem to lean backwards? This is called keystoning and it's caused by tilting the camera to get the whole building into the frame. Some keystoning can look natural, as we're used to looking up at buildings, but you may want to reduce excessive keystoning.

The horizon can be straightened using the Crop tool (page 129), and we'll use the tools in the Geometry panel to make more complex corrections (page 225).

RETOUCHING

Removing distractions from the photo allows your viewer to focus on the content. Some unnatural distractions, such as sensor dust spots, stand out more than the litter we see around us every day.

Are there any sensor dust spots?

Small spots that are most noticeable in the sky are caused by dust on the sensor. If you have a camera with interchangeable lenses, it's worth keeping your camera's sensor clean. Spots on blank areas on the sky are easy to clean up in Lightroom, but when they fall on more detailed areas, they can be tricky to remove.

LOOK FOR SPOTS

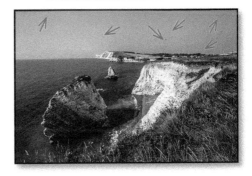

Dust spots on the sensor can be distracting

We'll use Lightroom's Healing Brush to remove these distractions, or pass the photo to Photoshop for more advanced retouching (page 235).

OUTPUT

Finally, the intended output will affect some of your editing choices, such as...

Does the photo need to fit a specific aspect ratio, for example, a frame?

If a photo will be placed in a specific frame, the aspect ratio used when cropping will be important. You'll need to bear in mind the shape of the frame when cropping the photo (page 129).

Does it need to match the color of another photo?

If the photo is part of a collection that will displayed together on the wall, consistency across the group will be a high priority.

How big is the photo going to be?

If it's a quick snap to email to Granny, you may decide to spend less time editing than you would for a poster-sized print.

ANALYZING THE IMAGE—ARTISTIC INTENT

Photography is a form of visual communication. It's not "just a pretty picture." It's up to you to decide what you're trying to communicate through your photo, and ensure that the viewer gets the right message.

The composition, the lighting and the subject of the photo are essential, of course. You can't make a bad photo great through editing, but thoughtful editing can enhance a good photo and turn it into a great photo.

It's easy to look at a photo and say "I like it" but ask yourself WHY you like it. Once you've answered that question, you're well on the way to knowing what needs to be enhanced, to ensure that your viewer sees it the same way. Not sure how to answer? Let's break it down into a series of questions about the purpose of the photo, the story you want to tell, the mood you want to convey, and where you want the viewer's eye to go.

THE PURPOSE

Why did you capture the photo? Or why did you keep the photo? What was it you wanted to show the viewer? For example:

- To capture a specific moment in time.

- To tell a story.

- A specific subject caught your eye.

- The way the light was falling caught your eye.

- Someone commissioned you to shoot it. (What was their purpose?)

- Something else?

What's important in the photo? What's interesting about it? For example, in a photo of a thunderstorm the clouds are most important, or in a portrait, it's the eyes.

THE STORY

They say a picture speaks a thousand words, so what are you trying to communicate through this photo? What kind of story are you trying to tell? What do you want the viewer to think of when they see it? If it's a portrait, does it show the subject's personality?

For example, a portrait of an older man can be edited as a gritty B&W to accentuate the weathered wrinkles on his face, showing that he's worked hard outdoors all his life, or as a soft low contrast color image, showing his softer side.

THE MOOD/EMOTION

How did you feel when shooting the photo, and how do you want the viewer to feel? What emotion are you trying communicate? And then, how can you communicate that mood through your editing?

For example, a high contrast B&W shot of stormy seas may communicate drama, power and a feeling of awe, whereas the colorful blue sky and yellow sand on a paradisaic beach makes us think of relaxation.

Or a country village looks better in peaceful calm tones, whereas edgy architecture looks great with a strong, contrasty look, and a factory can look great with a gritty grainy look.

USING EDITING TO COMMUNICATE MOOD

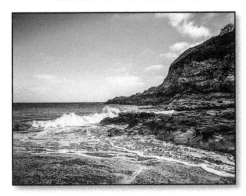

Was it a bright sunny day at the beach?

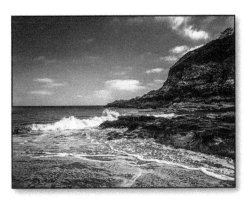

Or would you prefer a more moody look?

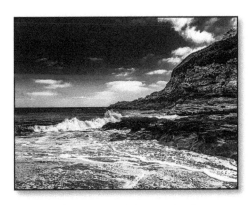

Or do you want to emphasize the drama of the crashing waves and rocky cliffs?

Words to Describe the Feel of a Photo

Light	airy, bright, clear, dainty, fluffy, glowing, hopeful, radiant, shining, sunny	dark, dull, gloomy, heavy, hopeless, mysterious, sinister, somber
Contrast	dramatic, energetic, gritty, hard, stormy, turbulent, wild	calm, delicate, gentle, mellow, mild, peaceful, smooth, soft
Color	cozy, fresh, happy, summery, rosy, upbeat, warm, yellow	bleak, blue, cold, frosty, icy, miserable, wet, wintry
Saturation	bright, cheerful, colorful, excited, gaudy, lively, loud, rich, vibrant, vivid	calm, dull, delicate, faded, mellow, muted, pale, pastel, sober, subdued

Think of words you'd use to describe the photo, and the brightness, contrast and colors you associate with those words.

SIMPLIFYING THE SCENE

So far we've been talking about the overall feel of the image, but now, let's think about the content.

In a confused scene, your eyes don't know where to look, so it's important to simplify the scene.

What caught your eye, making you take the

photo—and is that the first thing that will catch your viewer's eye? Or will their eye wander off to distractions?

If the eye doesn't go straight there, careful cropping and selective editing can draw the viewer's eye away from the distractions to the right spot.

DRAWING THE EYE USING VISUAL MASS

Once you've removed everything that isn't necessary, think about how your eyes move around the photo. Consider:

• Where does the eye go currently, and in what order?

• Where do you want the viewer's eye to go?

• How can you use editing to draw your viewer's eye along that same path?

In the world of photography and art, there's a concept called Visual Mass. It simply means that some elements attract the eye more than others, and you can use that to draw your viewer's eye around the photo. For example, we're drawn to:

• **People** (especially faces, particularly eyes). Even in landscapes, having a person in the scene creates a sense of scale or draws your eye to a specific spot. This also applies to animals, to a lesser extent.

• **Size**—We look at large objects before small.

• **Contrasts of Brightness**—We're drawn to light things in a mainly dark image, or dark things in a main light image.

• **Color**—We drift towards warm colors before cool colors (unless the scene is primarily warm, then we're drawn to the contrasting cool color), and saturated colors before dull colors.

• **Recognizable Objects**—We look at recognizable objects before those that are less recognizable.

• **Sharpness**—We see sharp objects before soft ones (which is why out of focus backgrounds work so well).

• **Lines**—We follow diagonal or curved lines before straight lines. Diagonal lines are more dynamic, whereas our eyes meander along curved lines.

• **Text**—We always try to read it!

This is massively over-simplified, and these elements are often combined, but you can use this concept to your advantage when editing, as well as when shooting.

Starting on page 207, we'll learn to use the selective adjustment tools to enhance these contrasts, but for now, just start noticing where your eye goes in photos, and where you want the viewer's eye to go to tell your story.

VISUAL MASS TO DRAW THE EYE

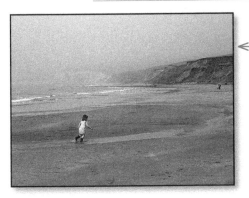

← People first

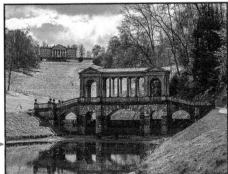

Large before Small →

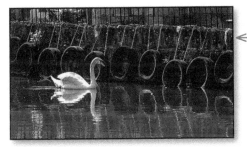

← Bright spots in a dark scene

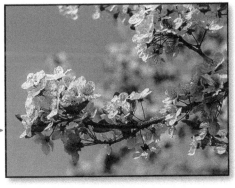

Sharp before Soft →

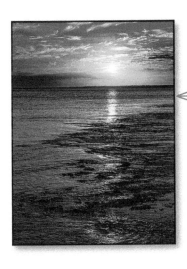

← Warm before cold

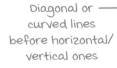

Diagonal or → curved lines before horizontal/ vertical ones

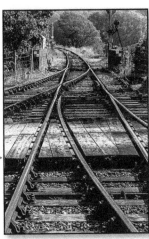

DEVELOPING YOUR OWN STYLE

One of the biggest differences between seasoned photographers and newer photographers is consistency in editing. Would all of your pictures look good hung on the wall together, or are they "all over the place"? Could someone identify a photo as yours, just by looking at it?

THE IMPORTANCE OF EDITING STYLES

If you look at the work of any famous photographer, you may know who the photographer is, long before you see their name. As you scroll through their website or Instagram feed, all of their photos work together as a consistent set.

This is partly due to their choice of subject, lighting, posing, lens, composition and so forth, but their editing style can make or break the consistency. If they applied a different preset to every photo, the photos would no longer be identifiable as theirs.

Professional photographers gradually develop a style and they stick to it. It may change over time, but it's a gradual shift.

If you're an amateur photographer, you don't have to go that far, but any improvement in consistency will make your photos look better together.

HOW DO YOU START TO DEVELOP YOUR STYLE?

To start to define your own preferences, look at lots of people's photos. Notice what you consistently like, and what you consistently don't like, but don't just copy them, because you're unique.

Experiment with different presets to help you learn too, but remember that they're someone else's style.

Start to analyze *what* it is you like or don't like about a photo. Look out for things like:

• Do you love high contrast, or do you prefer photos that look soft and dreamy?

• Do you like highly saturated colors, or softer muted shades?

• How important are creamy skin tones?

• Do you prefer specific color palettes, such as muted greens and blues?

• Do you prefer the darkest tones blocked to pure black, or do you prefer more shadow detail?

When you edit a photo and love the result, add it to a "my style" album. Over time, a theme will start to become apparent. The style you prefer for landscapes may not be identical to the style you prefer for portraits, but there will be similarities.

It won't happen overnight, and as you start to improve your editing, you might find your photos even become a little inconsistent for a while, as you're experimenting. That's part of the learning process. I've edited more than a million photos for professional photographers in their own styles, but I'm still figuring out my own preferences too. That's part of the fun of editing!

EDITING TOOLS   10

In the previous sections, we've discussed the theory of photo editing. Now let's get down to the practicalities of editing in Lightroom.

NON-DESTRUCTIVE EDITING

Lightroom's Editing tools are non-destructive. This simply means that the edits are saved as a series of text instructions. If you make an edit one day in Lightroom, and change your mind the next day, you can simply move the slider back, without degrading the image quality.

Non-destructive editing also means that you can make adjustments in whatever order you like, skipping from one tool to the next. However, there are more efficient ways of working, so we'll discuss the editing tools in a logical workflow order. Remember, you don't have to use every tool and slider!

To **show the main Edit sliders** on the desktop, click the Edit button in the right panel bar, or press the E key.

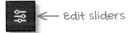 ← Edit sliders

On a mobile device, tap on a photo to open into a Detail view, then select the Edit view from the pop-up at the top of the screen on a phone, or the icons down the sidebar on a tablet.

WORKFLOW TOOLS

As you start to get better at editing, Lightroom offers tools that can help improve efficiency and consistency over groups of photos, and allow you to experiment with more freedom. They're handy to know about before you get started, so we'll discuss these tools next.

IN THIS SECTION, WE'LL CONSIDER:

• Where to find the global and local editing tools.

• How to undo and reset edits.

• How to compare the photo with the unedited original.

• How to create multiple versions of the same photo.

• How to copy edits to other photos.

EDITING WORKFLOW

It's time to start editing, but we don't want to waste time going in circles, so we've analyzed the photo (page 99) and made a plan, just like the pros.

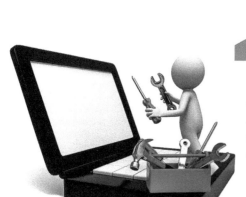

There's a whole array of editing tools which can look overwhelming (page 115), but we'll work through them in a logical order.

Don't worry about making mistakes, as Lightroom's a non-destructive editor, so you can always undo or start over (page 123).

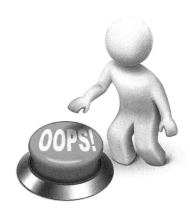

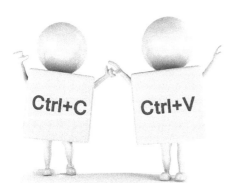

And if you do something you love, you can copy the same edits to other photos (page 126) or save them as a preset (page 146).

Start by cropping and straightening the photo (page 129) to remove distractions and improve composition.

Then decide on your "look" (page 137). Do you prefer bright punchy photos? Or soft and subdued? Perhaps you miss the "good old" film days.

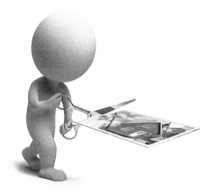

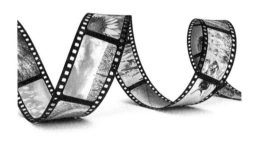

Then it's time to balance the light and contrast (page 151).

And perfect the color (page 175).

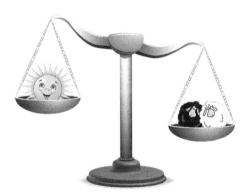

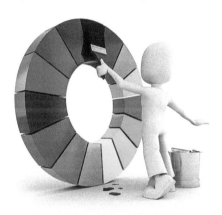

Or perhaps you'd prefer a B&W or tinted monochrome image (page 185).

How about adding some special effects (page 193), like a vignette to draw the eye, film-like grain, or split toning effects.

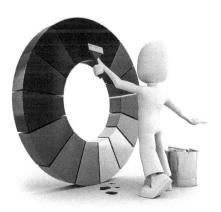

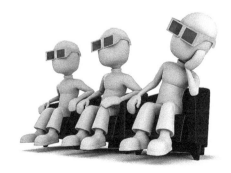

Then we need to optimize the detail (page 201) in the photo by sharpening and reducing digital noise.

Most photos benefit from selective adjustments (page 207), like dodging and burning, to minimize distractions and draw the eye around the photo.

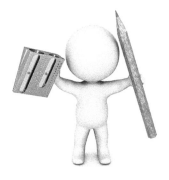

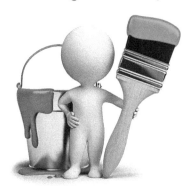

There might also be some distortion (page 225) that needs correcting, and of course you'll probably need to tweak the crop again after fixing it.

There's sure to be some distractions that need cleaning up, whether using Lightroom's Healing tools (page 236) or jumping to Photoshop for more advanced editing (page 244).

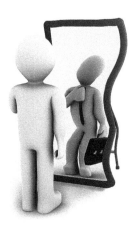

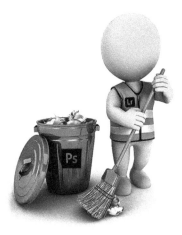

Done? Give yourself a pat on the back, and keep practicing!

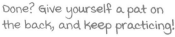

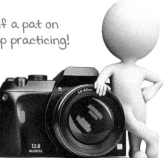

THE EDITING TOOLS (WINDOWS/MAC)

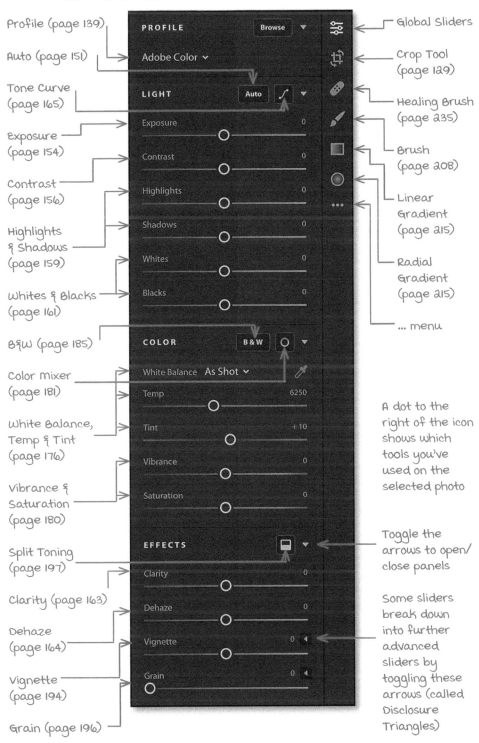

Profile (page 139)

Auto (page 151)

Tone Curve (page 165)

Exposure (page 154)

Contrast (page 156)

Highlights & Shadows (page 159)

Whites & Blacks (page 161)

B&W (page 185)

Color Mixer (page 181)

White Balance, Temp & Tint (page 176)

Vibrance & Saturation (page 180)

Split Toning (page 197)

Clarity (page 163)

Dehaze (page 164)

Vignette (page 194)

Grain (page 196)

PROFILE   Browse ▼

Adobe Color ⌄

LIGHT   Auto ⌄ ▼

Exposure   0

Contrast   0

Highlights   0

Shadows   0

Whites   0

Blacks   0

COLOR   B&W ○ ▼

White Balance As Shot ⌄

Temp   6250

Tint   +10

Vibrance   0

Saturation   0

EFFECTS   ▼

Clarity   0

Dehaze   0

Vignette   0 ◄

Grain   0 ◄

Global Sliders

Crop Tool (page 129)

Healing Brush (page 235)

Brush (page 208)

Linear Gradient (page 215)

Radial Gradient (page 215)

... menu

A dot to the right of the icon shows which tools you've used on the selected photo

Toggle the arrows to open/close panels

Some sliders break down into further advanced sliders by toggling these arrows (called Disclosure Triangles)

Sharpening (page 202)

Noise Reduction & Color Noise
Reduction (page 205)

Remove Chromatic
Aberration & Enable Lens
Corrections (page 226)

manual Transforms (page 232)

Upright (page 229)

Presets (page 146)

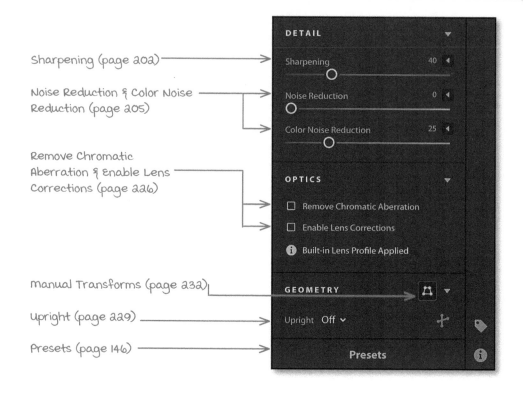

... menu

Copy/Paste Edit Settings
(page 126)

Before/After Preview (page 125)

Reset (page 123)

Histogram (page 103)

On a small screen, select Single-
Panel mode to automatically close
panels as you open another

Edit in Photoshop (page 244)

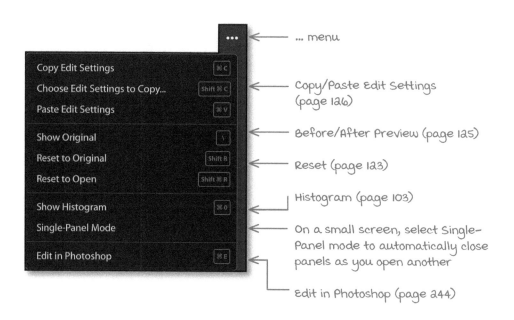

THE EDITING VIEW (IOS)

Tap to switch between Edit, Info, Keywords, Rate & Review and Activity views

Share menu incl. Edit in other apps

Sync Status incl. download full size original (if available)

Back to Grid view

Tap to undo, hold to redo

Two finger tap anywhere to switch between metadata overlay, histogram or neither. One finger tap on metadata cycles metadata views

Swipe left <> right on the photo with one finger to view the next/previous photo

Drag left <> right on slider to adjust value

Scroll up/ down to show additional sliders

Swipe row left <> right to show all sets of sliders

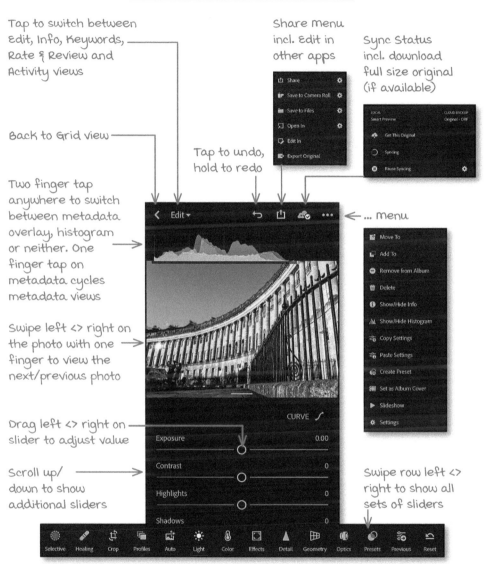

To view clipping warnings, hold two fingers while dragging slider handle

Hold finger on photo to preview without recent edits

Double-tap slider handle to reset slider

Double-tap anywhere or pinch/spread to zoom in and out

Tap on photo to hide controls

THE EDITING VIEW (ANDROID)

Tap to switch between
Edit, Info and Rate
& Review views

Sync Status
incl. download
full size original
(if available)

Share menu
incl. Edit in
other apps

Back to Grid view

Tap to
undo, hold
to redo

Enable metadata
or histogram
in the menu

One finger tap on
metadata cycles
metadata views

Swipe left <> right on
the photo with one
finger to view the
next/previous photo

Drag left <> right on
slider to adjust value

Scroll up/down to
show additional
sliders

← ... menu

Swipe row left <>
right to show all
sets of sliders

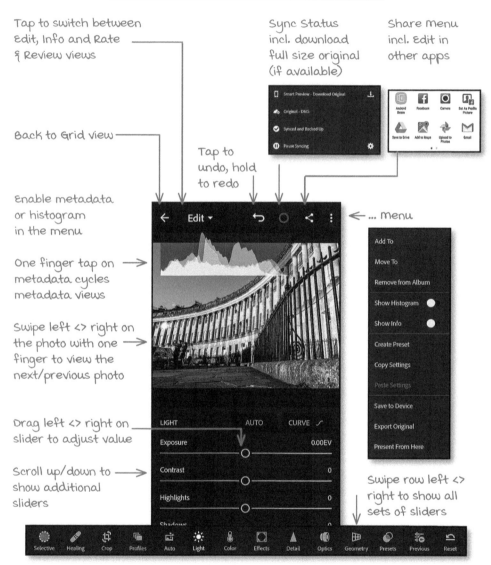

To view clipping
warnings, hold two
fingers while dragging
slider handle

Hold finger on photo
to preview without
recent edits

Double-tap
slider handle to
reset slider

Double-tap anywhere
or pinch/spread to
zoom in and out

Tap on photo to
hide controls

UNDOING MISTAKES & RESETTING EDITS

Lightroom is a non-destructive editor. It doesn't apply the settings to the original image data, but just stores your edits as a list of text instructions (*Exposure* +1.2, *Highlights* -40, *Shadows* +40, etc.). This means you can easily undo any edits you've made to your photo in Lightroom, even if it was edited months ago, so you can experiment without fear and try new things. It's a great way of learning.

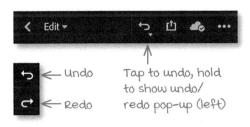

Tap to undo, hold to show undo/redo pop-up (left)

If you don't like a slider setting, the most obvious solution is to simply move the slider to a new value, but there's also a variety of undo and reset options.

UNDOING / REDOING ACTIONS

To **undo your last action** on the desktop (or the one before that, or the one before that), just keep hitting Ctrl-Z (Windows) / Cmd-Z (Mac) to step back in time.

This doesn't just apply to edits on the selected photo. It remembers most things you've done in chronological order—including adding star ratings, flags, metadata and even switching photos—for as long as Lightroom's open. When you quit Lightroom, the undo history is cleared.

If you go too far, use Ctrl-Y (Windows) / Cmd-Shift-Z (Mac) to redo the last undone action.

On mobile, undo/redo only applies to the edits you've applied since you last switched photos. To undo, tap the undo button at the top of the screen, and just keep tapping to undo previous actions. To redo an action, hold your finger on the undo button to show the redo button.

RESETTING THE EDITS

If you made the change you want to undo some time ago, then the reset options are a better choice. These reset a single slider, a whole section of sliders, a selective adjustment or all of the edits applied to a photo back to their default settings.

To **reset a single slider**, float over the slider label, which changes to a *Reset* button, then click on it. On mobile, double-tap on the slider handle.

To **reset a whole panel of sliders**, hold down the Alt key (Windows) / Opt key (Mac) and click on the section label (desktop only).

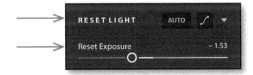

To **reset the entire photo** back to default settings on the desktop, click the ... menu in the right panel bar to show the fly-out menu, then select *Reset to Original*, or use the keyboard shortcut Shift-R.

If you only want to reset the edits from the current editing session (since you switched to the selected photo), select *Reset to Open* from the same menu, or use the keyboard shortcut Ctrl-Shift-R (Windows) / Cmd-Shift-R (Mac).

On mobile, tapping the **Reset** button at the right-hand end of the edit toolbar offers a series of options:

Adjustments resets everything except the Crop.

All resets all settings to the default settings.

To Import resets all of the settings to the settings selected when the photo was first imported to the mobile device or synced to the cloud.

To Open resets the photo to the settings used when you switched to the photo.

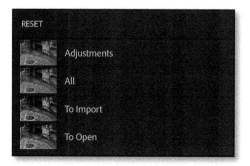

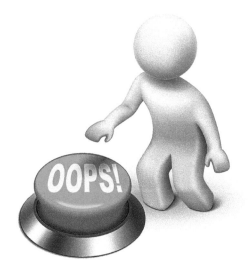

COMPARING VERSIONS & CREATING COPIES

While you're learning how to edit your photos, you'll want to compare your edits against earlier versions and experiment without losing the edits you're happy with. Lightroom provides the tools you need.

VIEWING A BEFORE/AFTER PREVIEW

While you're working on editing your photos, you can **compare your edited version with the original**. To do so on the desktop, click the *Show Original* icon in the toolbar beneath the photo, press the \ key on your keyboard, or use the **Show Original** command in the ... menu in the right panel bar. Repeat to show the edited version again.

Fit Fill 1:1 🖼 ⫶ ← Show Original

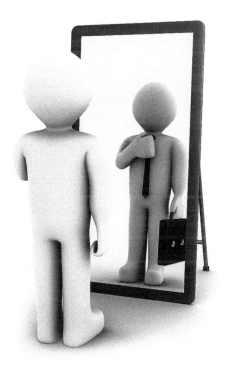

On mobile, hold your finger on the photo in Edit view to display the Before view. Unlike the desktop apps, this Before view is not necessarily the original. Instead, it shows the photo before you starting editing on the current device.

CREATING COPIES

Sometimes you'll want to create two different versions of the same photo. Perhaps you want to try it in color and in B&W, or you want to try a couple of different presets and compare them.

To **create a copy of a photo** on the desktop, right-click and select **Make a Copy**. You'll also find it in the *Edit* menu. Copies do take up additional space in the cloud and on your hard drive, so you may want to delete ones you no longer need.

At the time of writing, you can't create a copy using the mobile apps.

Remember, you don't need to create a copy before editing, because you can just reset the photo to get back to the unedited version.

COPYING & PASTING EDITS

If you're shooting a series of photos in similar light, they're likely to need similar edits. To save time and improve consistency, you can copy and paste the settings.

COPY/PASTE ON THE DESKTOP

On the desktop, you can paste the edit settings from one photo to multiple photos. To do so:

1. Go to the ... menu in the right panel bar and select *Choose Edit Settings to Copy...* or use the keyboard shortcut Ctrl-Shift-C (Windows) / Cmd-Shift-C (Mac).

2. In the Copy Settings dialog, check the specific panels, sliders or tools you want to copy to the clipboard. In the pop-up above the checkboxes:

All checks all of the sliders, and *None* unchecks the sliders, so you can pick specific sliders yourself.

Default checks the sliders Adobe thinks you'll want to include, or the sliders you've set as defaults. (We'll come back to setting custom defaults shortly.)

Modified checks only the sliders you've edited.

3. Click *Copy* to place the checked settings on the clipboard.

4. If you only want to paste to a single photo, you can stay in Detail view and go to the ... menu > *Paste Edit Settings* or use the shortcut Ctrl-V (Windows) / Cmd-V (Mac).

If you want to apply the settings to multiple photos, switch back to the Grid view, select the photos, and then use the same shortcut.

There's a secret shortcut that allows you to paste the settings to multiple selected photos in Detail view, but be careful if your Filmstrip is hidden, as you might not realize that multiple photos are selected. The secret shortcut is Ctrl-Shift-V (Windows) / Cmd-Shift-V (Mac).

DEFAULT COPY SETTINGS ON THE DESKTOP

You can **skip the Copy Settings dialog** by going to ... menu > *Copy Edit Settings* or using the shortcut Ctrl-C (Windows) / Cmd-C (Mac). This copies the default copy settings.

Adobe's own defaults copy the Profile, Light panel, Color panel, Effects panel, Detail panel and Chromatic Aberration checkbox. It skips the Crop, Healing, Brush and Gradient tools, as well as the Lens Profile and Geometry adjustments, as these are more likely to be in different positions on different photos.

You can **change the copy defaults** by checking your chosen checkboxes in the Copy Settings dialog, clicking the ... icon on the right and then selecting *Set as Default*.

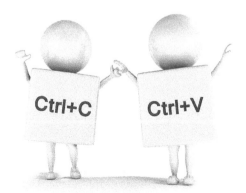

COPY/PASTE ON MOBILE

Copying on mobile is more limited, as you can only paste to one photo at a time. To do so:

1. Tap the ... menu and select *Copy Settings*.

2. In the Copy Settings menu, check the groups of settings you want to copy, or tap the arrow to check/uncheck individual sliders. Tap *OK* to place the settings on the clipboard.

3. Switch to the target photo.

4. Tap the ... menu and select *Paste Settings*.

COPY FROM PREVIOUS ON MOBILE

There's an additional *Previous* button at the right hand end of the Edit view toolbar, which copies some or all edits from the previously selected photo onto the current photo, without having to go through the Copy Settings dialog.

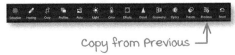

Copy from Previous

At the time of writing, there are some slight inconsistencies between operating systems, but I'd expect the Android app to be updated to match the iOS behavior in due course.

Adjustments copies everything except for the crop (iOS) / copies the Light panel settings (Android).

All copies all of the settings from the previous photo, including the crop (iOS) / excluding the crop (Android).

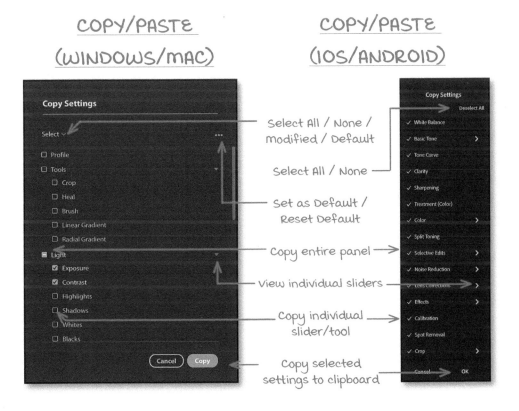

CROPPING & STRAIGHTENING 11

In an ideal world, you'd have the time to make sure a photo was perfectly composed in the camera at the time of shooting. Unfortunately, few of us live in an ideal world, and by the time you've perfected the shot, you've missed the moment.

Cropping is the removal of the outer parts of a photo. Most photos benefit from cropping, whether to remove distractions from the frame, to straighten horizons, to improve the composition, to draw the viewer's eye to the subject, to fit a specific paper or frame shape, or simply to zoom in closer on the subject, if you were unable to move closer at the time of shooting.

Any cropping you do within Lightroom is non-destructive. No pixels are deleted from the original files. They're just hidden. If you later change your mind, you can return to the Crop tool to adjust or reset the crop markings.

IN THIS SECTION, WE'LL CONSIDER:

• Some basic rules to help your composition.

• How to crop photos to specific aspect ratios, to fit standard print sizes or frames.

• How to straighten wonky horizons.

• How to rotate photos by 90°, if the camera didn't do it for you.

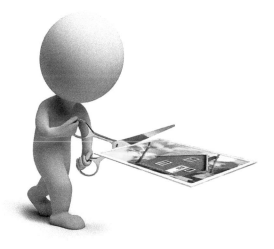

COMPOSITION BASICS

Entire books are written on the subject of composition, so we won't attempt to cover the subject in detail in this book. However, the principles learned from composition books apply to cropping photos in Lightroom, as much as they apply to framing the photo in the camera.

If you're new to photography, there are a few basic principles to bear in mind when learning to crop your photos. They're not hard and fast rules, and as you grow in experience, you can break them, but they're a good place to start.

COMPOSITION TIPS

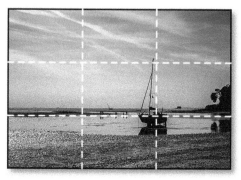

Use the Rule of Thirds to help you decide where to place the subject in the frame

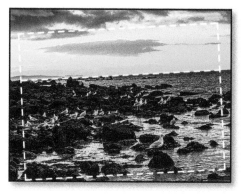

Straighten the horizon, and any other lines that should be vertical or horizontal, especially if they're near the edge of the frame

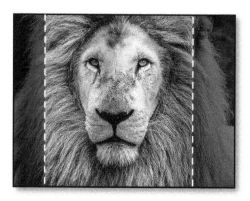

Crop to fill the frame, to simplify the image and remove distractions

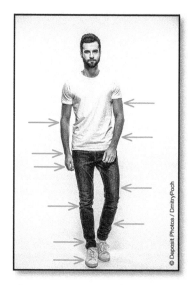

Avoid cropping at people's joints as it looks unnatural. Crop mid-way between joints wherever possible

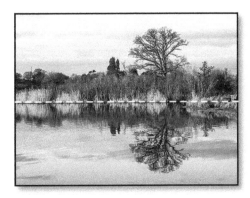

Avoid putting the subject or horizon
dead center (unless there's symmetry)

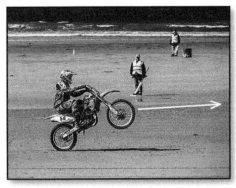

If the subject is moving, leave space
for the viewer's eye to follow

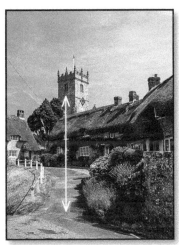

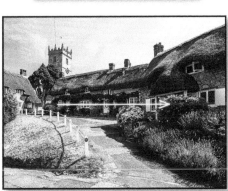

The orientation can affect the
direction the viewer's eye travels,
so select a vertical or horizontal
crop with that in mind

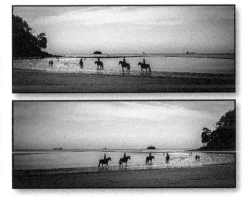

If a person or animal isn't looking
at the camera, leave space to
follow the subject's gaze

Flip a photo if it helps the viewer's eye
travel more smoothly from left to right

UNDERSTANDING ASPECT RATIO

Images on screen can be any shape you like, but if you're printing or framing a photo, you'll need to match the photo's aspect ratio to the paper or frame. If you don't crop to the right ratio, you'll either end up with white paper showing along two edges, or the printer will cut off more of the photo than you intended.

The same principle applies to other aspect ratios, not just cropping to square. Imagine trying to fit a panoramic photo into a normal rectangular frame, and you'll have the same choices to make.

We'll learn how to crop to a specific ratio in the next lesson.

WHAT IS ASPECT RATIO?

The aspect ratio is simply the proportional relationship between the width and height of a photo, in other words, it's the shape of the photo. You'll often see it written with a colon (2:3) or with an x (2x3).

Some aspect ratios are long and thin, whereas others are closer to square. A square is 1x1, which means the height and width are equal, whereas a 16x9 widescreen shape is a long and thin rectangle.

CROPPING FOR PRINTS/FRAMES

Imagine you have a rectangular photo and a square frame. Clearly it's not going to fit, so what are your options?

1. Squash the photo to fit. This never looks good, so Lightroom doesn't let you do it.

2. Keep the rectangular shape, but add white borders along the other edges.

3. Crop the top and bottom (or sides), so that it will fit.

4. Buy another frame that's closer to the aspect ratio of the photo, so you don't need to crop as much.

STANDARD ASPECT RATIOS

1 x 1

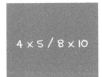
4 x 5 / 8 x 10

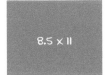
8.5 x 11

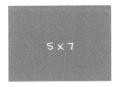
5 x 7

2 x 3 / 4 x 6

The shape of standard print ratios varies. 4x5 is quite square, whereas 2x3/4x6 is longer and thinner

Screen sizes vary from traditional rectangular ratios to newer widescreen formats

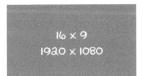
4 x 3
1024 x 768

16 x 9
1920 x 1080

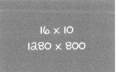
16 x 10
1280 x 800

CROPPING FOR PRINT

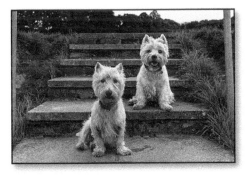

A rectangular photo and a square frame... how do you make the photo fit?

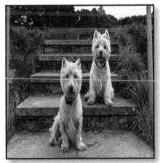

Squash it?

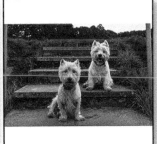

Add borders?

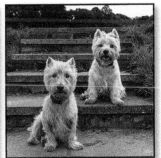

Crop it!

CROPPING & STRAIGHTENING PHOTOS

In the last couple of lessons, we've learned about composition and aspect ratios, but now let's focus on the practicalities of cropping using Lightroom.

To **select the Crop tool** and show the crop options, click the icon in the right panel bar (desktop/tablet) / Edit view toolbar (phone) or press the C key (desktop).

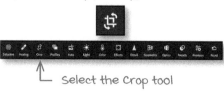

Select the Crop tool

STRAIGHTENING WONKY HORIZONS

Logically, our eyes expect the horizon to be horizontal, but most photographers have trouble getting it perfectly level at the time of capture. The Crop tool allows you to correct the rotation in a few different ways:

To let Lightroom attempt to **automatically straighten the horizon**, click the *Auto* button (desktop) / *Straighten* button (mobile) in the Crop panel.

To **straighten the photo by eye** on the desktop, float the cursor outside the bounding box (the edge of the crop) so the cursor turns into a double-headed arrow, then click and drag to rotate the photo. A grid displays to help you judge the rotation. On a mobile device, drag your finger anywhere outside the bounding box.

As you rotate the crop, the photo remains level, so you don't have to turn your head to see how the photo will look once it's cropped.

To **manually draw the correct horizon line** on the desktop, hold down the Ctrl

key (Windows) / Cmd key (Mac), click on the horizon and drag further along the horizon, then release the mouse. Lightroom straightens the line, and in the process, straightens the photo too.

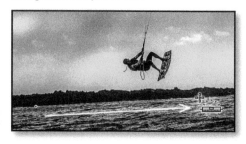

To **straighten the photo using the slider**, adjust the *Straighten* slider in the Crop panel (desktop) / under the photo (mobile). While you're dragging the slider, a grid overlay displays to help.

To **reset the rotation**, click on the slider label (desktop) / double-tap the curved slider under the photo (mobile). This only resets the rotation and doesn't expand the crop back to the edges of the original photo.

CROPPING PHOTOS

To **crop a photo**, drag the edges or corners of the bounding box (that's the edge of the crop). Occasionally, you'll try to drag the edge of the bounding box, but it won't move. This is because the photo is slightly rotated and it's bumping up against the edge. Move the crop boundary away from the edge of the photo or reset the *Straighten* slider to fix it.

To **crop a vertical rectangle out of a horizontal photo**, or vice versa, click/tap the *Rotate Crop Aspect* button or on the desktop, you can also press the X key. You can also drag the corner of the bounding box at a 45° angle.

To **move the photo** under the crop overlay, click (desktop) / hold (mobile) and drag within the crop boundary.

To completely **reset the crop**, click the main *Reset Crop* button at the top of the Crop panel (desktop) or double-tap on the photo (mobile).

SELECTING AN ASPECT RATIO

If you're planning to print your photo using a standard print size or put it in a standard shape frame, you'll need to crop the photo to the right ratio, as we learned in the previous lesson (page 132). Lightroom offers the most frequent ratios as presets in the **Aspect** pop-up. The first set are standard print ratios, and the second set are standard screen shapes.

The **Original** and **As Shot** options are identical for most photos. Some cameras (including Lightroom's own camera) allow you to crop the photos to a specific ratio at the time of shooting, or display crop lines on the screen. *As Shot* respects the in-camera crop setting, whereas *Original* uses the full sensor data (where available).

To **constrain your crop** to a specific aspect

CROP PANEL (WINDOWS/MAC)

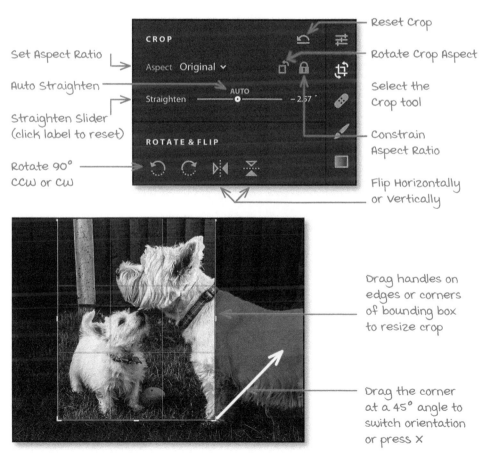

Set Aspect Ratio

Auto Straighten

Straighten Slider (click label to reset)

Rotate 90° CCW or CW

Reset Crop

Rotate Crop Aspect

Select the Crop tool

Constrain Aspect Ratio

Flip Horizontally or Vertically

Drag handles on edges or corners of bounding box to resize crop

Drag the corner at a 45° angle to switch orientation or press X

ratio, click/tap the *Constrain Aspect Ratio* lock icon so that the lock is closed (desktop/mobile), or hold down the Shift key while adjusting the crop (desktop).

To **allow a freeform crop**, click to unlock the lock icon.

ROTATING & FLIPPING PHOTOS

If your camera doesn't automatically rotate vertical photos, you can manually **rotate by 90°** using the circular arrow buttons.

You can also **rotate multiple photos by 90°** on the desktop by selecting the photos in Grid view and going to *Photo menu > Rotate Left/Right* or using the keyboard shortcuts Ctrl-[(Windows) / Cmd-[(Mac) to rotate counter-clockwise/left and Ctrl-] (Windows) / Cmd-] (Mac) to rotate clockwise/right.

Occasionally you may want to flip a photo horizontally or vertically, because we read photos from left to right. To **flip the photo**, click/tap the *Flip Horizontal* or *Flip Vertical* buttons.

CROP TOOL (IOS/ANDROID)

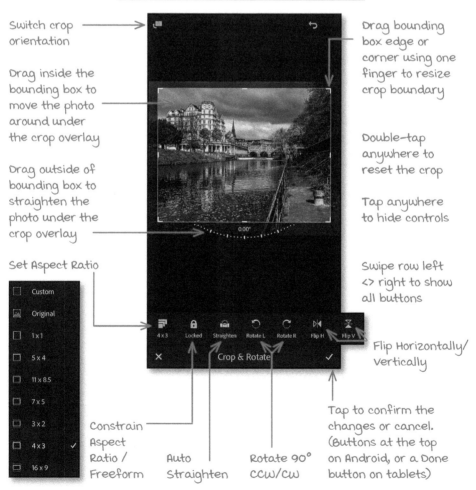

Switch crop orientation

Drag inside the bounding box to move the photo around under the crop overlay

Drag outside of bounding box to straighten the photo under the crop overlay

Set Aspect Ratio

Custom
Original
1 x 1
5 x 4
11 x 8.5
7 x 5
3 x 2
4 x 3 ✓
16 x 9

Constrain Aspect Ratio / Freeform

Auto Straighten

Rotate 90° CCW/CW

Drag bounding box edge or corner using one finger to resize crop boundary

Double-tap anywhere to reset the crop

Tap anywhere to hide controls

Swipe row left <> right to show all buttons

Flip Horizontally/ vertically

Tap to confirm the changes or cancel. (Buttons at the top on Android, or a Done button on tablets)

4 x 3 | Locked | Straighten | Rotate L | Rotate R | Flip H | Flip V

Crop & Rotate

SELECTING YOUR LOOK

12

Over the last few years, presets and filters have become a popular way of editing photos. On page 95, we said that when used alone, they can be a bit of a blunt instrument. However, in combination with other editing skills, they can be a valuable addition to your workflow.

FILM STOCK

The idea of starting to build your photo from a base profile isn't a new concept. In the world of film photography, each film has its own characteristics, and a photographer chooses their film stock based on the kind of look they desire.

Kodak's Portra range is popular for portraits, with it's natural skin tones, realistic color saturation and fine grain, whereas their Ektar film offers much more vivid and highly saturated colors.

Slide films like Kodak's now-retired Kodachrome and Ektachrome, and Fuji's Provia and Velvia, have long been popular with landscape photographers for their vibrant, punchy colors and high contrast.

For B&W, the iconic Kodak Tri-X has lots of contrast and a distinctive grain, making it popular for street and documentary photography, whereas Kodak's T-Max had a finer grain for a cleaner look.

In the same way, you can build your photo edits from a specific base profile, depending on the look you desire.

PROFILES VS. PRESETS

Lightroom uses three different types of profiles and presets, each with their own advantages and disadvantages.

Camera-specific profiles only work on raw files and are designed to be a starting point for your own editing. They're found in the Profile panel, above the editing sliders.

Creative profiles can be applied to all sorts of photos to add a distinctive look, and they're designed to not need additional editing, beyond corrections for exposure, lens distortion, sharpening, etc. They can also be faded or exaggerated using an *Amount* slider, depending how strong an effect your prefer. These are also found in the Profile panel.

Presets, found in the Presets panel (opened using the button below the editing sliders), save sets of slider values to easily apply to other photos. They're ideal for saving your favorite vignette settings, or the sharpening settings you use for portraits, or the starting edits you apply to every photo.

The main differences are shown in the table overleaf, but in summary, they're slightly different tools for different jobs. Presets are best used for your own creations, and for modular systems (for example, to use one preset for sharpening and a different one for grain), whereas profiles are ideal for commercial developers to create special effects and film emulation.

WHEN TO APPLY PRESETS & PROFILES

You'll generally need to select your profile or preset before you start moving sliders, as profiles change the overall look, and presets move sliders, overwriting your changes.

The exception are presets that only move a few sliders, such as your favorite vignette settings.

IN THIS SECTION, WE'LL CONSIDER:

- The different types of profiles.

- How to preview and apply profiles.

- How to preview and apply presets.

- How to create your own presets.

DIFFERENCES BETWEEN PRESETS & PROFILES

Presets	Camera-Specific Raw Profiles	Creative Profiles
.lrtemplate or .xmp file extension	.dcp or .xmp file extension	.xmp file extension
Works on all photo formats, unless they call a raw-only profile	Work on raw files only (usually camera-specific)	Most work for all photo formats
Create them yourself using Lightroom	Mostly created by third-party developers using DNG Profile Editor (.dcp format) or Profiles SDK (.xmp format)	Mostly created by third-party developers using Profiles SDK
Moves sliders, so you can see how the adjustments were created	Separate layer of adjustments, which doesn't move visible sliders, so they're more difficult to learn from	Separate layer of adjustments, which don't move visible sliders, so they're more difficult to learn from
Can only adjust visible Lightroom tools such as sliders	Applies normal Lightroom edits behind the scenes, plus 3D LUT's for more advanced color adjustments	Applies normal Lightroom edits behind the scenes, plus 3D LUT's for more advanced color adjustments
Increase/decrease effect by moving the individual sliders	Can't be faded	Exaggerate/fade effect using *Amount* slider, then edit from there
Best for your own settings, to improve consistency and efficiency	Best as a starting point, like film stock	Best for special effects

BROWSING, APPLYING & IMPORTING PROFILES

Camera-specific and Creative profiles are found in the Profile panel, at the top of the Edit slider panels (desktop/tablet) or near the left of the Edit view toolbar (phone).

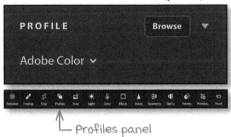

Profiles panel

To view the full range of profiles, click the **Browse** button, or on the desktop, use the shortcut Shift-B.

BROWSING & APPLYING PROFILES

When you first open the Profile Browser, you'll see a series of small thumbnails, grouped into sets. We'll come back to the difference between the sets on page 143.

To **apply a profile** on a desktop or tablet, click/tap on it and then click the *Back* button to return to the normal Edit sliders (or on the desktop, double-clicking on the profile

will do both at once). On a mobile phone, tap on the profile and then tap the checkmark to return to the normal Edit view.

If you change your mind, you can return to the Profile panel and select a different profile at any time.

On the desktop, the thumbnails may be a little small to preview properly, so float your cursor over the profile thumbnail or name to **preview the profile** on the larger image. To briefly stop previewing the profile, to compare it with your current profile, hold down the Alt key (Windows) / Opt key (Mac). You can change the thumbnail Grid view to a List view or Large thumbnail view by clicking the ... icon in the top right corner.

SETTING FAVORITES

Over the course of time, you're likely to use some profiles more than others. This is a good thing, because the profile becomes part of YOUR distinctive style. If you mix and match too many different profiles, your work will lack consistency.

List view   Grid view →

Large view

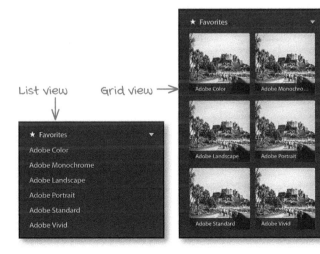

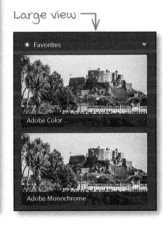

THE PROFILE BROWSER (WINDOWS/MAC)

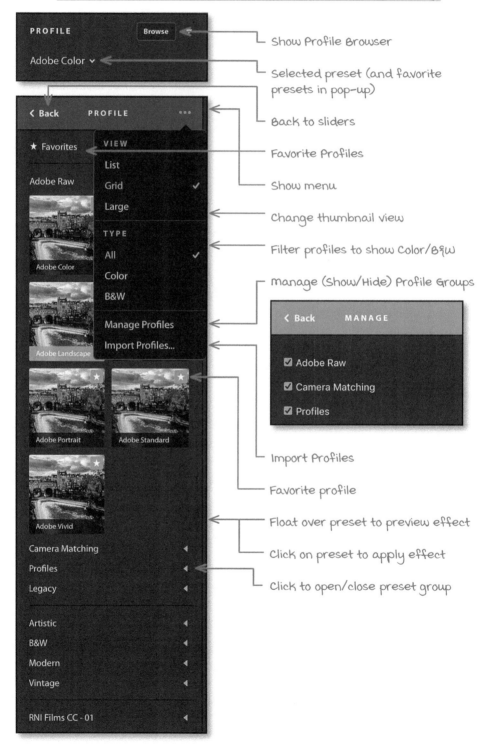

Show Profile Browser

Selected preset (and favorite presets in pop-up)

Back to sliders

Favorite Profiles

Show menu

Change thumbnail view

Filter profiles to show Color/B&W

Manage (Show/Hide) Profile Groups

Import Profiles

Favorite profile

Float over preset to preview effect

Click on preset to apply effect

Click to open/close preset group

THE PROFILE BROWSER (IOS/ANDROID)

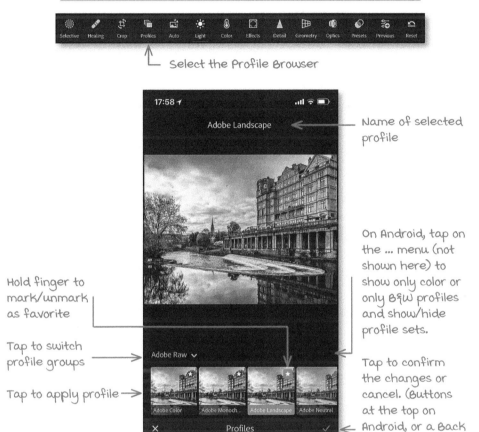

Select the Profile Browser

Name of selected profile

On Android, tap on the ... menu (not shown here) to show only color or only B&W profiles and show/hide profile sets.

Hold finger to mark/unmark as favorite

Tap to switch profile groups

Tap to apply profile

Tap to confirm the changes or cancel. (Buttons at the top on Android, or a Back button on tablets)

To **mark/unmark a profile as a favorite** on the desktop, click the star icon in the corner of the thumbnail, or to the right in List view. On mobile, hold your finger on the thumbnail.

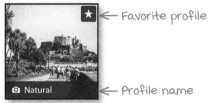

← Favorite profile

← Profile name

These profiles then show in the Favorites set at the top of the Profile Browser. On the desktop, they also show in the pop-up, so

you don't have to open the Profile Browser every time you want to switch profiles.

MANAGING PROFILES

If you know you want to create a color or B&W photo, you can **temporarily filter the profiles** on Windows, Mac or Android by clicking/tapping the ... button and selecting *Color* or *B&W* from the menu. Select *All* to show all of the profiles again. (This filtering is not currently available on iOS.)

There will likely be some profiles that you

don't use, and the number of profiles will grow over time as you download new ones, so Lightroom allows you to hide entire sets of profiles.

To **show and hide profiles** on the desktop, click the ... icon at the top of the Profile Browser panel and select *Manage Profiles*. Check or uncheck profile sets, and then click the *Back* button to return. If you right-click on a profile set in the Profile Browser, there's quick access to the *Hide* and *Reset Hidden Items* commands.

On Android, tap the ... menu in the Profile Browser and select *Manage Profiles* to check/uncheck profile sets. (This isn't currently available on iOS.)

INSTALLING & SYNCING PROFILES

Some third-party profiles are starting to become available for purchase and download.

To **install downloaded profiles** on the desktop, go to *File menu > Import Profiles and Presets* or click the ... icon at the top of the Profile Browser and select *Import Profiles*. Navigate to the folder or zip file containing the presets and click *Import*.

Profile import is currently only available in Windows/Mac apps, not on mobile or web, but once profiles are imported into the desktop app, they sync to your other devices.

MISSING PROFILES

If you've used other versions of Lightroom (such as Lightroom Classic), or you've used Adobe Camera Raw in Photoshop, you may have used camera-specific profiles (DCP format) without realizing. For example,

VSCO presets automatically select a camera-specific profile. These camera-specific profiles need to be imported into Lightroom CC, so they can be stored safely and synced to your other devices.

On first launch, Lightroom automatically imports any camera-specific (DCP format) profiles installed on your computer. However, if the profiles can't be automatically imported into Lightroom, it displays a missing profile warning on affected photos, to remind you to import the profile or select a different one.

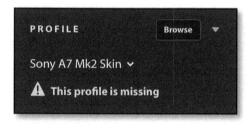

SETS OF PROFILES

When you open the Profile Browser, you'll notice that the profiles are grouped into sections with a line between (called clusters), and into folders (called sets) too.

BASIC

The Basic set appears for rendered photos (JPEG/TIFF/PSD/PNG format), as they don't have Adobe Raw profiles. There are simple *Color* and *Monochrome* profiles for these file types.

ADOBE RAW

The Adobe Raw profiles aim to make photos from different cameras look as similar as possible, so if you change your camera or shoot an event with multiple camera brands, they'll blend well. They're available for raw photos from most (but not all) supported cameras.

Adobe Color is Adobe's default profile. The aim is to look great on a wide range of photos, so it adds a little contrast and saturation, while attempting to protect the skin tones.

Adobe Portrait is optimized for a wide range of skin tones, including very pale skin and very dark skin, so it's ideal for portraits and family shots. It has a little less contrast than *Adobe Color*, but you can add contrast if you prefer a bit more punch.

Adobe Landscape automatically compresses the tones to give a little more headroom for outdoor photos which often have a wide dynamic range, and the blues and greens are enhanced.

Adobe Vivid has a very punchy and saturated effect. It's great for sunsets and other very colorful photos, but may be a little over the top for portraits.

Adobe Neutral is a very flat starting point, ready for you to edit in your own way. It's ideal for photos with very tricky colors and gradients that just don't quite work with the other profiles.

Adobe Standard is an older profile that all of the other Adobe Raw profiles are based on. It's similar to *Adobe Color*, but it has a little less contrast and saturation.

Adobe Monochrome is the default profile for B&W photos, and is automatically assigned when you click the *B&W* button in the Color panel.

CAMERA MATCHING

The camera matching profiles are designed to mimic your camera JPEG, so your raw files more closely match the image you saw on the back of the camera. In addition to the *Camera Default* or *Camera Standard* profiles, these profiles also try to emulate the other picture styles that your camera manufacturers offers. The names of these vary by manufacturer, for example, Canon calls them Picture Styles, Nikon named them Picture Control, Fuji has Simulation Modes, Olympus has Picture Modes and Sony calls them Creative Styles. These camera matching profiles are available for most current DSLR's, but may be missing from compact or older cameras, and they won't be available for rendered files.

PROFILES

If you've created camera-specific DCP

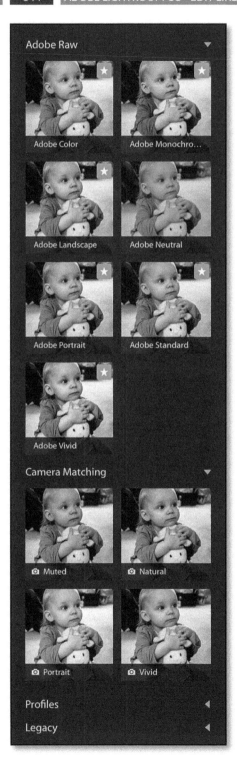

Camera-Specific Profiles

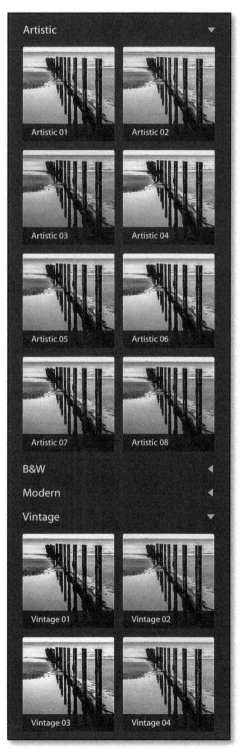

Creative Profiles

format profiles using Adobe's DNG Profile Editor tool or the X-Rite ColorChecker Passport plug-in for Lightroom Classic, or installed camera-specific profiles created by third-parties such as VSCO or RNI Films, they'll be found in a Profiles set.

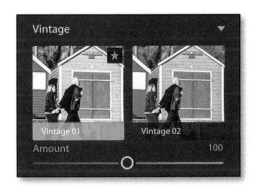

LEGACY PROFILES

The Legacy Profiles set contains B&W versions of some camera-specific profiles. As the set name suggests, these are just to maintain compatibility with edits applied using previous Lightroom versions.

CREATIVE PROFILES

The next cluster of sets contains a selection of creative profiles. These are primarily designed to apply special effects or a specific "look" to your photo, and they'll work for rendered files (JPEG/TIFF/PSD/PNG) as well as raw photos.

The **Modern** profiles represent current fashions in photography, while the **Vintage** profiles are designed to look more like film photos. The **Artistic** profiles are designed to be more edgy, with stronger color shifts.

The **B&W** profiles are optimized for high impact black and white work, offering a range of color channel mixes and tonal adjustments. In addition to the selection of numbered B&W profiles, there are profiles to imitate the effect of adding a red, orange, yellow, green or blue filter. These are traditionally used at the time of capture when shooting B&W on film. The B&W profiles are a great starting point for B&W editing.

The effect of the Creative profiles can be faded or exaggerated using the **Amount** slider that appears immediately below the profile thumbnail, or in the main Profile panel. 100 applies the effect as the developer intended, moving the slider to the left reduces the effect of the profile, and moving it to the right exaggerates the effect.

Creative Profiles can contain any normal slider adjustments to be applied "behind the scenes," but they can also include LUT's (Look Up Tables) for much more advanced color adjustments. 3D LUT's can, for example, tell Lightroom to make this shade of blue yellower and make this shade of blue more saturated and another shade of blue lighter. The tables allow profile developers to apply specific adjustments in very precise, targeted ways that are not possible through any of Lightroom's sliders.

Creative profiles created by third-party profiles are added as additional sets at the bottom of the Profile Browser.

SAVING SETTINGS AS PRESETS

Whereas profiles are created by third-party developers, you can create presets yourself. They can help you to:

Improve Efficiency—For example, perhaps you find yourself selecting a camera matching profile, decreasing *Highlights*, increasing *Shadows* and adding a little *Clarity* and *Vibrance* to most photos. Rather than having to move multiple sliders, you can select a single preset.

Improve Consistency—Presets (especially those you've created yourself) can help to ensure consistency over a group of photos, or over your entire portfolio by saving and applying the same settings.

Presets move visible sliders, so unlike profiles, you can apply multiple presets that do different things. For example, you may apply a preset that you use as a starting point, and another one that applies a vignette to some photos, and another that applies your landscape sharpening settings.

PREVIEWING & APPLYING PRESETS

To **show the Presets panel** on the desktop, select the Edit view then click the *Presets* button in the bottom right corner or use the shortcut Shift-P. On mobile, tap the Presets button in the toolbar.

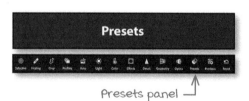

Presets panel

To **show the individual presets** on a desktop or tablet, click/tap the arrows to open/close the preset groups. On a phone, select the preset group from the pop-up to switch sets.

To **preview a preset** on the desktop, float the cursor over the preset name. The effect is previewed on the photo in the main preview area, and the sliders move temporarily to their preset positions. On mobile, tap on the preset thumbnail (as the preset isn't applied on mobile until you confirm).

To **apply a preset to the selected photo** on the desktop, click on the preset name. On mobile, tap on the preset and then tap the checkmark/*Done* button.

To **close the Presets panel** on the desktop, click the X in the corner or the *Presets* button again.

CREATING PRESETS

As you start to find combinations of sliders that you like or use frequently, you can create your own presets.

To **create a preset**, click the ... button at the top of the Presets panel and select **Create Preset**, then give the preset a name.

In the *Group* pop-up, select an existing preset group or select *New Group* to create a new one.

Check the panels or individual slider values you want to include in your preset and click *Save*.

If you frequently save the same sliders in presets, click the ... button in the Create Preset dialog (desktop only) and select **Set as Defaults** to automatically check those sliders in future.

If you later change the sliders and want to **update the preset**, you can right-click on the preset (desktop) / tap on the ... menu to the right of the preset (mobile) and select *Update with Current Settings*.

INSTALLING & SYNCING PRESETS

A large cottage industry has grown up around Lightroom, with a huge number of free and paid presets and profiles available.

Presets designed for Lightroom 4 or later work with Lightroom CC. These may be marked PV2012 or PV3/PV4.

To **install presets** on the desktop, go to *File menu > Import Profiles and Presets* or click the ... icon at the top of the Presets panel and select *Import Presets*. Navigate to the folder or zip file containing the presets and click *Import*.

Preset import is currently only available in the Windows/Mac apps, but any profiles or presets you import on the desktop (or create on any of your devices), are automatically synced to the cloud, so they're available everywhere.

ORGANIZING PRESETS

Over time, your collection of presets will grow, so you'll need to organize them. It's easy to end up with too many presets, and then you can't see the wood for trees.

To **rename a preset**, right-click on it (desktop) / tap on the ... menu to the right of the preset (mobile) and select *Rename.*

To **delete a single preset**, right-click on it (desktop) / tap on the ... menu to the right of the preset (mobile) and select *Delete* (but take care as it will be deleted from all of

your devices).

To **move a preset into another group**, right-click on the preset and select *Move to Group > [the name of the new group]* (desktop only). While you're moving or creating a preset, you can also **create a new group**.

To **rename an existing preset group**, right-click on it and select *Rename Group* (desktop only).

To **delete an entire preset group**, right-click on it and select *Delete Group* (but it will be deleted from all of your devices, and entire preset groups can only be deleted from the desktop, not mobile).

To **hide a preset group** without deleting it, click/tap the ... menu at the top of the Presets panel and select *Manage Presets*. Uncheck the preset group and click the *Back/Done* button to return to the Presets panel. To show them again, repeat the process and check the preset group. On the desktop, you can also right-click on the preset group and select *Hide* or *Reset Hidden Presets*. This visibility status is local, so you can have all of your presets available on the desktop, but only your favorite groups visible on your smaller mobile screen.

As your preset creation skills improve, you may want to **share a preset** with other photographers. To do so (desktop only), right-click on a preset and select *Export*, then navigate to a folder on your hard drive.

PRESETS (WINDOWS/MAC)

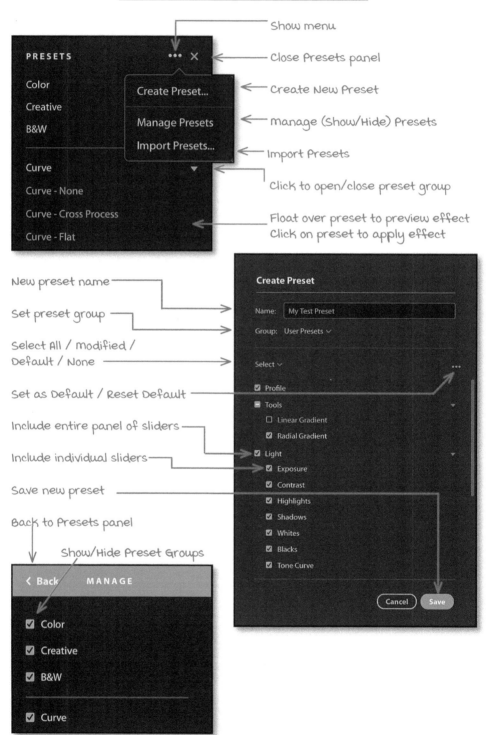

Show menu

Close Presets panel

Create New Preset

Manage (Show/Hide) Presets

Import Presets

Click to open/close preset group

Float over preset to preview effect
Click on preset to apply effect

New preset name

Set preset group

Select All / Modified /
Default / None

Set as Default / Reset Default

Include entire panel of sliders

Include individual sliders

Save new preset

Back to Presets panel

Show/Hide Preset Groups

PRESETS (IOS/ANDROID)

Tap to select preset group from menu →

Tap to preview → preset on photo

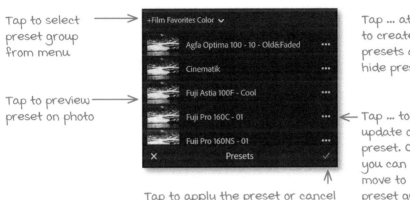

Tap ... at the top to create new presets and show/ hide preset groups

← Tap ... to rename, update or delete preset. On Android, you can also move to a new preset group.

Tap to apply the preset or cancel
(Buttons at the top on Android,
or a Done button on tablets)

Save new preset

New preset name →

Set preset group →

Select All / None →

Select Modified / Default also available on Android

Include entire panel of sliders →

View checkboxes for individual sliders

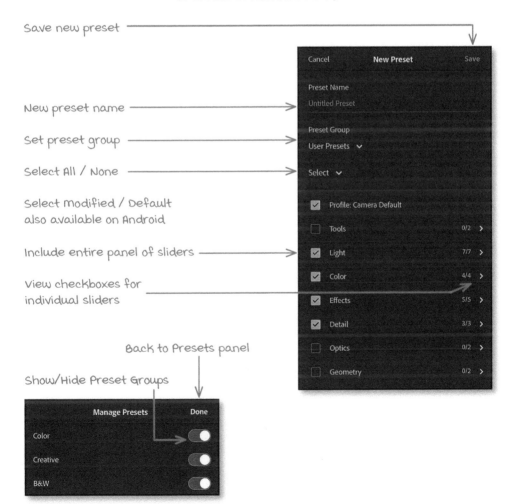

Back to Presets panel

Show/Hide Preset Groups

BALANCING LIGHT & CONTRAST 13

Photography is all about balancing light, shade and the contrast between them. These adjustments are made using the sliders in the Light and Effects panels, and are the focus for this section.

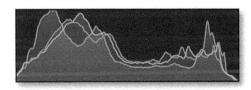

IN THIS SECTION, WE'LL CONSIDER:

• How to set the *Exposure* slider to optimize the overall image brightness.

• How the *Contrast* slider increases or decreases the overall (or global) contrast.

• When to use *Highlights* & *Shadows* to lighten or darken the highlight or shadow tones in your photo.

• How the *Whites* & *Blacks* sliders can be used to increase the dynamic range or clip the highlight and shadow tones.

• How to use *Clarity* to add local contrast, giving the photo punch without compressing the highlight or shadow detail.

• How to use *Dehaze* to reduce or emulate atmospheric haze.

• When to use the Tone Curve instead of, or along with, the Light panel sliders.

• The best order to adjust the Light panel sliders.

LIGHT	AUTO		
Exposure			0
Contrast			0
Highlights			0
Shadows			0
Whites			0
Blacks			0

COLOR

EFFECTS

Clarity			0
Dehaze			0

ADJUST FROM THE TOP... MOSTLY

You may have read articles and watched videos by numerous Lightroom users on editing photos, and they all have different opinions.

Some will tell you to start at the top and always work down. Others will tell you to always set *Whites* and *Blacks* first. Some will tell you skip the Light panel (a.k.a. the Basic panel in Lightroom Classic) and use a Tone Curve instead. So who is right?

They're all right—and they're all wrong. It's impossible to set hard and fast rules because Lightroom's Light sliders are image-adaptive (intelligent). The range and effect of the sliders changes based on the content of the photo and the values of the other Light panel sliders.

In this book, we'll discuss how the sliders were *designed* to work, as explained by the engineers who created them, because they know the tools better than anyone.

WORK TOP DOWN... SORT OF

The Light sliders were designed to be used top down, because the first few Light sliders affect the range of the lower Light sliders. For example, if you change *Highlights* and *Shadows* before *Exposure*, the sliders won't move far enough. It'll be ok for little tweaks, but you'll want to get *Exposure* in the right ballpark first.

The *Contrast* slider is the exception. It can be used at any time as it doesn't affect slider range, and it's usually easiest to set it after you've set the other Light sliders.

SKIPPING SOME SLIDERS

The top-down principle doesn't mean you have to adjust every slider. For example, a photo with a low dynamic range (one that doesn't stretch to pure white/black but should do so) is still best adjusted from top to bottom, but skip the *Highlights/Shadows* and go straight from *Exposure* to *Whites/Blacks*.

In the following lessons, we're going to look at the principles behind the "normal" use of each slider, as well as examples of when you might want to do things slightly differently, for example, if specific tonal ranges are more important than others, or where you want a softer look (without adding local contrast).

APPLYING AUTO ADJUSTMENTS

If you just need a quick way to improve photos, try the **Auto** button. You'll find it in or near the Light panel, depending on which device you're using. On the desktop, the shortcut Shift-A applies the *Auto* adjustments, and if you hold down the Shift key while floating over the slider label, you can apply *Auto* settings to that single slider.

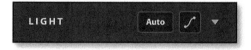

Like your camera's exposure meter, it's not as intelligent as you, so it doesn't know what's in the photo or how it's meant to look. Sometimes it works great, sometimes it's a reasonable starting point for adjusting sliders further, and sometimes the result is awful.

LIGHT PANEL WORKFLOW

High or Normal
Dynamic Range

Exposure always goes
first as other sliders
won't work well with
incorrect Exposure

If the White Balance
is way off, you may
need to roughly fix
it before continuing

Low Dynamic
Range

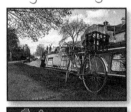

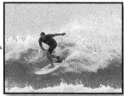

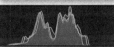

− Highlights
+ Shadows
to pull back
highlight and
shadow detail

+ Whites
− Blacks to
extend tonal
range

+ Whites
− Blacks to bring
back contrast lost
by the Highlights/
Shadows
adjustments

Ignore
Highlights
and Shadows,
as they won't
work well

Exception: Highlights/
Shadows add local
contrast. In some
cases, you might
want the softer
look of a tone
curve instead of
Highlights/Shadows

+ Clarity and/or
+ Contrast to bring
back midtone
contrast if needed

Exception: In some
cases, you might
want to use +
Highlights and/
or − Shadows to
brighten highlights
or crush shadows

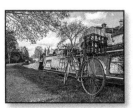

White Balance

Adjust Vibrance
/ Saturation

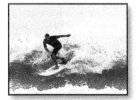

SETTING OVERALL EXPOSURE

At the top of the Light panel, the **Exposure** slider sets the overall image brightness, and it uses the same f-stop increments as your camera, so +2.0 of *Exposure* is the equivalent of opening the aperture on your camera by 2 stops.

The *Exposure* slider attempts to maintain a gentle transition to pure white to avoid harsh digital clipping.

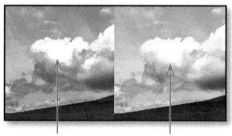

Clipped   Gentle Transition

It's important to get the *Exposure* setting about right before moving on to the other Light panel sliders, as the range of other sliders are affected and they won't work well if your *Exposure* slider is set incorrectly.

SETTING EXPOSURE

So how do you know where to set the *Exposure* slider? Try these tips:

Squint Your Eyes—If you screw your eyes up, you won't be able to see the detail in the photo, and you'll be left with the overall impression of how bright it is. You're aiming for a mid-gray.

The Only Slider—Pretend it's the only control you have available. If there weren't any other sliders, how bright would you make the photo?

Confuse Your Brain—Your eyes adjust to the original camera exposure, making it difficult to judge the correct exposure. It can help to confuse your brain by swinging the *Exposure* slider to the left and right like a pendulum and then settle somewhere in the middle, wherever it looks right.

Focus on the Midtones—Don't worry if the highlights are a bit bright or the shadows a bit dark, or if there are clipped highlights or shadows at this stage (white/black areas with no detail), as you'll pull them back using the *Highlights* and *Shadows* sliders.

You can hold down the Alt key (Windows) / Opt key (Mac) / two fingers (mobile) to view the clipping warnings, but don't worry about them at this stage.

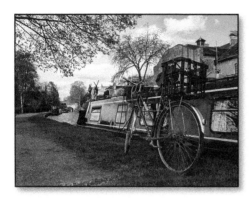

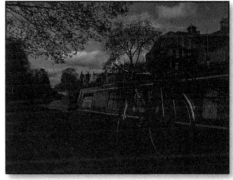

To illustrate the effect of the Exposure slider, let's start with a photo set to 0. It's a little dark

Set to Exposure –2.5, we can see there's loads of detail available even in the brightest clouds, which can be pulled back using the Highlights slider, but it's way too dark overall

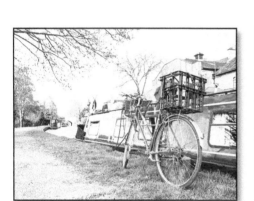

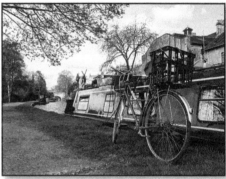

Set to Exposure +2.5, it's way too bright and we've lost all the detail in the clouds, but we can see there's loads of detail in the dark areas, which can be pulled back using the Shadows slider

I've settled on +0.43 as a good overall Exposure value, and I'll pull the clouds back later using the Highlights slider

GLOBAL VS. LOCAL CONTRAST

Contrast is defined as the difference in tone or color that makes an object distinguishable from its surroundings. In real terms, this means that all of the detail we see in the world around us—or in a photo—depends on contrast.

Contrast also affects the feel of a photo, with high contrast adding drama and excitement, commanding your attention. Since our eyes are drawn to the highest contrast, you can use it to draw the viewers eye away from distractions and toward the subject.

Enhancing these contrasts is, therefore, one of the most important things we can do when editing photos.

The second slider in the Light panel is called **Contrast**, so it would be an obvious choice, but it's a bit of a blunt instrument, and there are better tools to use. Why?

INCREASING MIDTONE CONTRAST

Normally, to increase midtone contrast, you have to make light pixels lighter and dark pixels darker. This is called global contrast, and it's what the *Contrast* slider does. The problem is, you lose highlight and shadow detail in the process.

Fortunately, our eyes are more interested in local contrast—small contrasts in similar

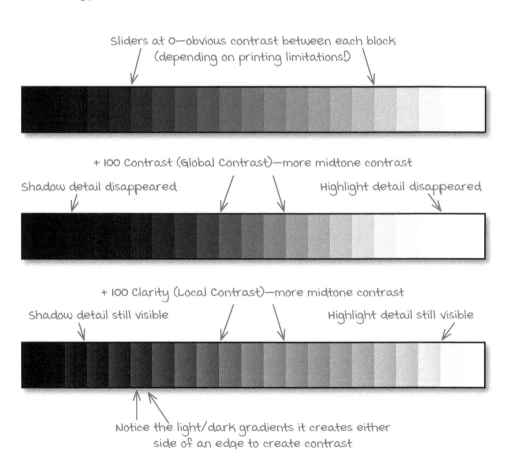

Sliders at 0—obvious contrast between each block
(depending on printing limitations!)

+ 100 Contrast (Global Contrast)—more midtone contrast
Shadow detail disappeared   Highlight detail disappeared

+ 100 Clarity (Local Contrast)—more midtone contrast
Shadow detail still visible   Highlight detail still visible

Notice the light/dark gradients it creates either
side of an edge to create contrast

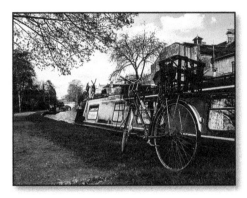

Adding midtone contrast using the Contrast slider loses the highlight and shadow detail

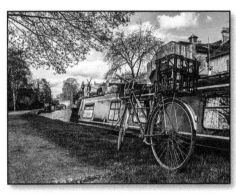

Adding local contrast using the Clarity slider, enhances the highlight and shadow detail

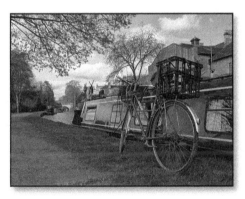

Reducing contrast using the Contrast slider recovers the highlight and shadow detail, but the whole photo ends up really dull and flat

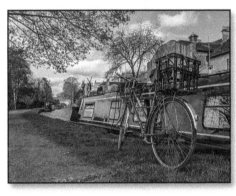

– Highlight brings back the cloud detail and + Shadows brings back the shadow details, but the photo still retains its punch thanks to the local contrast it applies

tones—than they are in big global contrast. Local contrast adjustments look for small changes in contrast and enhances them. This adds contrast without sacrificing as much detail in the highlights and shadows. Lightroom mainly adjusts local contrast using *Clarity* slider, but it's also affected by the *Highlights*, *Shadows* and *Dehaze* sliders.

It can sound complicated, so let's illustrate the difference using the step wedges, and photos. (The step wedge is just an image created in Photoshop, with 21 blocks of gray

in different shades, ranging from pure black to pure white, which makes it easier to see the differences.)

Once you've adjusted all of the other Light panels sliders, you can tweak the midtone contrast using the *Contrast* slider, but in many cases, it won't need adjusting at all.

DECREASING GLOBAL CONTRAST

But what if you have the opposite problem?

If a photo has too much contrast (too wide a dynamic range), you can darken highlights and lighten the shadows using -*Contrast* to see more detail in those tones, but then you lose midtone contrast, making the photo look really flat. The *Highlights/Shadows* sliders are usually better at reducing dynamic range as they add local contrast at the same time, so it's often best to skip the *Contrast* slider altogether if you have too much contrast.

There may be exceptions, however. On a soft dreamy image, the extra local contrast may not be desirable, so you might want to use a negative *Contrast* adjustment in that case. Or if the *Highlights/Shadows* sliders don't go far enough, some negative *Contrast* can be useful to compress the tones.

CONTRAST VS. TONE CURVE

If you want to add or reduce global contrast, a Tone Curve is a better choice than the *Contrast* slider, because it allows you to control which tones gain or sacrifice contrast. To learn how to use curves to add or reduce contrast, turn to page 165.

RECOVERING HIGHLIGHT & SHADOW DETAIL

After setting *Exposure*, the *Highlights* and *Shadows* sliders are next in line for adjustment.

The **Highlights** slider mainly adjusts the brighter tones in the photo and barely touches the darker tones. It's generally intended to be dragged to the left (-) to recover highlight details, such as fluffy clouds in the sky or detail on a bride's dress.

Shadows does the opposite, mainly affecting the darker tones in the photo. It's generally intended to be moved to the right (+) to lighten shadow details, such as shadowed areas on people's faces or detail in a groom's suit.

Brightening shadows and darkening highlights usually comes at the cost of midtone contrast, making the photo look flat. Unlike a simple highlights or shadows control, Lightroom's *Highlights* and *Shadows* also add local contrast (page 156) and saturation to help to compensate for the loss of global contrast.

In most cases, the additional local contrast is beneficial, but you don't have any control over how much is added. For average

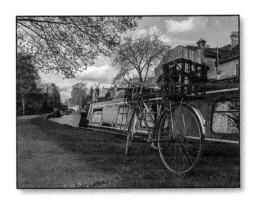

– Highlights brings back cloud detail
without darkening the shadows

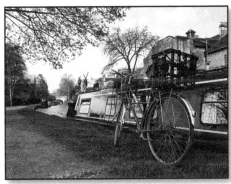

+ Highlights lightens the highlight
tones without affecting the shadows

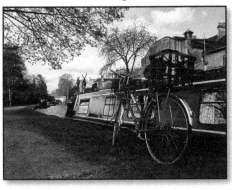

– Shadows darkens the shadows
without affecting the highlights

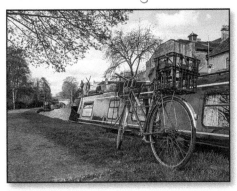

+ Shadows lightens the shadow tones
without lightening the highlights

photos, that's not a problem, but for some photos you may want a softer look, so you might prefer to use the Tone Curve to reduce the contrast in those cases.

SETTING HIGHLIGHTS/SHADOWS

So how do you know where to set the *Highlights* and *Shadows* sliders?

Amount—How much highlight and shadow detail you choose to recover will depend on the results of your photo analysis. For example, if the photo is of a stormy beach, the detail in the clouds will be essential, so you'll use more highlight recovery. Likewise, if the photo is a woodland scene, you'll need more shadow detail in the leaves and bark. In contrast, you won't need as much shadow recovery if the shadow detail is unimportant, such as the bushes in the background of a portrait.

Clipping—While you're moving the *Highlights* slider, hold down the Alt key (Windows) / Opt key (Mac) / two fingers (mobile) to see the clipping warnings, to ensure your adjustment is recovering any clipped highlights.

Keep It Natural—The effect on local contrast gets stronger as you move the sliders further. Both sliders look fairly natural up to 50, but beyond that, the effect becomes more surreal and halos can become noticeable, which can make photos look over-processed if not used carefully.

Slider Direction—Due to the local contrast and saturation changes applied by the *Highlights/Shadows* sliders, they usually work best when they're fairly symmetrical, for example, -50 *Highlights* and +50 *Shadows*. There are always exceptions, for example, you may only want local contrast in the clouds but softer shadows.

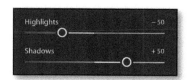

If you need to swing both sliders in the same direction, it's usually (but not always) a sign that the *Exposure* slider needs moving in that direction.

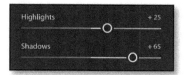

Follow with Whites/Blacks—Darkening highlights and lightening shadows decreases the midtone (global) contrast, so you'll usually need to adjust the *Whites/Blacks* sliders after *Highlights/Shadows*. We'll look at these sliders in the next lesson.

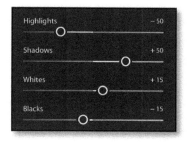

CONTROLLING WHITE & BLACK CLIPPING

The **Whites** and **Blacks** sliders affect the clipping point and roll off at the extreme ends of the tonal range. If you've used other image editing software, they're similar to the black and white points in Levels.

In most cases, the *Whites* slider is pulled to the right (+) and *Blacks* is pulled to the left (-) to expand the tonal range.

If a photo was captured in flat light, and therefore has a low dynamic range, use +*Whites* and -*Blacks* to stretch image data to fill the entire histogram, making a few pixels black and a few pure white.

The sliders adapt to the range of the photo, so even a foggy white photo can be stretched to fill the entire tonal range. This becomes even more useful when working with scans of old faded photos, as it allows you to create a bright white and deep black point in even the lowest contrast photos if you need to do so.

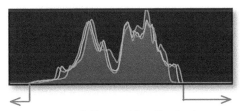

Use + Whites and – Blacks to stretch the histogram to the ends to fill the whole dynamic range

SETTING WHITES & BLACKS

So how do you know where to set the *Whites* and *Blacks* sliders?

Auto Adjust—On the desktop, hold down the Shift key and click on the slider name to automatically set the clipping points. This is an automatic setting that Lightroom often calculates correctly.

Check the Clipping Warnings—Hold down the Alt key (Windows) / Opt key (Mac) / two

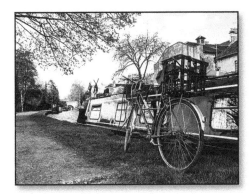

+ Whites clips light pixels to pure white, but we've pushed it too far and lost detail in the clouds. Try to only clip small specular highlights like the shiny mudguard

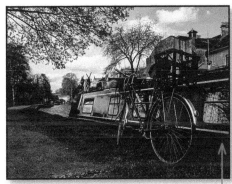

– Blacks clips dark pixels to pure black. We've pushed it way too far and lost too much detail in the shadows. It's ok to clip dark pixels to black, but avoid creating large areas of solid black like this

fingers (mobile) while dragging the *Whites* or *Blacks* sliders to view the clipping warnings, so you can check you're not clipping important details (making large areas pure white or pure black). The colored overlay shows whether the clipping only affects one channel, multiple channels, or all channels.

What to Clip—Turn back to page 105 for a reminder of what's ok to clip and what to avoid.

Deep Blacks—Deep blacks, caused by clipping larger numbers of dark pixels, is a popular choice to enhance contrast. Just be careful not clip too far and lose important shadow detail. This is more frequently done with a tone curve (page 165), as it compresses the dark tones with gentler transitions.

Clipping Studio Backgrounds—If you're

shooting against a white studio background, which you want to keep pure white, the *Whites* slider allows you to clip highlights that would otherwise be protected by the *Exposure* slider's gentle roll off. If the photo was correctly exposed, with the whites close to clipping, a small value such as +15-25 is enough to blow the white background without having a noticeable impact on the overall exposure. The same principle applies using the *Blacks* slider with a black studio background.

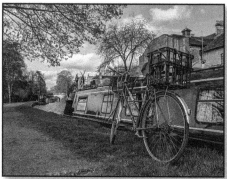

After –100 Highlights and + 100 Shadows, the full range of detail is back but the photo looks very flat

If we use +21 Whites and –61 Blacks (below left), we can add back contrast without losing it anywhere important

On the Blacks clipping warning we can see we're just clipping the blacks in areas where the detail doesn't matter

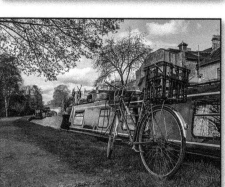

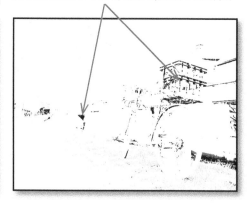

ADDING 'POP' USING CLARITY

The **Clarity** slider is found in the Effects panel, but it affects brightness and contrast, so we're including it in this section.

As we learned on page 156, *Clarity* creates local contrast in the midtones by searching for edges and other areas of local contrast and enhancing that contrast. You might also use words like definition, punch, pop or texture.

SETTING CLARITY

Positive Clarity—As a general rule, it's best to use a very low setting for portraits, if you use it at all, as it can accentuate lines and wrinkles.

It's very good at emphasizing texture, so it works well on architecture and landscapes, adding a distinctive crisp feel, and it can also look great on high contrast B&W photos. Although the slider goes to 100, that's almost always too strong.

Clarity doesn't increase saturation, so if you use high *Clarity* values, you may find that the colors start to look a little muted. Adding a little *Vibrance* or *Saturation* (page 180) can make the effect look more natural.

Negative Clarity—Set to a negative amount, *Clarity* creates a diffuse soft-focus effect. It gives a gentle glow to the photo, so it can look good on B&W, vintage style or infrared photos. On faces, it softens the eyes too much when applied using the main slider, but it works well for skin softening when applied using a brush (page 224).

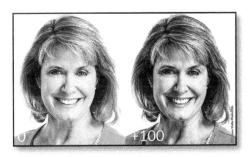

Wrinkles on faces create local contrast, so avoid adding more the Clarity slider. I know of very few women who appreciate having their wrinkles exaggerated!

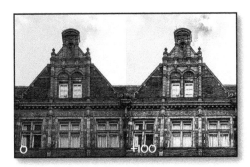

The Clarity slider helps to add 'pop' to buildings, landscapes and other textured scenes, which naturally have small contrasts between similar tones

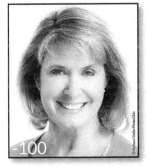

Negative Clarity has softened everything in this example, but applying it using the brush protects the eyes/hair

REMOVING HAZE USING DEHAZE

Like *Clarity*, the **Dehaze** slider is found in the Effects panel. It's designed to remove (or add) haze, for example, atmospheric haze over a landscape or city smog. It also works well on photos of the night sky, backlit photos, underwater photos, reflections, scans/photographs of old faded photos, and more. It's also brilliant for adding a high contrast gritty feel to B&W photos.

It runs complex calculations to try to estimate the light lost as it passes through the atmosphere, adapting to the content of each photo to get a good result as quickly as possible.

SETTING DEHAZE

To get the best result, adjust the white balance first (page 176), as it uses the color of the light in its calculations, then adjust the *Dehaze* slider until your photo looks great.

It's best used in combination with the normal adjustment sliders. Use *Dehaze* to remove the worst of the haze, and then use the other sliders as normal to finish editing the photo.

Dehaze is a magical slider, but it can have negative side effects such as unwanted color shifts and halos, stronger noise, and more noticeable sensor dust and lens defects. As a result, you may need to adjust the Light panel sliders, *Vibrance* or *Saturation*, *Noise Reduction*, *Vignette* and remove additional sensor dust spots after applying the *Dehaze* slider. It has fewer side effects when applied to a localized area using the selective editing tools (page 207).

Because *Dehaze* adapts to the content of each photo, it's best avoided when doing timelapse photography.

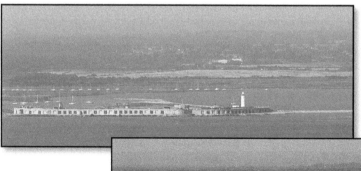

Atmospheric haze can be reduced using the other Light and Color sliders, but it's far easier with Dehaze!

USING TONE CURVES

Tone curves are primarily used for controlling brightness and contrast in specific tonal ranges, but you can do that with the Light panel sliders, so why use a tone curve?

In the Contrast lesson (page 156), we said that when you add contrast in one tonal range (e.g., the midtones), you lose contrast in other tonal ranges (e.g., the highlights and shadows). There's always a trade-off.

The Light panel sliders adjust broad ranges of tones, whereas a tone curve allows you to carefully control where you're willing to sacrifice contrast to gain it in other areas. For example, the *Contrast* slider adds contrast using a simple S curve, with almost equal compression in the highlights and shadows. However, you may decide that you're willing to lose more shadow detail in the deepest shadows but you want to keep

more contrast in the highlights.

Likewise, if you have a photo with too much contrast, if you lighten the shadows and darken the highlights to see more detail, you lose contrast in the midtones. The *Highlights* and *Shadows* sliders compensate by adding local contrast, but the resulting halos can be too strong, especially on photos that benefit from a softer look. The tone curve doesn't add local contrast or saturation, leaving you to decide whether to add it yourself.

As a rule of thumb, the Light and Color panel sliders are designed for the heavy-lifting—the major adjustments—and the Tone Curve is usually used for fine tuning, but rules are made to be broken, so feel free to experiment!

READING A TONE CURVE

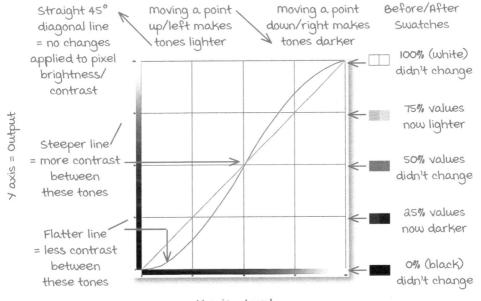

Straight 45° diagonal line = no changes applied to pixel brightness/ contrast

moving a point up/left makes tones lighter

moving a point down/right makes tones darker

Before/After Swatches

100% (white) didn't change

75% values now lighter

Steeper line = more contrast between these tones

50% values didn't change

25% values now darker

Flatter line = less contrast between these tones

0% (black) didn't change

Y axis = Output

X axis = Input

CURVES VS. SLIDERS

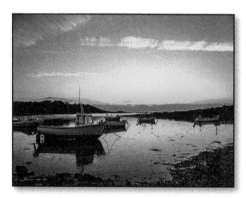 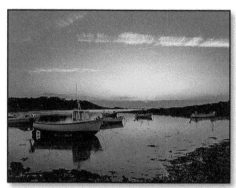

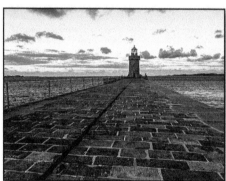 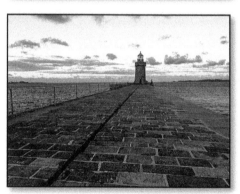

Highlights and Shadows (left) add local contrast, which may not be desirable in a photo shot in lovely soft light, whereas the Tone Curve (right) allows you to reduce excessive contrast without adding local contrast

READING A TONE CURVE

Along each axis are all the possible tones, with pure black (0%) in the bottom left and pure white (100%) in the top right. The tone curve starts as a straight 45° diagonal line, with no changes being applied to the photo. Moving the line up/left makes the tones lighter, and moving down/right makes the tones darker. The line getting steeper means contrast is increased, and getting flatter means contrast is reduced.

PARAMETRIC VS. POINT CURVES

To display the Tone Curve in Lightroom, click/tap the button at the top of the Light panel.

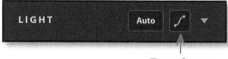

Tone Curve

Lightroom offers two different types of tone curve: a parametric curve and a series of point curves. These are toggled using the circles above (desktop) / below (mobile) the curve grid.

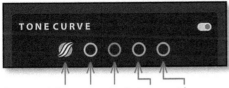

Parametric RGB Red Green Blue

The parametric tone curve is the default view, and it allows you to adjust four different regions of the curve called *Highlights*, *Lights*, *Darks* and *Shadows*, rather than individual points. This protects the photo from extreme adjustments, so it's a great way to start experimenting with curves.

The point curve interface, represented by the colored circles, is usually used by more advanced users or those familiar with Photoshop's curves dialog. It gives you full control over the curve, including the individual RGB channels.

Point curves aren't necessarily an alternative to the parametric curves. You may be more comfortable with one or the other, but both types of curves are active at the same time and the effect is cumulative.

USING THE PARAMETRIC CURVE

Let's start experimenting with the parametric curve by selecting the parametric tone curve icon.

The most frequently used curve is a basic contrast curve which is an S shape. Click/ tap on the white line in the *Shadows* or *Darks* regions and **drag down to darken** the shadow tones, then click/tap on the white line in the *Lights* or *Highlights* section and **drag upwards to lighten** the highlight tones.

How far you drag away from the center line controls how much you brighten or darken those tones. As you drag, the highlighted

section shows the **maximum range of movement** for that region of the curve. It's limited in order to maintain smooth transitions between tones and protect your photo from banding/posterization.

If you change your mind, double-click on the line to **reset a section** of the curve (desktop only), or right-click and select *Reset* to **reset the whole parametric curve** (desktop only). For some unknown reason, there isn't currently a way to reset the parametric curve on mobile! To **reset both the parametric and point curves** at once, hold down the Alt key (Windows) / Opt key (Mac) and click on the Tone Curve label.

You can **fine tune the curve using the split point markers** at the bottom.

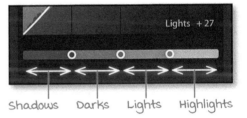

Shadows Darks Lights Highlights

They define the tonal range for the regions. For example, if you've used the *Shadows* and *Highlights* regions to create strong midtone contrast, you may move the 25% and 75% split points out to restrict the flattened contrast to the lightest highlights and the deepest shadows. They're also useful if you've got the shape of the curve about right, but it's a little light or dark overall. There are some examples on page 171. On the desktop, double-clicking on any of those split points resets it to the default position at 25%/50%/75%.

USING THE POINT CURVE

If you need greater control, click the gray circle to display the RGB point curve. Click/ tap anywhere on the curve line to **add a**

PARAMETRIC TONE CURVE (WINDOWS/MAC)

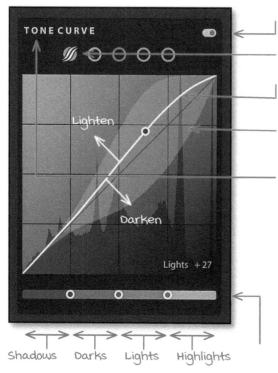

Enable/disable tone curve

Select parametric curve

Drag line to adjust curve

Highlighted area shows maximum range of movement

Alt-click / Opt-click on Tone Curve label to reset all curves

Double-click or right-click on line to reset single region. Right-click on curve to reset parametric curves

To show/hide histogram, go to ... menu > Show Histogram

Split points control the range of each adjustment

Shadows   Darks   Lights   Highlights

PARAMETRIC TONE CURVE (IOS/ANDROID)

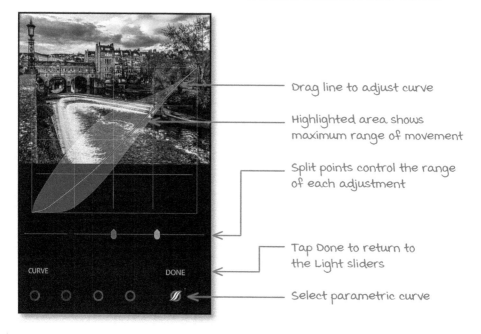

Drag line to adjust curve

Highlighted area shows maximum range of movement

Split points control the range of each adjustment

Tap Done to return to the Light sliders

Select parametric curve

PARAMETRIC SPLIT POINTS

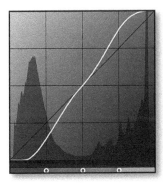 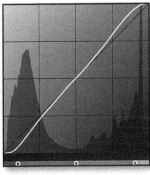 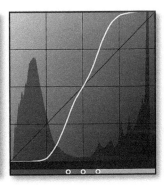

The shape of the curve changes depending on whether the split points are at their defaults (left), far apart (center) or close together (right), so you can use it to fine tune the curve

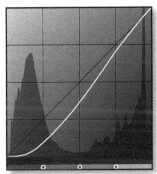 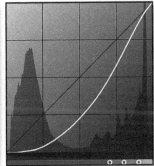

Dragging all of the split points to the left or right can change the overall brightness without changing the relative shape of the curve

control point, and then drag it up or down to adjust the curve. Control points can make adjustments or lock the curve in position, so you can adjust other tonal ranges without those changing.

You'll usually want to keep the curve to a smooth line, without any sharp bends, otherwise you may introduce posterization (banding).

On the desktop, holding down the Alt key (Windows) / Opt key (Mac) slows down the movement for greater accuracy, or holding the Shift key

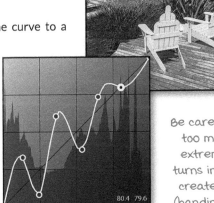

80.4 79.6

Be careful not to place too many points as extreme twists and turns in the curve can create posterization (banding) in the photo

POINT TONE CURVE (WINDOWS/MAC)

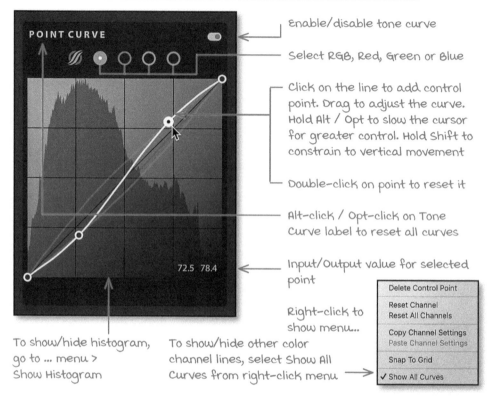

Enable/disable tone curve

Select RGB, Red, Green or Blue

Click on the line to add control point. Drag to adjust the curve. Hold Alt / Opt to slow the cursor for greater control. Hold Shift to constrain to vertical movement

Double-click on point to reset it

Alt-click / Opt-click on Tone Curve label to reset all curves

Input/Output value for selected point

Right-click to show menu...

Delete Control Point
Reset Channel
Reset All Channels
Copy Channel Settings
Paste Channel Settings
Snap To Grid
✓ Show All Curves

To show/hide histogram, go to ... menu > Show Histogram

To show/hide other color channel lines, select Show All Curves from right-click menu

POINT TONE CURVE (IOS/ANDROID)

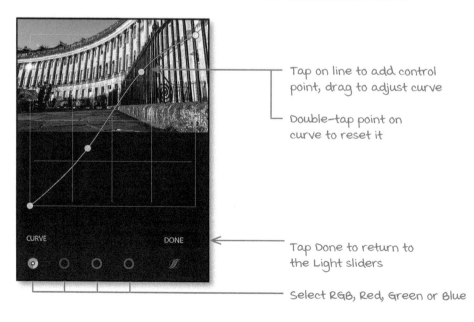

Tap on line to add control point, drag to adjust curve

Double-tap point on curve to reset it

Tap Done to return to the Light sliders

Select RGB, Red, Green or Blue

SAMPLE POINT CURVES

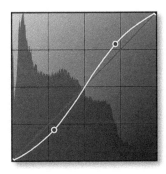

A standard S-curve adds midtone contrast, like the Contrast slider

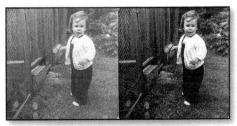

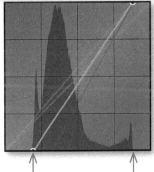

To roughly correct color casts in scans, move the ends of the point curve to the ends of the histogram on each color channel

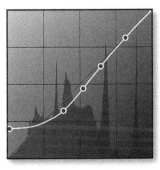

Locking most of the curve in place and then lifting the deepest shadows creates the flat shadows effect popular in film-effect presets

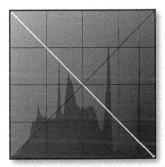

Reversing the tone curve inverts scanned negatives, although it doesn't remove the orange mask of color film, and the Light panel sliders go "the wrong way"

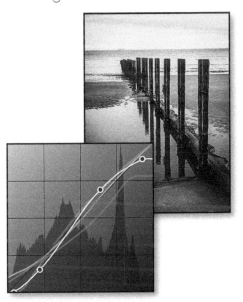

RGB point curves are used for cross-processing effects, creating a different result to the split toning sliders

constrains the movement to vertical only. If you're a little OCD and like everything perfectly lined up, there's also a **Snap to Grid** option in the right-click menu, which locks the control points to the intersections of a 20x20 grid, rather than the standard 4x4 grid.

If you change your mind, you can **delete a control point** by double-clicking/double-tapping on it. To **reset the selected channel** or **reset the whole point curve**, right-click on the curve (desktop only).

The point curve interface also gives you access to the red, green and blue channels that make up your photo. These are often used for cross processing effects, or for correcting scans or other tricky white balance situations. For example, where color casts differ between the highlights and shadows—perhaps where the overall color is correct but the shadows have a magenta tinge—normal white balance adjustments would be unable to fix it, but RGB curves allow you detailed control over each channel.

There are some example point curves on page 171 to give you some ideas of how they can be useful.

CURVES FOR ILLUSTRATING SLIDERS

Once you're familiar with reading tone curves, they're also useful to illustrate and compare the effect of different Light panel sliders on the brightness and contrast of different image tones. These are shown on page 173.

CURVES ILLUSTRATING LIGHT PANEL SLIDERS

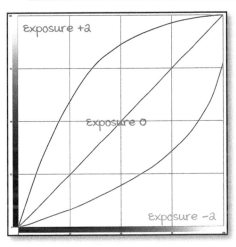

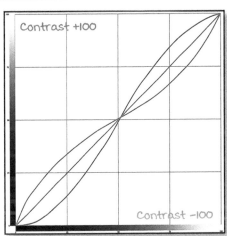

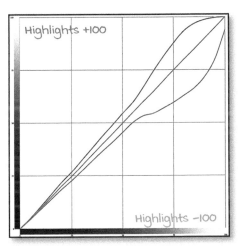

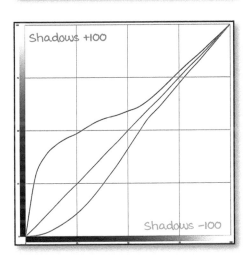

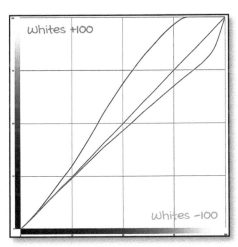

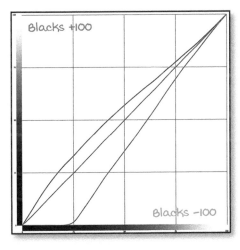

PERFECTING COLOR

14

We see the world around us in color, and since the advent of color film, it's been an important part of photography. The Color panel allows us to correct colors to match the scene we remember, or to make more creative artistic choices.

IN THIS SECTION, WE'LL CONSIDER:

• How to use the White Balance sliders to correct color casts, which can cause the photo to look dull and muddy.

• How to adjust the saturation of the colors throughout the whole photo to influence the viewer's mood.

• How to use the Color Mixer to optimize the brightness and saturation of specific color ranges, to draw the eye.

• How to shift the hue of specific color ranges, for example, reducing ruddy cheeks or tweaking memory colors.

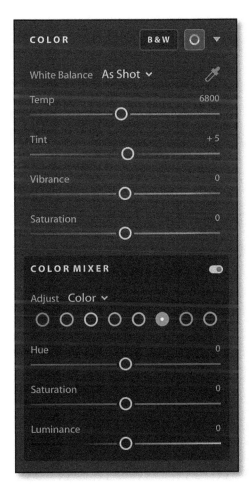

PERFECTING WHITE BALANCE

The color of light varies depending on its source. It can range from cool (blue sky) to warm (candlelight or tungsten), and the color temperature is measured using the Kelvin scale.

Our eyes and brain automatically compensate for different lighting conditions, which is why a white object looks white to us whether it's viewed in sunlight, shade or indoors using artificial lighting.

Cameras aren't quite so smart. A camera's auto white balance works fairly well in a narrow range of daylight with "average" image content, but it doesn't take much to confuse it. Capture a scene of autumn leaves, and the camera's likely to make the photo a little cold and blue. Shoot a snow scene, and the camera will probably try to warm it up.

Lightroom's White Balance sliders are designed to compensate for the color of the light in which the photo was taken. When you get the white tones right, everything else falls into place.

Most of the time, you'll want the colors in the scene to be rendered as accurately as possible, but sometimes you'll want to warm or cool the scene to suit the mood of the photo.

If you look outside on a cold winters day, the light is cool and blue, but during a beautiful sunset, it may be warm and orange. If you neutralize these colors, you lose the atmosphere.

WHITE BALANCE

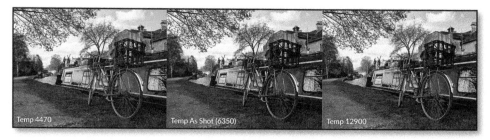

Temp 4470   Temp As Shot (6350)   Temp 12900

- Temp makes the photo cooler/bluer

↑ The camera's auto white balance did pretty well on this photo! ↓

+ Temp makes the photo warmer/yellower

- Tint makes the photo greener

+ Tint makes the photo more magenta (pinker)

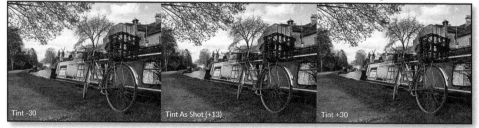

Tint -30   Tint As Shot (+13)   Tint +30

SETTING WHITE BALANCE

White balance adjustments are made using the **Temp** *(Temperature)* and **Tint** sliders in the Color panel, but there are a few ways of deciding on the best values.

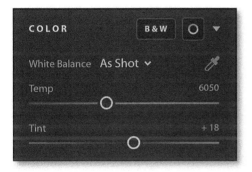

Auto—In the *White Balance* pop-up, select **Auto**. It attempts to neutralize the photo, but like the camera's auto white balance, it's not as intelligent as your eyes, so the results may not be perfect.

Presets—If you're working on a raw file, the **White Balance** pop-up includes presets for standard lighting conditions. They include *As Shot, Daylight, Cloudy, Shade, Tungsten, Fluorescent* and *Flash* settings. Select the right preset for the lighting conditions, for example, if the photo was captured on a cloudy day, select the *Cloudy* preset.

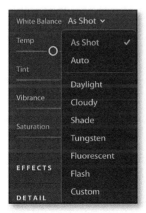

Eyedropper—For more control, the White Balance Selector allows you to click in the photo to automatically neutralize any color cast.

On the desktop, click the eyedropper icon in the Color panel or press the W key, then click on something in the photo that *should* be neutral, for example, the shadows on a white t-shirt.

On a mobile device, tap the eyedropper icon in the Color panel, then drag the eyedropper to something that should be neutral, such as this lighthouse, and tap the checkmark to confirm your selection. On a small screen, it may help to zoom in before selecting the eyedropper.

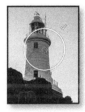

Using white or light gray subjects gives a more accurate result than darker shades, but avoid whites that are too bright, as some of the color data may be clipped.

When you click with the eyedropper, the pop-up changes to *Custom* and the sliders automatically adjust. If it still doesn't look right, click somewhere else to try again or tweak the sliders by eye. The eyedropper's often a good way to get the white balance in the right ballpark before fine-tuning the sliders.

If you regularly shoot in difficult lighting or you struggle to select the right white balance, a WhiBal, ColorChecker or other calibrated neutral light gray card is an easy way to guarantee correct white balance. Simply shoot a photo of the card in the same lighting conditions as the subject and

SETTING WHITE BALANCE USING THE EYEDROPPER

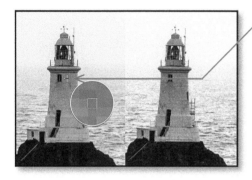

Select the White Balance eyedropper and click on something that SHOULD be white or light gray, like this lighthouse

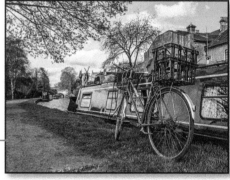

Oooops, clicking on the stone path turned the photo too blue

Clicking on the window made it a bit too warm and pink because it's reflecting the surroundings

What else might be neutral in this picture?

Darker areas of clouds may work if they weren't partially clipped (white with no detail), but results can vary depending on where you click

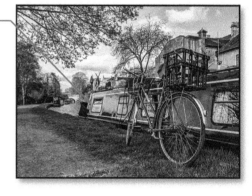

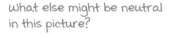

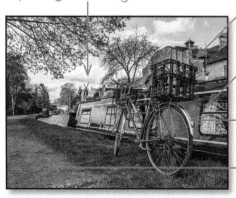

The satellite dish gave the best result, but it's still a bit cold, so try an extra 200K-400K on Temp

Paintwork and white fabrics often yellow over time

Shiny objects are no good, as they'll reflect surroundings

Stone sometimes works, but it's rarely perfectly neutral

click the eyedropper on that photo to get an accurate white balance setting. You can then copy these values to other photos shot in the same conditions.

Adjust Sliders By Eye—As you gain experience, you can go straight to the *Temp* and *Tint* sliders. If the photo's too yellow or warm, move the *Temp* slider to the left to compensate, and if it's too blue or cold, move the slider to the right. Likewise, the *Tint* slider adjusts from green on the left to magenta on the right.

If you're working on a raw file, the *Temp* slider uses the Kelvin scale to measure the color of the light. For JPEGs and other image formats, the scale runs from -100 to 100, because the white balance compensation has already been applied to the image data (e.g., by the camera), and now you're simply warming or cooling the photo.

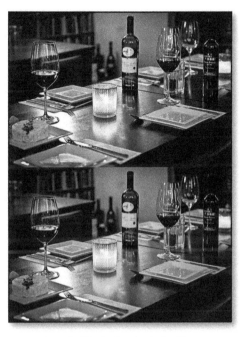

Candlelit photos look better warm. Some photos just aren't meant to be perfectly neutral!

ADJUSTING FOR MOOD

Once you've made the photo neutral, you can tweak the white balance to enhance the mood. For example, indoor photos often look better with a *Temperature* value 200-400K higher than neutral, to bring back a pleasant warmth. Or a sunset shot may need warming up to reflect the lovely warm light usually seen at that time of day.

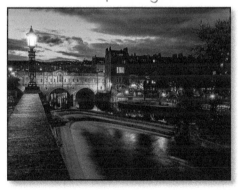

Photos shot in mixed lighting can be tricky to correct

HANDLING MIXED LIGHTING

Sometimes your photos will be shot with light from two or more sources. For example, a photo shot at night may have moonlight and street lighting, a photo shot near a window may have warm tungsten light and cooler daylight, or a photo shot outdoors may have bright sunlight and shade.

In this case, you have three choices:

• Pick a white balance in the middle that looks ok for both.

• Get the lighting right for one light source and don't worry about the other.

• Use Lightroom's Selective Editing tools to apply a different white balance to each area of the photo (page 221).

VIBRANCE VS. SATURATION

Saturation describes the intensity or purity of a color. Lightroom offers two different global saturation controls, with slightly different behaviors:

Saturation is quite a blunt instrument which adjusts the saturation of all colors equally. This can result in some colors clipping as they reach full saturation.

Vibrance is more intelligent as it adjusts the saturation on a non-linear scale, increasing the saturation of lower-saturated colors more than highly saturated colors. It also aims to protect skin tones from becoming over-saturated.

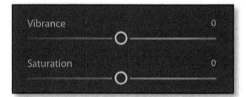

SETTING VIBRANCE OR SATURATION

Our eyes are drawn to vivid saturated colors, but if you go too far, it becomes garish and cartoon-like. This is particularly true on skin tones, which look ridiculous when heavily saturated.

The saturation of colors affects the mood of the photo. For example, you may want bright, saturated colors for a kid's party, but calm, muted colors may be better suited to a newborn photo.

In practice, you may use a little of both sliders, or just stick to the *Vibrance* slider for more natural colors.

If you need even more control over the saturation of specific tones, you can use the Color Mixer tool (page 181) or selective editing (page 207).

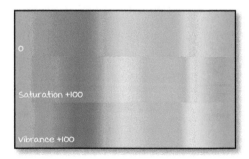

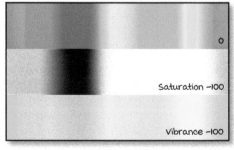

| + Vibrance enhances the blue tones (sky!) more than Saturation | + Vibrance keeps reds/oranges (skin!) looking more natural than Saturation | – Saturation completely desaturates to B&W (but there are better B&W tools) | – Vibrance is much more gentle, fading colors to pastel tones |

ADJUSTING COLOR RANGES USING THE COLOR MIXER

When your white balance is perfect, you can enhance specific colors using the Color Mixer. The sliders are hidden by default, but appear when you click the color wheel icon in the Color panel.

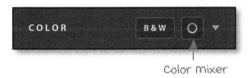

Color mixer

SETTING THE HSL SLIDERS

The Color Mixer panel can look slightly daunting to start with, as there's a multitude of sliders covering different color ranges. You may also hear these referred to as HSL sliders:

H stands for **Hue**, which is the shade of a color, for example, a red jumper may lean towards orange or pink.

S stands for **Saturation**, which is the purity or intensity of the color.

L stands for **Luminance**, which is the brightness of the color.

The default view is *Color*, which displays circles for each color range, and the *Hue*, *Saturation* and *Luminance* sliders for the selected color range below.

If you prefer, you can select *Hue*, *Saturation* or *Luminance* in the **Adjust** pop-up. They're exactly the same sliders, just presented in a different format.

The sliders are tinted to help you remember how the color will change, for example, moving the *Red Saturation* slider to the left reduces the saturation of the reds in the photo. There are some examples to follow.

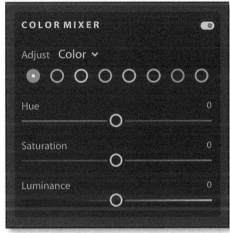

The Color mixer can be displayed in two different ways

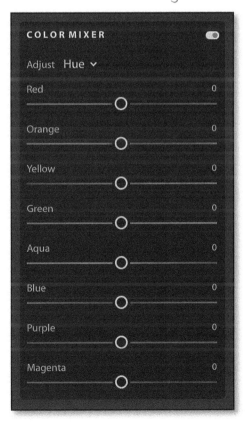

TARGETED ADJUSTMENT TOOL

On mobile, there's a particularly useful tool called the Targeted Adjustment Tool, or TAT tool. It allows you to adjust the Color Mix visually by dragging directly on the photo, while it figures out which sliders to move.

Tap the TAT tool, which is displayed above the colored dots, and hold your finger on the tone you wish to adjust (e.g. the blue sky) and drag up/down to move in large increments or left/right to move in smaller increments.

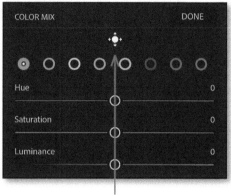

Select the TAT tool and drag on the photo itself to adjust the HSL sliders

EXAMPLE COLOR MIX IMAGES

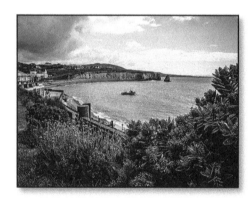
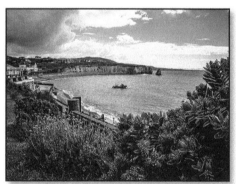

memories—Imagine you've been shooting on the coast, but in your photos, the sea's just not as turquoise as you remember. Try moving the Aqua Hue slider to the right, and perhaps add a little Aqua Saturation

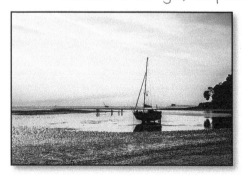
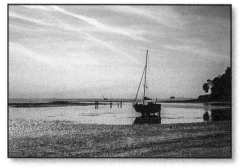

Blue Skies—Unless it's truly overcast, there's often some blue sky hidden among the clouds. Try reducing the Blue Luminance and increasing the Blue Saturation to enhance it. Don't go too far on either slider, as you'll start to introduce noise

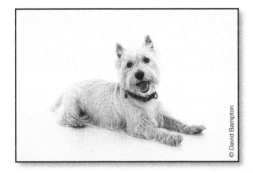 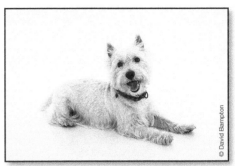

Fix Colors—Due to allergies, Charlie isn't quite as white as he should be. Reducing the Saturation and increasing the Luminance of the orange tones reduces the brown tones without losing the color in his tongue

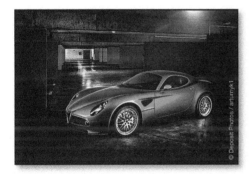 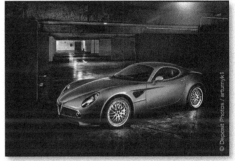

Changing Colors—The Hue slider allows you to shift the colors toward a nearby color, for example, from red toward pink or orange. If you need to completely change colors, you'll need the Brush tool (page 221)

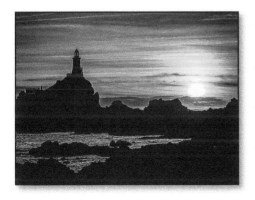 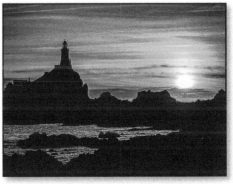

Sunsets—If the sunset isn't quite the color you need for your room's color scheme, shifting the Hue and Saturation of colors can create a whole new look

GREAT B&W CONVERSION 15

Black and white photography is an art in its own right. Some photographers consider it more creative than color photography, because it doesn't match the reality we see around us.

In the days of film, you generally had to make the decision at the time of capture, and add filters to change the appearance. For example, you'd use a red filter to create a dark dramatic sky. Today, you can make the decisions while editing the photos.

Lightroom offers great control over the contrast between light and dark, and between the different colors that made up the original scene.

HOW DO YOU DECIDE WHICH PHOTOS TO CONVERT TO B&W?

A good color photo usually also makes a good B&W photo, so how do you decide which photos to convert? Do you have to test a B&W conversion on every single photo?

If you're not sure, think back to the decisions you made when you were analyzing the photo, and ask yourself...

• Does the color add anything to the photo? For example, if the photo's of a sunset, the answer's probably yes, but in bad weather, the photo may be better without color.

• Is the color distracting? For example, is the color drawing your eye to the wrong spot?

• How would conversion to B&W affect the story and mood of the photo? The way we respond emotionally to color may conflict with the story we're trying to tell.

Also look out for a few features that make particularly good B&W photos, including:

• Contrasts of brightness, especially the beams of light and strong shadows caused by directional light.

• Contrasts of color (light vs. dark, saturated vs. unsaturated, warm vs. cold.)

• Shapes, textures, patterns and compositional features like leading lines. By removing the color, your eye is drawn to these elements.

IN THIS SECTION, WE'LL CONSIDER:

• How to do a simple B&W conversion using pre-mixed Profiles.

• How to enhance contrasts between colors when converting to B&W.

• Which other tools you might want to use to optimize your B&W photo.

SOME REASONS YOU MIGHT CONVERT TO B&W

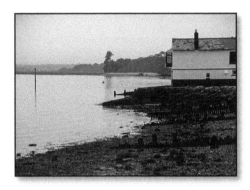 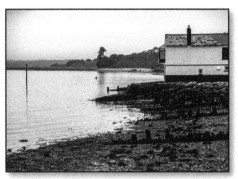

Photos that don't have much color often look more striking in B&W

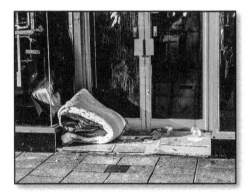 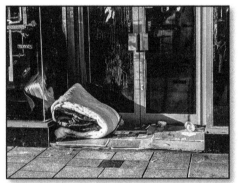

The bright colors in this photo detract from the somber story of homelessness

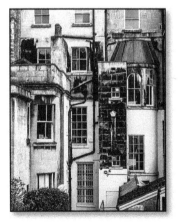 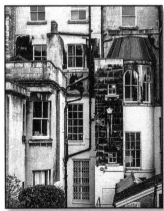

Color can be a distraction, drawing your eye to the wrong spot, like the warm tones in this photo. By removing the color, we notice the lines and textures

UNDERSTANDING B&W CHANNEL MIX

Before you convert the photo to B&W, take a close look at the subtle contrasts between the different colors in your photo. These different shades become varying levels of brightness in the B&W photo, and by mixing the colors to make some colors lighter and others darker, you can control the contrast (or tonal separation) in your B&W photo.

In the color wheels below, you can see that the first B&W conversion makes all of the tones a similar brightness, and it lacks contrast as a result. You don't know where to look first. However, when adjusting the brightness of the different colors, we can create some interesting contrasts and start to control how the viewers eye travels around the photo.

Now let's put this into a simple real world situation. If you look at a landscape on a sunny day, the sky may be vibrant blue and the grass and bushes a vibrant green, so there's an interesting contrast, however the default conversion may make them a similar shade of gray. Instead, you might darken the blue sky to contrast with the white fluffy clouds, and lighten the greens and yellows to move these into the midtones, enhancing the texture and details. We'll take a look at how in the next lesson.

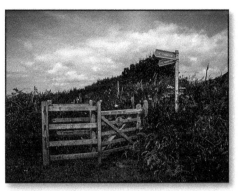

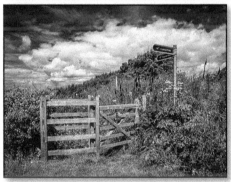

The way you mix the colors can add contrast and draw your eye to different areas of the photo

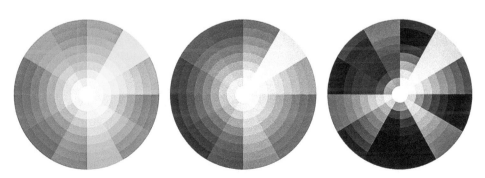

The default B&W conversion (center) lacks contrast, but adjusting the B&W mix (right) allows you to lighten some colors and darken others

CONVERTING TO B&W

Having discussed the theory, let's move on to the practicalities of B&W conversion using Lightroom.

CORRECT COLOR FIRST

Before you convert a photo to B&W, first adjust the photo in color. This removes any color cast or other problems, so you can accurately judge the best B&W settings. You may even want to create a copy (page 125), so you retain your color version as well as the B&W rendition.

CONVERSION OPTIONS

There are numerous ways to convert a photo to B&W, including:

• Shoot using the B&W mode on your camera with the JPEG file format. This isn't a great option as it limits your editing options later. (Shooting in B&W mode in raw, however, can be helpful in visualizing how a photo would look in B&W. As it's raw, it'll be imported into Lightroom as a color photo, ready for you to convert to B&W yourself.)

• Move the *Saturation* slider to -100. It's a very limited way of converting to B&W, because you can't control the ways the color channels are mixed.

• Select a B&W profile from the Profile panel, or a preset from the Presets panel. These profiles and presets are "pre-mixed," so you can pick one that suits your photo and tweak it from there.

• Click the B&W button in the Color panel and manually mix the color channels to suit the photo.

Let's take a closer look at two of these options that give you control over the look of the photo.

STEP-BY-STEP USING PROFILES

On page 137, we introduced the Profile panel. B&W film photographers select a specific film stock and filters, depending on the look they desire. Profiles allow you to do the same when editing your digital photos. Let's give it a try:

1. On a desktop or tablet, select *Browse* in the Profile panel to open view the available profiles. On a phone, select the Profiles view.

2. Open the B&W folder to view the B&W profiles. If you've installed third-party profiles, there may be more B&W profiles in other folders too. On Windows, Mac or Android, you can temporarily filter to show just the B&W profiles by clicking the ... button and selecting *B&W* from the menu. (This filtering is not currently available on iOS.)

3. Once you've found a profile that suits the photo, apply it on a desktop or tablet by clicking/tapping on it and then clicking the *Back* button to return to the normal Edit sliders. On a phone, tap on the profile and then tap the checkmark to return to the normal Edit view.

STEP-BY-STEP USING B&W MIX

If you prefer to "blend your own" B&W mix, you can use the B&W Mixer sliders to control how the color channels are mixed.

1. Click the **B&W** button in the Color panel.

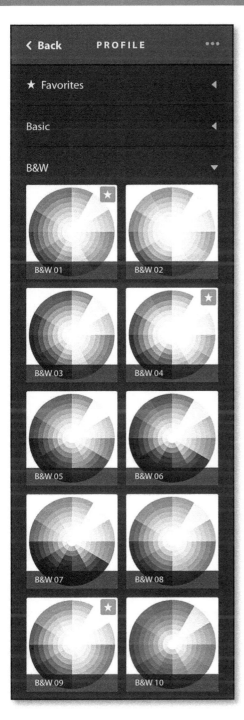

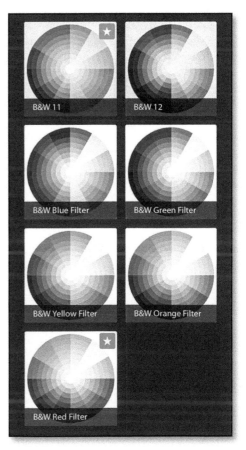

There's a range of B&W
profiles built into Lightroom

This automatically selects the default *Adobe Monochrome* profile for raw photos, or the default B&W profile for rendered (JPEG/TIFF/PSD/PNG) photos.

2. Open the B&W Mixer by clicking the color wheel icon to the right.

3. There is an **Auto** button, and while the computer can't evaluate the scene as accurately as your eyes and brain, it can be a good starting point.

4. Adjust the sliders for each color range, for example, move the blue slider to darken the sky. As you move a slider to the left, the color channel is darkened, and as you move to the right, the color channel is lightened.

The colors overlap, for example, adjusting the orange slider also affects red and yellow tones in the photo.

On mobile, the Targeted Adjustment Tool, or TAT tool, is available. We've already used this tool previously in the Color Mixer panel (page 182). Tap the TAT tool, hold your finger on the tone you wish to adjust (e.g., the blue sky) and drag up/down to move the slider.

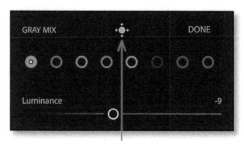

Select the TAT tool and drag on the photo itself to adjust the B&W mix

Toggle Color/B&W   B&W mix

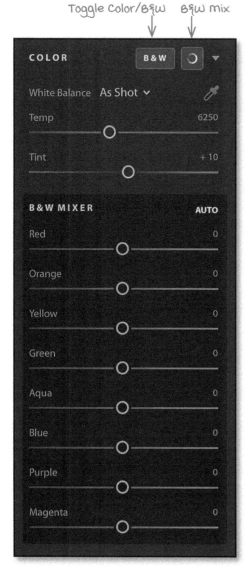

As you're adjusting the sliders, concentrate on increasing tonal separation (the contrast between different colors, which we discussed on page 187) and don't worry about the overall brightness and contrast initially. Ansel Adams, who is famous for his B&W photos, frequently used a dark sky to contrast with white fluffy clouds, and lightened the greens and yellows. On portraits, lightening the skin can make it seem smoother, whereas darkening it enhances wrinkles.

As with most things, moderation is key. Pushing the blue tones too far can introduce noise into your photo, and extreme adjustments between contrasting colors can create halos.

FINE TUNING B&W

Most B&W photos need a full range of tones, from a deep black with detail to a bright white with detail, and all the shades in between, so once you've selected your profile or adjusted the B&W mix, you'll likely need to fine tune the overall contrast using the Light panel sliders (page 151) or the Tone Curve (page 165).

The Linear Gradient (page 215) can be useful for darkening the sky in a B&W photo, like an ND Grad filter, and you can add *Clarity* to bring out contrast in the clouds. A Radial Gradient can darken the edges of the photo to draw your eye into the center, especially if there are bright areas around the edge that draw the viewer's eye out of the photo.

You may also want to use the Brush tool (page 208) to dodge and burn to add emphasis, or add local contrast. Be careful not to go overboard, or the changes will stand out. You can also damp down the contrast in some areas to draw the viewer's eye away from distractions.

Many people love the grain inherent in many popular B&W film stocks, so turn to page 196 to learn to add grain to your B&W photos.

You can also try adding a Sepia or Selenium tint to the photo, like many monochrome photos from years ago. In the Split Toning panel (page 197) set the *Hue* sliders to around 40 to 50 for Sepia or around 215-225 for Selenium, and then adjust the *Saturation* sliders to increase or decrease the strength of the effect. You can create your own mix of colors if you prefer, and even have different tints in the highlights and shadows.

ADDING EFFECTS 16

In previous sections, we've focused on correcting and optimizing the brightness, contrast and color of your photos, but the Effects panel is designed to add special effects.

We've already discussed the *Clarity* and *Dehaze* sliders along with the Light panel sliders on page 163, as they affect the tone and contrast in the photos.

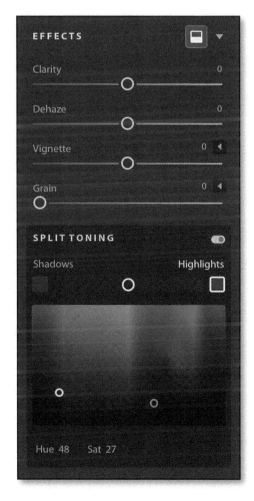

IN THIS SECTION, WE'LL CONSIDER:

• How to add a vignette to draw the viewer's eye into the photo.

• How to add grain for a film-like old-fashioned look.

• How to use Split Toning to tone monochrome photos.

• How to add cross-processed special effects.

• How to do cinematic color-grading to paint a particular mood.

ADDING A VIGNETTE

Vignetting is the darkening or lightening of the corners of a photo. It helps to draw your eye into a photo and focus on the main subject, rather than being distracted by the edges.

It may seem silly to remove the vignetting created by the lens and then add it back using the sliders in the Effects panel, but the Effects sliders are tied to the crop boundaries, whereas any lens vignetting may be partially cropped away.

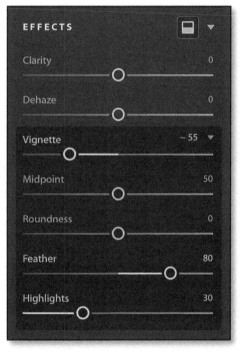

VIGNETTE SLIDERS

The main **Vignette** slider controls how dark or light the vignette should be, with 0 not applying a vignette at all. Most photos look better with a dark vignette, rather than a white one.

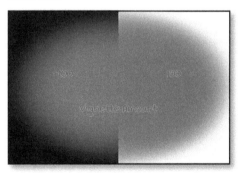

For many photos, the main *Vignette* slider is the only one you'll need to adjust, but if you want more control, there some additional sliders. These are hidden behind a disclosure triangle on the desktop.

The **Midpoint** slider controls how close to the center of the photo the vignette affects. The vignette created by the Effects panel is always centered within the crop boundaries, but if you need an off-center vignette,

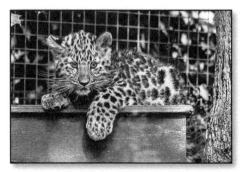

A vignette helps to draw the eye to the center of the photo

you can use the Radial Gradient instead (page 215).

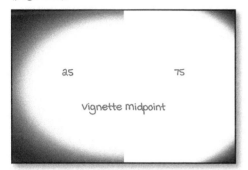

The **Roundness** slider controls how round or square the vignette is. -100 is almost rectangular and barely visible whereas +100 is circular. Most vignettes look great with the default of 0, which matches the ratio of the photo.

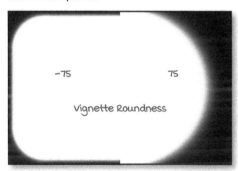

The **Feather** slider runs from 0 to 100, with 0 showing a hard edge, and 100 being so soft it almost disappears. The default of 50 is a great starting point, with most vignettes ranging from 35 to 65.

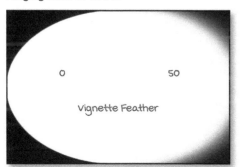

The **Highlights** slider runs from 0, which has

no effect, to 100, which makes the highlights under a dark vignette brighter. This allows you to darken the edges without the photo becoming too flat and lacking in contrast.

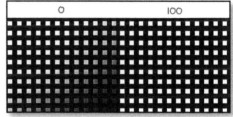

STEP-BY-STEP

Ready to give it a try? You can use the sliders in any order, but this works well:

1. Move the *Amount* slider to -100, so you can easily see the effect of the other sliders.

2. Adjust the *Midpoint* slider, so the vignette doesn't cover important areas of the photo.

3. Adjust the *Feather* slider so the edge of the vignette disappears.

4. Move the *Vignette Amount* back towards the center, until you're drawn into the photo, but the vignette isn't immediately obvious.

5. Adjust the *Highlights* slider if the corners look too flat and lacking contrast.

ADDING GRAIN

We spend a lot of time trying to reduce the noise in our photos... and then put grain back! However, some photos look great with a little extra grain, particularly if they're B&W, toned, or have a film emulation preset applied. It can also help to hide the plasticky look that results from high noise reduction.

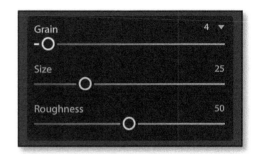

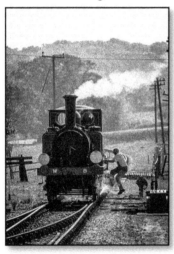

Size affects the size of the grain, just as grain on film came in different sizes, and it gets softer as it gets larger. More expensive film usually had smaller grain. (This may be hard to see in the paperback!)

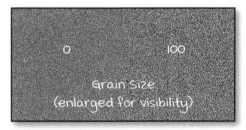

Grain Size
(enlarged for visibility)

GRAIN SLIDERS

The main **Grain** slider in the Effects panel affects the amount of grain applied. The noise is applied equally across the photo, giving a much more film-like quality than digital noise, which tends to be heavier in the shadows.

Roughness affects the consistency of the grain, so 0 is uniform across the photo, whereas higher values become rougher and less "digital."

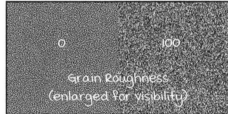

Grain Roughness
(enlarged for visibility)

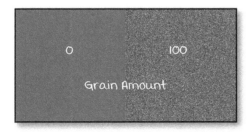

Grain Amount

There are additional sliders for fine-tuning the quality of the grain. These are hidden by a disclosure triangle on the desktop.

You'll need to zoom into 1:1 view to get an accurate preview. Grain is very sensitive to resizing, sharpening and compression, so if you're going to downsize the photo when saving it, you'll need stronger grain than looks right on screen.

SPLIT TONING

Split Toning is primarily designed for toning monochrome photos (such as selenium and sepia tones) but it also works well for cross-processed color effects, or simply enhancing the lighting on a color photo. It allows you to apply a single color tone across the entire photo, or different color tints to the highlights and to the shadows.

SPLIT TONING CONTROLS

The Split Toning controls are hidden by default, but appear when you click the Split Toning icon in the Effects panel.

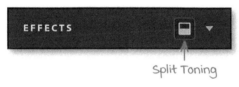

Split Toning

There are only three decisions to make:

• The *Hue* and *Saturation* of the **Shadows**.

• The *Hue* and *Saturation* of the **Highlights**.

• The circle in the middle (desktop) / **Balance** slider (mobile) sets the balance between the highlight tint and the shadow tint, defining which tones qualify as shadows or highlights.

So how do you know which colors to use? There are no set rules, but some combinations typically go well together.

COLOR COMBINATIONS FOR B&W PHOTOS

Traditionally, sepia (a brown tone) or selenium (a blue tone) were used to tone B&W photos to increase the longevity of the prints, and while this is no longer the aim, these tones are still popular choices, adding a soft warm look or a crisp cool look. A mix of these tones can also look great, with sepia highlights and selenium shadows.

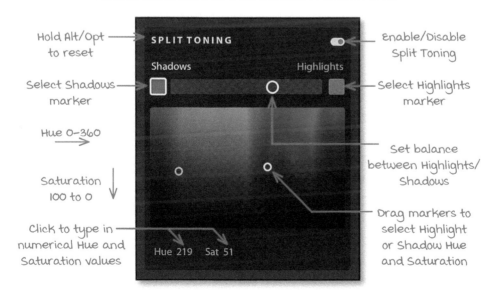

SPLIT TONING (WINDOWS/MAC)

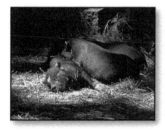
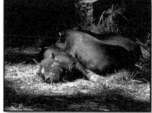
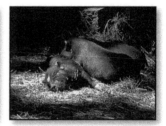

Sepia tone   Selenium tone   Split tone

COLOR COMBINATIONS FOR COLOR PHOTOS

On color photos, it gets a little more tricky, because there are already colors in the image that you don't want to conflict with.

As a rule of thumb, pairs of complementary colors—those opposite each other in the color wheel—look great together. While there can be exceptions, you generally want warm tones in the highlights and cool tones in the shadows, as this reflects the way we see the world around us.

CINEMATIC COLOR GRADING

Do you have a specific color palette in mind? You may have heard of cinematic

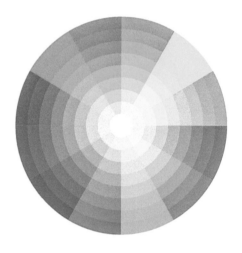

Complementary colors are opposite each other in the color wheel.

SPLIT TONING (IOS/ANDROID)

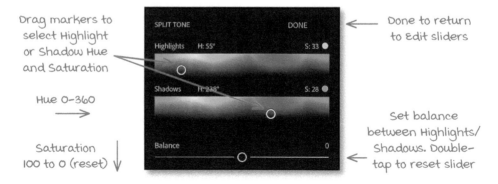

Drag markers to select Highlight or Shadow Hue and Saturation

Hue 0-360

Saturation 100 to 0 (reset)

Done to return to Edit sliders

Set balance between Highlights/ Shadows. Double-tap to reset slider

color grading, which is often used by movie editors to convey a specific look or mood. Next time you're watching a movie, especially summer blockbuster movies, look out for the color palette they've used and how it makes you feel.

Orange and teal/blue is popular in Hollywood, because the teal shadows contrast with people's skin tone, making the actors stand out from the background. This is an effect you can replicate on your own photos, but you have to be quite subtle with the orange saturation if there are people in the photos, or you'll make them look seriously ill.

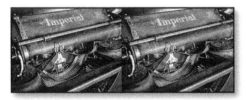

Yellow highlights and blue shadows is also flattering to a range of photos if not overdone, or a softer combination of sepia (brown) and selenium (blue) can add a little color contrast without being obvious.

Watch out for memory tones in the images and ensure these remain natural. We're particularly quick at spotting unnatural skin tones.

Although I've exaggerated the effects in this book so you can see the difference, the key in real life is to be subtle, enhancing the existing colors rather than blowing them away, unless you're aiming for a quirky cross-processed effect.

ENHANCING COLORS USING SPLIT TONING

The Split Toning controls can also be used to enhance the tones in a photo to tell your story.

As a simple example, adding yellow to the highlights and blue to the shadows can give an "golden hour" feel to photos that weren't shot in ideal lighting.

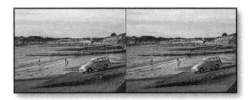

Likewise, adding blues and purples to the shadows can make your nighttime photos crisp and clean.

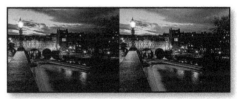

You can also use Split Toning to play with the colors of a sunset.

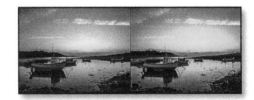

STEP-BY-STEP

1. Click/tap the Split Toning icon in the Effects panel to open the Split Toning panel.

2. On the desktop, click on the *Highlights* icon and drag the highlighted color picker circle to your chosen color. On mobile, drag the circular marker in the *Highlights* section.

3. Repeat for the *Shadows* color picker, but don't overdo the saturation on the shadows.

4. Drag the *Balance* slider to the left to

apply the *Highlights* color to more tones, or
to the right to extend the *Shadows* color into
the midtones.

OPTIMIZING DETAIL

17

Our eyes can see an incredible amount of detail in our surroundings (at least when we're young!) and adjust for very low-light conditions.

Cameras have made incredible progress, but they still can't match the human eye. A little editing is required to optimize the detail in a photo, allowing the viewer to focus on the content of the photo rather than being distracted by false detail (noise). These adjustments are made using the Detail panel.

IN THIS SECTION, WE'LL CONSIDER:

- How sharpening works.

- How to sharpen your photos effectively but without over-sharpening.

- How to reduce digital noise without creating a plastic effect.

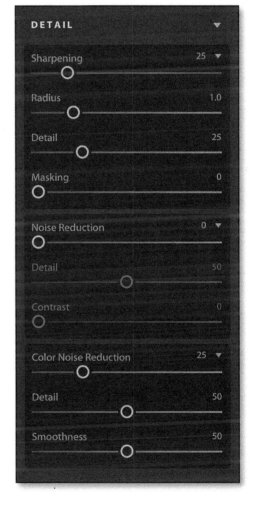

SHARPENING PHOTOS

Most photos benefit from some sharpening, because it highlights the detail in the photo and makes edges look more defined by adding local contrast on a very small scale.

It's easy to get carried away and apply too much sharpening, especially if the photo is slightly out of focus. No amount of sharpening will recover the detail lost in a blurry photo. It can only enhance detail that has been captured.

Over-sharpening can often look worse than too little sharpening. In this lesson, we'll learn how to adjust the Sharpening sliders to get the balance just right.

TYPES OF SHARPENING

Digital image sharpening works in two ways:

USM, or unsharp mask, works by creating small halos along edges to make them appear sharper. On the dark side of an edge it creates a darker halo, and on the light side of an edge it makes a lighter halo.

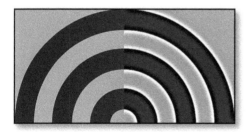

Deconvolution sharpening attempts to calculate and reverse the cause of the blurring.

Lightroom uses both kinds of sharpening, balanced using the *Detail* slider.

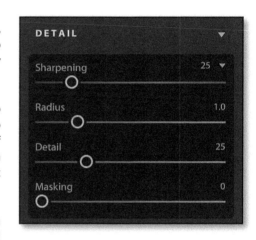

SHARPENING SLIDERS

Lightroom has four sharpening sliders, three of which are hidden under the disclosure triangle on the desktop. Although most of the hidden sliders in Lightroom can remain hidden, these sliders are important.

The number of Sharpening sliders can look overwhelming to start with, but the principles are simple:

• Only sharpen real detail, not noise.

• Avoid making the sharpening halos obvious.

• Always judge sharpening at 1:1 zoom.

Let's take a closer look at how the individual sliders work, and then we'll put it into practice:

Sharpening works like a volume control, running from 0-150. The higher the value, the more sharpening is applied. If you're shooting JPEG, the photos are usually sharpened by the camera, so you'll need less sharpening than a raw file.

You won't usually want to use the slider

at 150 unless you're combining it with the *Masking* or *Detail* sliders, which suppress the sharpening.

If you hold down the Alt key (Windows) / Opt key (Mac) / two fingers (mobile) while moving the *Sharpening* slider, you can see the amount of sharpening being applied without being distracted by color.

Radius affects the width of the sharpening halo. It runs from 0.5-3, with a default of 1.0. Photos with fine detail need a smaller radius, as do landscapes, but a slightly higher radius can look good on portraits.

Hold down the Alt key (Windows) / Opt key (Mac) / two fingers (mobile) while moving the *Radius* slider to see the width of the halos.

Detail and *Masking* are both dampening sliders, allowing you to control which areas of the photo get the most sharpening applied and which areas are protected, but there's a difference in the way they behave.

Detail is very good at controlling sharpening of textures. Under the hood, low values use the USM sharpening methods, and as you increase the slider, it gradually switches to deconvolution methods. In the real world, this means your *Detail* setting will depend on the content of the photo.

The default of 25 is a good general *Detail* setting for most raw files. A low value is ideal for large smooth areas, such as portraits (skin) or sky, where you don't want to sharpen pores or noise. A high value works well for landscapes or other shots with lots of fine detail, where you want to sharpen details like the leaves on the trees.

As you increase *Detail*, it also starts to amplify the noise in the image, so you may need to reduce the *Sharpening* slider and increase the *Masking* and *Luminance Noise Reduction* sliders (page 205) to compensate.

If you hold down the Alt key (Windows) / Opt key (Mac) / two fingers (mobile) while

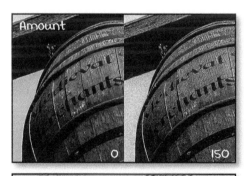

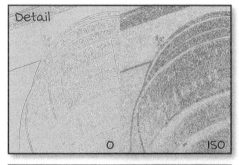

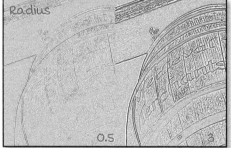

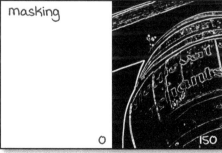

moving the *Detail* slider, you can preview the effect in more detail. The white areas of the mask will be sharpened and the gray areas will be protected. (It's much easier to see on screen than in print.)

The **Masking** slider creates a soft edge mask from the image, so that only the edge details are sharpened. Hold down the Alt key (Windows) / Opt key (Mac) / two fingers (mobile) while moving the *Masking* slider to see the mask it's creating.

The aim is to move the *Masking* slider until only the detail you want to sharpen is white, and everything else is black.

STEP-BY-STEP

That's all very interesting, but how do you know where to set the sliders to get a crisp result without over-sharpening? Try this:

1. Zoom out to Fit view so you can see the entire photo.

2. Hold down the Alt key (Windows) / Opt key (Mac) / two fingers (mobile) and drag the *Masking* slider to the right. You're aiming to make areas of low detail, such as the sky, turn black so the noise in these areas will be protected from your sharpening.

3. Zoom into 1:1 view to accurately preview your further adjustments. (On mobile, tap on the photo to zoom in, but remember it won't be a perfectly accurate 1:1 view if the original is not available/downloaded.)

4. Increase the main *Sharpening* slider to easily preview the effect of your adjustments. Try around 75-100 temporarily.

5. Hold down the Alt key (Windows) / Opt key (Mac) / two fingers (mobile) and drag

the *Detail* slider to the left for portraits or to the right for detailed shots such as landscapes. The aim is to enhance the detail, shown in white, without sharpening the noise, protected in gray.

6. Hold down the Alt key (Windows) / Opt key (Mac) / two fingers (mobile) and drag the *Radius* slider to the left for detailed shots such as landscapes or slightly to the right for portraits. Watch the size of the black and white halos you're creating along the edges, as you don't want them to overwhelm the image detail.

While viewing the *Radius* mask, take note of where the halos are most visible. You'll usually notice them most along high contrast edges.

7. Hold down the Alt key (Windows) / Opt key (Mac) / two fingers (mobile) and drag the *Sharpening* slider to the left until the halos almost disappear.

REDUCING NOISE

Noise in your photos can be distracting. You'll particularly notice it in photos shot at a high ISO, for example, shot without flash in a darkened room, or photos shot using a small sensor. If you've increased the exposure considerably within Lightroom, that can also increase the appearance of noise. Fortunately, Lightroom's Noise Reduction tools are excellent.

NOISE REDUCTION SLIDERS

There's an array of noise reduction sliders, but just because they exist doesn't mean you need to use them on every photo. Most photos only require the main *Noise Reduction* and *Color Noise Reduction* sliders. Additional sliders are available for more extreme cases, and can be left at their default settings most of the time. They're hidden under a disclosure triangle on the desktop.

The **Noise Reduction** slider controls the amount of luminance noise reduction applied. 0 doesn't apply any noise reduction, but at 100, the photo has a soft, almost

painted effect.

If you hold down the Alt key (Windows) / Opt key (Mac) / two fingers (mobile) while moving the *Noise Reduction* slider, you can see the amount of noise reduction being applied without being distracted by color.

The aim is to reduce the noise, without losing the detail or making the subject look like plastic, so don't push it too far.

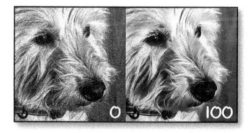

The **Color** slider tries to suppress single pixels of random noise without losing the edge detail. I've zoomed in on Charlie's eye to make the small colored pixels more visible, but you'll see them more clearly at 1:1 view in your own photos.

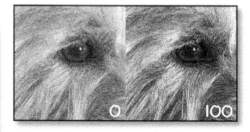

EXTREME NOISE REDUCTION

The other noise reduction sliders only make a noticeable difference to extremely noisy images, such as those produced by the highest ISO rating that your camera offers, or where a high ISO file is extremely underexposed. You're unlikely to see a difference at lower ISO ratings, for better or

Noise Reduction	20 ▼
Detail	50
Contrast	0
Color Noise Reduction	25 ▼
Detail	50
Smoothness	50

for worse, so in most cases you won't need to change these settings from their defaults. I haven't included screenshots, because the difference is so small, you wouldn't be able to see it. Like the main *Noise Reduction* slider, holding down the Alt key (Windows) / Opt key (Mac) / two fingers (mobile) shows a grayscale preview.

The luminance **Detail** slider sets the noise threshold, so higher values preserve more detail but some noise may incorrectly be identified as detail.

The luminance **Contrast** slider at 0 is a much finer grain than 100. Higher values help to preserve texture, but can introduce a mottling effect, so lower values are usually a better choice.

The color **Detail** slider refines any fine color edges. At low values it reduces the number of color speckles in these edges but may slightly desaturate them, whereas at high values, it tries to retain the color detail but may introduce color speckles in the process.

The color **Smoothness** slider is similar to the main *Color Noise Reduction* slider, but it aims to remove larger areas of color mottling or splotchiness. You're most likely to see this on very underexposed images, where you've brightened an area considerably, or extreme contrast images that you're tone-mapping (using maximum - *Highlights* and + *Shadows* adjustments). The default is 50, which works very well on most images. Moving the slider to the right increases the smoothing, but can slow Lightroom down.

STEP-BY-STEP

Let's put this into practice on an "average" photo:

1. Zoom in to 1:1 view, as this provides the most accurate preview.

2. Check for color noise. For most raw files, the default *Color Noise Reduction* setting of 25 is spot on. It's set to 0 for JPEGs, but if there's still colored noise in your photo, particularly in the dark shadows, try increasing it slightly.

3. Adjust the *Noise Reduction* slider to reduce the noise without losing too much detail. If you're working on raw files, try a setting of around 15-20 on the main *Noise Reduction* slider as a starting point.

4. Leave the other sliders at their defaults unless you have an extremely noisy photo that will be printed as a billboard!

SELECTIVE NOISE REDUCTION

If your noise reduction is too strong in some areas, select the Brush tool (page 208), set the *Noise* sliders to between 0 and -100 and brush over those areas to reduce the noise reduction. Don't remove it entirely, as it'll look too grainy in comparison with the rest of the photo.

Likewise, if you only want to paint the noise reduction into certain areas, a brush set to + *Noise* applies additional noise reduction. (Contrary to the name of the slider, it doesn't really add noise!)

SELECTIVE EDITING

18

Most of Lightroom's sliders apply to the whole photo, but the selective adjustment tools allow you to apply settings to specific areas. This isn't a new concept. Photographers have been dodging and burning photos in the darkroom for years. The selective editing tools can be used for things like:

Dodging & Burning—The *Exposure* adjustment is similar to dodging and burning in a traditional darkroom, lightening and darkening areas of the photo.

Enhancing Faces—Settings such as *Sharpness*, *Clarity* and *Noise Reduction* can be used for softening skin on portraits without softening the eyes.

Mixed Lighting—*Temp* and *Tint* are useful when adjusting for mixed lighting situations, or changing the color of specific regions.

Enhancing Sunset Skies—Settings can be combined, so a combination of - *Exposure*, + *Saturation* and + *Clarity* can enhance a sunset.

But how do you decide what to adjust, and where to draw the eye? It comes back to the decisions you made when you were analyzing the photo. Did you find any distractions that need to be minimized, for example, bright areas in a dark scene, or warm saturated colors in the wrong spot? And what did you decide to enhance, to draw the viewer's eye around the photo?

Before you start applying settings, however, you need to create a selection, and there are three tools to do this:

• The **Brush** offers complete flexibility to correct uneven lighting, dodge and burn to draw the eye and enhance people's faces.

• The **Linear Gradient** is ideal for darkening skies and lightening foregrounds.

• The **Radial Gradient** creates off-center vignettes and can put a "spotlight" on certain areas of the photo.

IN THIS SECTION, WE'LL CONSIDER:

• How to create brushed selections.

• How to create linear selections.

• How to create radial selections.

• Examples of the adjustments you can make using selective adjustments.

MAKING SELECTIONS USING THE BRUSH

The Brush tool allows you to create a freeform selection by painting on the photo. Unlike the gradient tools, it's not constrained to a specific shape, so it's very flexible.

The brush is a powerful tool, with lots of useful tricks, so in this lesson we'll look at:

- The basics of creating a brush selection.

- How to choose the right brush for the job.

- How to manage multiple brush selections.

CREATING BRUSH SELECTIONS

To **open the Brush tool** on the desktop, click on the brush icon in the right panel bar or press the B key.

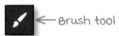
Brush tool

On mobile, select the Selective Editing tool, then tap the **+** button and select the brush icon.

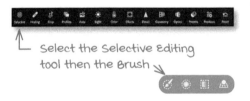
Select the Selective Editing tool then the Brush

When you select the brush, it's automatically ready to start a new selection. To **paint with the brush** on the desktop, hold down the mouse button and drag the cursor across the photo then release the mouse. On mobile, drag your finger or stylus/pen across the photo. Holding down the Shift key while you paint draws the stroke in a straight vertical or horizontal line (desktop only).

To **apply adjustments** to the selection, so you can see where you're painting, adjust the sliders. You can tweak them again later, when you've perfected your selection.

If you make a mistake when brushing, it's not a problem. To **erase part of the selection,** select the *Eraser* from the Brush panel (desktop) / icons (mobile).

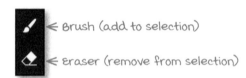
Brush (add to selection)
Eraser (remove from selection)

On the desktop, you can also hold down the Alt (Windows) / Opt (Mac) key to select the eraser temporarily, and brush away the selection. Of course, if you've only just painted a stroke, Ctrl-Z (Windows) / Cmd-Z (Mac) / undo icon (mobile) will also undo your last action.

By creating multiple selections, you can apply different edits to different areas of the photo, and they can be overlapped and layered to build up the effect. To **create an additional brush selection**, click the **+** button at the top of the Brush panel (desktop) / tap the **+** button and select the brush icon again (mobile).

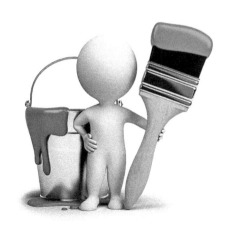

THE BRUSH TOOL (WINDOWS/MAC)

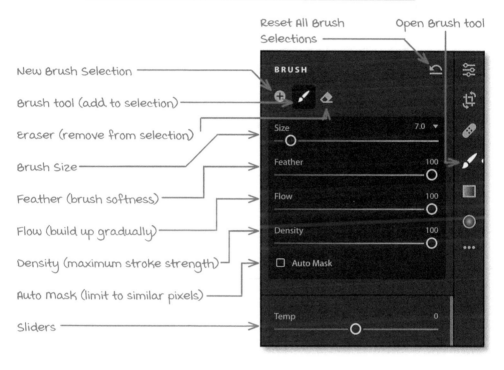

Reset All Brush Selections

Open Brush tool

New Brush Selection

Brush tool (add to selection)

Eraser (remove from selection)

Brush Size

Feather (brush softness)

Flow (build up gradually)

Density (maximum stroke strength)

Auto Mask (limit to similar pixels)

Sliders

BRUSH

Size   7.0

Feather   100

Flow   100

Density   100

☐ Auto Mask

Temp   0

CHOOSING THE RIGHT BRUSH

If you're doing some painting at home, you'll pick the right brush for the job. Perhaps a large brush for the wall, and a small brush to paint along the edges. Lightroom offers similar controls. On the desktop, these are selected using sliders in the Brush panel (some are hidden under a disclosure triangle), and the size and feathering are previewed on the cursor, with two lines close together for minimal feathering, and further apart for greater feathering.

On mobile, hold your finger on the *Size*, *Feather* or *Flow* icon and drag up or down

to increase or decrease the slider value. The numeric value displays at the top of the screen, and a red preview displays in the center of the screen, so you can see how big or hard the brush will be.

Size runs from 0.1, which is a tiny brush, to a maximum size of 100. You can use multiple different brush sizes on the same selection, perhaps using a large brush to cover a large area, then a small brush for detailed edges. On the desktop, you can also use the [and] keyboard shortcuts or your mouse scroll wheel to adjust the size.

Feather runs from 1, which is a hard edged brush, to 100 which is soft. A harder edged brush is useful when you're brushing up against the edge of an object in the photo, whereas a soft brush is better for blending your adjustments into the rest of the photo.

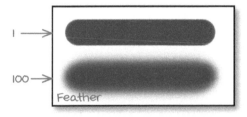

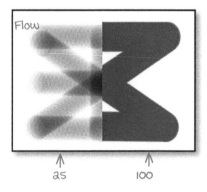

On the desktop, the Shift-[and Shift-] keys also adjust the feathering.

Flow controls the rate at which the adjustment is applied. With *Flow* at 100, the brush behaves like a paintbrush, laying down the maximum effect with each stroke.

With *Flow* at a lower value, such as 25, the brush behaves more like an airbrush, building up the effect gradually.

THE BRUSH TOOL (IOS/ANDROID)

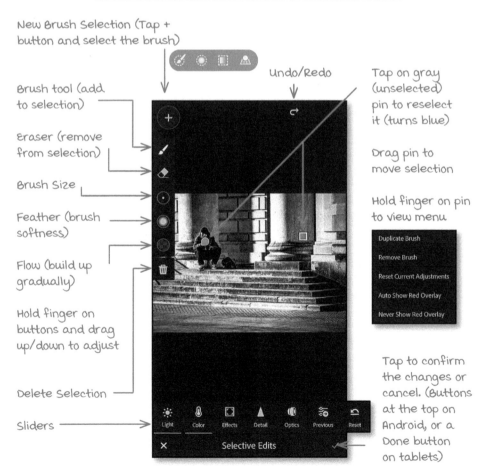

New Brush Selection (Tap + button and select the brush)

Undo/Redo

Brush tool (add to selection)

Eraser (remove from selection)

Brush Size

Feather (brush softness)

Flow (build up gradually)

Hold finger on buttons and drag up/down to adjust

Delete Selection

Sliders

Tap on gray (unselected) pin to reselect it (turns blue)

Drag pin to move selection

Hold finger on pin to view menu

Duplicate Brush
Remove Brush
Reset Current Adjustments
Auto Show Red Overlay
Never Show Red Overlay

Tap to confirm the changes or cancel. (Buttons at the top on Android, or a Done button on tablets)

Light Color Effects Detail Optics Previous Reset

Selective Edits

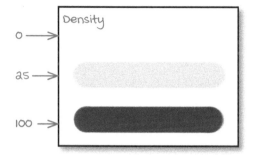

Density (desktop only) limits the maximum strength of the stroke. Regardless of how many times you paint, the mask can never be stronger than the maximum density setting. Unless you need the *Density* control for a specific purpose, I'd suggest leaving it set at 100.

If you're brushing over the photo and nothing seems to be happening, it's usually because either the *Flow* or *Density* sliders are set too low.

Some photographers like to use a graphics tablet/pen (desktop) / Apple Pencil (iOS) / stylus (Android) to paint on the photo. It can take some practice, but it's a more natural and accurate way of drawing. The flow/opacity of the stroke can be controlled by how hard you press, just like drawing with a pencil on paper.

The **Auto Mask** checkbox (desktop only) confines your brush strokes to areas of similar color, based on the tones that the center of the brush passes over. This helps to prevent your mask spilling over into other

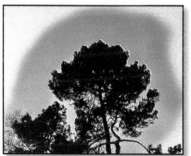

areas of the photo, for example, you can paint over a child's shirt to selectively adjust the color, without having to carefully brush around the edges.

It can cause halos, for example, trying to darken a bright sky with a silhouette of a tree in the foreground may leave a halo around the edge of the tree.

MASK & PINS

Each brush selection is marked with a small icon called a pin. On the desktop, they're all circular and the colors are reversed depending on whether the pin is selected or not.

Unselected Selected

On mobile, there's a different pin for each type of selective edit, and they have a blue center when selected, or a gray center when deselected.

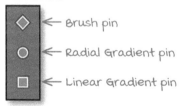

← Brush pin

← Radial Gradient pin

← Linear Gradient pin

To **hide the pins**, float the cursor away from the photo (desktop) / click *Done* to exit the Selective Editing tools (mobile).

The **mask overlay** is a colored tint that shows the location and opacity of your selection.

On the desktop, you can temporarily **show the mask overlay** by floating the cursor over a pin. If you can't see the pins and overlays on the desktop, press the O key or

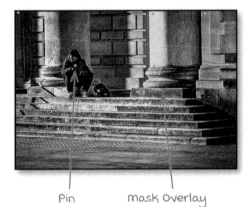

Pin   mask Overlay

go to *View menu > Edit Tools > Show Overlay*. The O key cycles through four states—*Hide Overlays* (pins), *Show Tool Overlay* (pins), *Show Mask Overlay* (red/green mask) and *Show Tool and Mask Overlays* (pins and mask). You can also use Shift-O to switch between a red overlay and a green one, which can be useful when you're painting over a red object.

On mobile, the mask shows automatically, but disappears when you apply edits to the selection using the sliders. To hide the red mask overlay, long press on the pin to show the menu and switch from *Auto Show Red Overlay* to *Never Show Red Overlay*.

EDITING SELECTIONS

To **reselect an existing brush selection**, click/tap on its pin.

If you've reached the limit of a slider, you can duplicate the selection without having to paint a new selection. To **duplicate a selection**, right-click (desktop) / long press (mobile) on the pin and select *Duplicate*. There isn't an easy way to access the bottom mask again, however. To do so, you must move the top pin, so get the first pin right before duplicating it.

Duplicating a selection is also useful if you want to replicate an effect somewhere else on the photo, for example, if you've enhanced the iris of one eye, you can duplicate the selection and move it to the other eye.

To **move the brush selection**, click/tap and drag the pin.

You can't **invert the brush selection**, but you can use a large brush to paint over everything, and then use a small brush to erase from that mask. For example, you can paint the entire photo using a negative *Saturation* brush to partially desaturate the background and then erase to show a small amount of the original color photo below, to draw the eye to that area.

To **fade the edits (desktop only)**, hold the Alt (Windows) / Opt key while dragging left<>right on the pin to move multiple adjustment sliders at once.

To **delete a brush selection** on the desktop, select the pin then press the Delete key or right-click on the pin and select *Delete*. On mobile, select the pin then tap the Delete icon or long press on the pin and select *Remove Brush*.

To **delete all brush selections**, press the *Reset* button in the Brush panel (desktop) / toolbar (mobile). On the desktop, this only deletes the brush strokes, whereas on mobile, choosing *Selective Edits* (iOS) / *Selection* (Android) clears all selective edits.

There's a multitude of keyboard shortcuts and modifiers for the Selective Editing tools on the desktop, so we won't list them all here. They're all listed on the Keyboard Shortcuts sheets available in the Members Area (see page 314).

MAKING SELECTIONS USING A DEPTH MASK ON IOS

If you own an iPhone 7+, 8+ or iPhone X (or a later iPhone with dual cameras), you can take advantage of the dual cameras to create a depth mask, which can be used for blurring and darkening backgrounds, creating a fake depth of field.

To **capture a photo with a depth mask**, you must either use the Apple Camera app (or similar) set to Portrait mode with *iOS Settings > Camera > Formats* set to *High Efficiency* mode so it captures in HEIC format, or select *Depth Capture* from the pop-up in Lightroom's camera.

To **use the depth mask**, select the Selective Editing tool, then tap the **+** button and select the depth mask icon. It only appears

for HEIC format photos that have a depth mask.

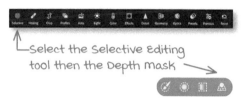

Select the Selective Editing tool then the Depth mask

The selected areas are shown using a red mask. To invert the selection, tap the *Invert* button.

At the bottom, the histogram shows the number of pixels at each depth, from distant pixels on the left to nearby pixels on the right.

THE DEPTH MASK TOOL (IOS)

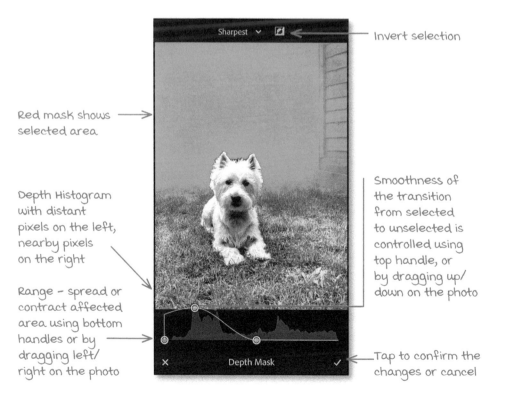

Invert selection

Red mask shows selected area

Depth Histogram with distant pixels on the left, nearby pixels on the right

Range – spread or contract affected area using bottom handles or by dragging left/right on the photo

Smoothness of the transition from selected to unselected is controlled using top handle, or by dragging up/down on the photo

Tap to confirm the changes or cancel

The curved line allows you to choose how many of the pixels should be included in the selection.

The range is selected using the handles at the bottom, and the smoothness of the transition from selected to unselected is controlled by the top handle. For example, moving the handles to the right selects the pixels closest to you.

When you tap the checkmark, the mask is turned into a normal brush mask, which you can edit further using the brush tools discussed in the previous lesson (page 208).

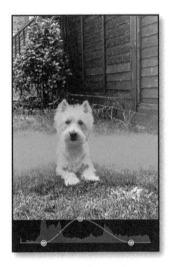

Dragged apart
widens the range

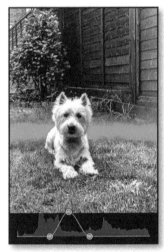

Dragged together
narrows the range

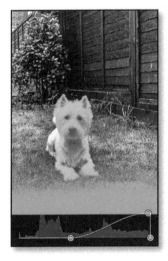

Dragged to the
right selects areas
near the camera

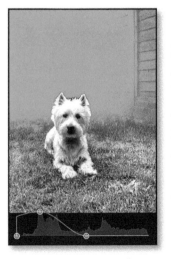

Dragged to the left
selects areas further
away from the camera

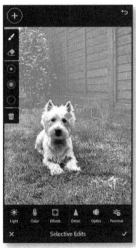

When you're done,
it becomes a normal
brush selection

MAKING SELECTIONS USING A GRADIENT

There are two kinds of gradients—Linear (straight) and Radial (round/oval). Since the behavior is similar, we'll discuss both at once.

LINEAR GRADIENT

The Linear Gradient is particularly useful for darkening the sky in a sunset photo or blurring a distracting foreground. It can also be useful if the lighting on one side of the photo is different to the other side.

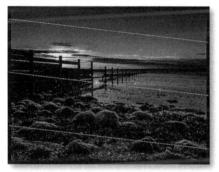

RADIAL GRADIENT

The Radial Gradient is particularly useful for off-center vignettes, to draw the eye to a specific area of the photo. It can also be used to lighten faces in photos or put a "spotlight" on one area of the photo, among other things.

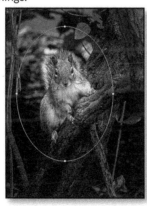

CREATING A GRADIENT

To **open the Linear and Radial Gradient tools**, click the buttons in the right panel bar or press the L key (Linear) or R key (Radial).

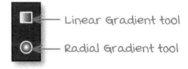

Linear Gradient tool

Radial Gradient tool

On mobile, select the Selective Editing tool, then tap the **+** button and select the Radial Gradient or Linear Gradient icon.

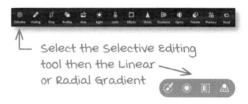

Select the Selective Editing tool then the Linear or Radial Gradient

To **create a linear gradient** on the desktop, click at the gradient starting point, and drag to the gradient end point before releasing the mouse button. To drag out from the center of the gradient, instead of setting the start/end points, hold down the Alt (Windows) / Opt (Mac) key while dragging. The gradient then expands equally from both sides of your starting point. If the horizon is straight, hold down the Shift key while creating the gradient to constrain it to a 90° angle.

On mobile, drag your finger or stylus/pen across the photo, from the start of the gradient to the end.

To **create a radial gradient** on the desktop, click in the center of your new circle/oval, and drag out towards the edge of the photo before releasing the mouse button. On mobile, drag your finger or stylus/pen out from the center of your radial gradient.

To **apply adjustments** to the selection, so

you can see the effect, adjust the sliders. You can tweak them again later, when you've perfected your selection.

By creating multiple gradients, you can apply different edits to different areas of the photo, and they can be overlapped and layered to build up the effect.

To **create an additional gradient** on the desktop, just click and drag again. On mobile, tap the **+** button and select the Linear or Radial Gradient icon again, then drag across the photo.

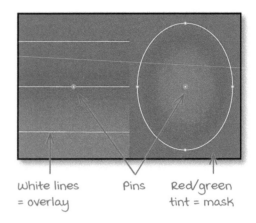

White lines = overlay   Pins   Red/green tint = mask

OVERLAYS, PINS & MASKS

The gradients are controlled using an overlay—three lines for the Linear Gradient and a circle with four small handles for the Radial Gradient. They allow you to adjust the size, rotation and position of the gradient.

Each brush selection is marked with a small icon called a pin. On the desktop, they're all circular and the colors are reversed depending on whether the pin is selected or not.

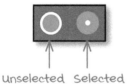

Unselected Selected

On mobile, there's a different pin for each type of selective edit, and they have a blue center when selected, or a gray center when deselected.

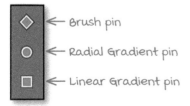

← Brush pin

← Radial Gradient pin

← Linear Gradient pin

To **hide the pins**, float the cursor away from the photo (desktop) / click *Done* to exit the Selective Editing tools (mobile).

The **mask overlay** is a colored tint that shows the location and opacity of your selection.

On the desktop, you can temporarily **show the mask overlay** by floating the cursor over a pin. If you can't see the pins and overlays on the desktop, press the O key or go to *View menu > Edit Tools > Show Overlay*. The O key cycles through four states—*Hide Overlays* (pins), *Show Tool Overlay* (pins), *Show Mask Overlay* (red/green mask) and *Show Tool and Mask Overlays* (pins and mask). You can also use Shift-O to switch between a red overlay and a green one, which can be useful when you're painting over a red object.

On mobile, the mask shows automatically, but disappears when you apply edits to the selection using the sliders. To hide the red mask overlay, long press on the pin to show the menu and switch from *Auto Show Red Overlay* to *Never Show Red Overlay*.

EDITING GRADIENTS

Like the Brush tool, you can go back and edit

the selection or settings later. To **reselect an existing gradient**, click/tap on the pin.

To **feather/stretch a linear gradient**, drag the outer lines further apart. Moving them closer together reduces the feathering.

To **feather a radial gradient**, adjust the *Feather* slider (desktop) / hold your finger on the *Feather* icon and drag up or down to increase or decrease the slider value (mobile).

To **resize a radial gradient**, drag the handles on the oval line.

To **rotate the gradient** on the desktop, float over ends of the central line (linear) / oval line (radial). The cursor changes to a curved double-headed arrow, then click and drag to adjust the rotation of the gradient. On mobile, simply drag the central line (linear) /

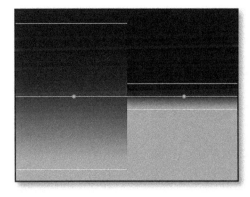

oval line (radial).

If the gradient is the wrong way round, for example, the effect is applied to the inside of a radial gradient instead of the outside, **invert the gradient** by clicking the *Invert* checkbox (desktop) / tapping the *Invert* icon (mobile).

To **move the gradient**, drag the central pin.

LINEAR & RADIAL GRADIENT (WINDOWS/MAC)

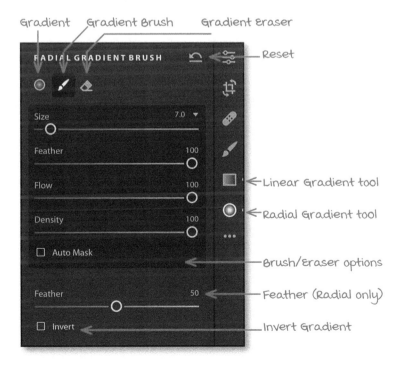

Gradient   Gradient Brush   Gradient Eraser

RADIAL GRADIENT BRUSH — Reset

Size 7.0

Feather 100

Flow 100 ← Linear Gradient tool

Density 100 ← Radial Gradient tool

☐ Auto Mask — Brush/Eraser options

Feather 50 — Feather (Radial only)

☐ Invert — Invert Gradient

If you've reached the limit of a slider, you may want to **duplicate the gradient**. To do so, right-click (desktop) / long press (mobile) on the pin and select *Duplicate* from the menu.

To **fade the edits** (desktop only), hold the Alt (Windows) / Opt key while dragging left<>right on the pin to move multiple adjustment sliders at once.

To **delete a gradient** on the desktop, select the pin then press the Delete key or right-click on the pin and select *Delete*. On mobile, select the pin then tap the Delete icon or long press on the pin and select *Remove Linear/Radial Gradient*.

To **delete all gradients**, press the **Reset** button in the Linear/Radial Gradient panel (desktop) / toolbar (mobile).

LINEAR GRADIENT (IOS/ANDROID)

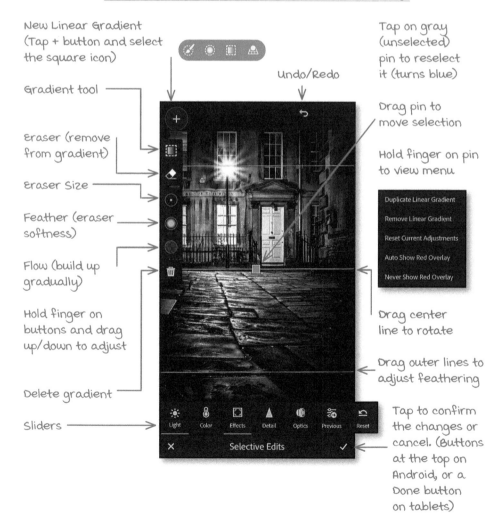

New Linear Gradient (Tap + button and select the square icon)

Gradient tool

Eraser (remove from gradient)

Eraser Size

Feather (eraser softness)

Flow (build up gradually)

Hold finger on buttons and drag up/down to adjust

Delete gradient

Sliders

Undo/Redo

Tap on gray (unselected) pin to reselect it (turns blue)

Drag pin to move selection

Hold finger on pin to view menu

Duplicate Linear Gradient
Remove Linear Gradient
Reset Current Adjustments
Auto Show Red Overlay
Never Show Red Overlay

Drag center line to rotate

Drag outer lines to adjust feathering

Tap to confirm the changes or cancel. (Buttons at the top on Android, or a Done button on tablets)

Light   Color   Effects   Detail   Optics   Previous   Reset

Selective Edits

ADDING TO OR ERASING PART OF THE GRADIENT

At times, you may want to prevent parts of the photo being affected by a gradient, or add an extra brush stroke to the gradient. For example, if you're darkening the sky, you may not want to darken the building on the horizon at the same time. In this case, you can brush away part of the gradient.

To **add to or erase part of the gradient**, select the **Brush** or **Eraser** icon in the Gradient panel (desktop) / sidebar (mobile), then click and drag across the photo. (On mobile, you can only erase from the gradient.) The brush/eraser options (size/ feather, etc.) in the gradients work like the main Brush tool (page 208).

RADIAL GRADIENT (IOS/ANDROID)

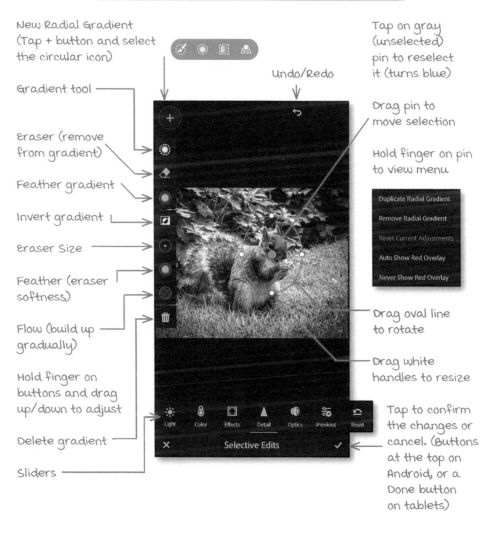

New Radial Gradient (Tap + button and select the circular icon)

Gradient tool

Eraser (remove from gradient)

Feather gradient

Invert gradient

Eraser Size

Feather (eraser softness)

Flow (build up gradually)

Hold finger on buttons and drag up/down to adjust

Delete gradient

Sliders

Undo/Redo

Tap on gray (unselected) pin to reselect it (turns blue)

Drag pin to move selection

Hold finger on pin to view menu

Duplicate Radial Gradient
Remove Radial Gradient
Reset Current Adjustments
Auto Show Red Overlay
Never Show Red Overlay

Drag oval line to rotate

Drag white handles to resize

Tap to confirm the changes or cancel. (Buttons at the top on Android, or a Done button on tablets)

Light   Color   Effects   Detail   Optics   Previous   Reset

✕   Selective Edits   ✓

LIGHT ADJUSTMENTS (INCL. DODGING & BURNING)

One of the most logical uses for local adjustments is tonal changes—**Exposure, Contrast, Highlights, Shadows, Whites, Blacks, Clarity** and **Dehaze**. They can be used for darkening skies, brightening shadows, reducing bright highlights, darkening edges like an off-center vignette, and many other adjustments.

The word 'dodging' comes from the

darkroom printing process and refers to lightening areas of the image. Many photos benefit from a little dodging, for example, lightening faces.

The opposite of dodging is 'burning in' or selectively darkening areas of the photo that are too bright, attracting your attention more than the main subject.

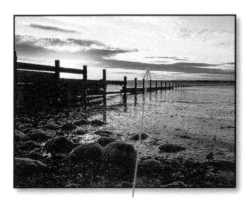 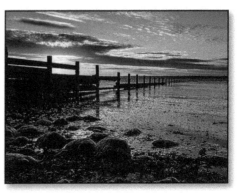

−1 Exposure & −39 Highlights on a linear gradient brings back the detail in the sky without darkening the foreground, like an ND Grad filter. For some skies, we might also add Clarity, Dehaze, Saturation or a different color tint

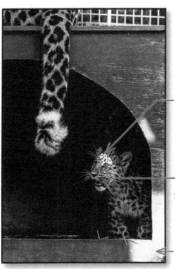

+0.6 Exposure & +45 Saturation lightens and warms up the cub's face & body

−1.0 Exposure & −80 Highlights darkens the light patch on the cub's face

−40 Temp & +20 Saturation enhances the cub's blue eyes

−3.2 Exposure evens out lighting on wall

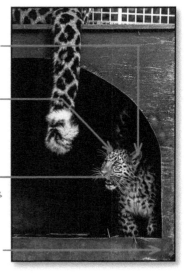

LOCAL COLOR ADJUSTMENTS

The *Temp*, *Tint* and *Saturation* sliders and the *Color* picker (mobile only) are useful for local color adjustments.

Temp makes the selected area warmer or cooler, while **Tint** moves between green and pink. The **Saturation** slider acts like the intelligent *Vibrance* slider when dragged to the right (+), but dragged to the left (-), it behaves like negative *Saturation*, allowing you to desaturate the selected area to B&W.

The **Color** option, only currently available on mobile, applies a specific color tint of your choice.

You can use the color controls to compensate for mixed lighting, enhance the color of the sky, draw the eye towards the subject or away from a distraction, or even do a selective color effect (a B&W or partially saturated photo with a small area of the photo in its original color).

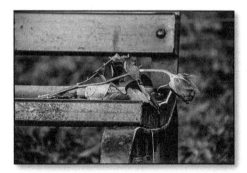
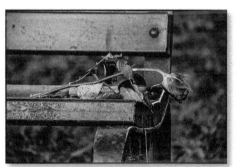

To create an effect known as B&W with Spot Color or Selective Color, we've used a brush to paint negative Saturation. I've exaggerated the effect for print, but aim for a more subtle touch rather than complete desaturation for a more natural look. Also, avoid desaturating skin when applying this effect, as it always looks odd!

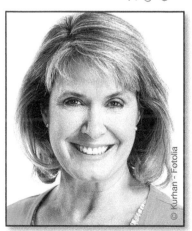
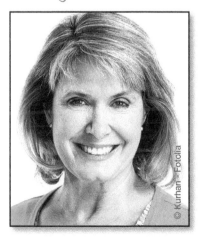

In this photo, we've used the Tint slider to apply some "pink lipstick." Saturation has also been used to subtly enhance the color of her eyes

LOCAL DETAIL

The *Sharpening, Noise Reduction, Clarity* and *Defringe* sliders are ideal for selectively sharpening, blurring, reducing noise and removing colored fringes.

Adding **Sharpening** can be useful for sharpening eyes and other facial features without over-sharpening the skin. Setting the *Sharpening* slider between -50 and -100 applies a blur similar to a lens blur, allowing you to blur the background of a photo.

Negative **Clarity** gives a slightly different softening effect, which works well for softening skin, while + values allow you to add local contrast (texture) to specific areas.

Contrary to the name, the **Noise** slider doesn't add noise, but decreases or increases any global noise reduction that you've applied, for example, the shadows may benefit from extra noise reduction.

On mobile, there's an additional **Defringe** slider, which can be used to remove color fringes along high contrast edges.

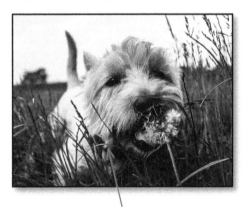

In this grab shot, the camera focused on the grass at the front, so the eyes are soft

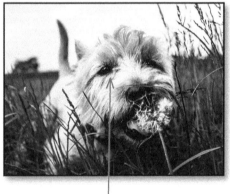

A high sharpness value just made it look "crunchy," but a combination of +35 Sharpness and +35 Clarity works

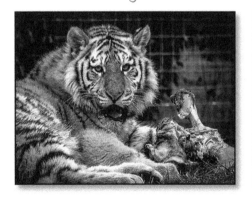

The wires of the enclosure walls in the tiger sanctuary are distracting

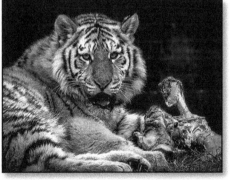

- Clarity, -Sharpness, -Saturation and -Exposure tone down the background, focusing attention on the tiger

REDUCING A MOIRÉ PATTERN

The **Moiré** removal slider in the Brush tool allows you to paint a moiré rainbow away. It can only usually remove the color rainbow, not any luminosity changes, but it works very well. It works on both raw and rendered photos, although the additional data in a raw file means that it is far more effective on raw files.

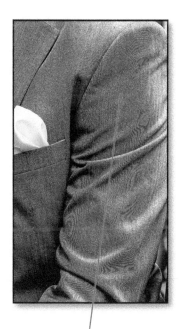

STEP-BY-STEP

1. Temporarily increase the Saturation slider in the Color panel (page 180) to make the moiré easier to see.

2. Open the Brush tool (page 208).

3. Set the *Feather* slider to 0 to create a hard edged brush, adjust the *Size* to suit and turn off *Auto Mask*.

4. Set the *Moiré* slider to +100. (If you set the *Moiré* slider to a negative value, it won't do anything—that's only used to reduce the effect of another brush stroke which already has positive moiré removal applied.)

5. Paint carefully over the photo. If you cross a boundary of another color in the photo, it can blur or smudge.

6. Set the Color panel's *Saturation* slider back to your preferred setting for the photo.

7. Reduce the brush selection's *Moiré* slider if the full +100 setting is too strong.

The rainbow-colored pattern sometimes found on fabrics is called moiré. It can't be removed completely, but it can be reduced

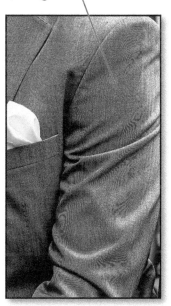

ENHANCING FACES

Most facial retouching can be done faster using a pixel-based editor such as Photoshop, but if you don't have access to such a tool, the brush tool allows you to do some enhancement. Here's a few examples, using a mix of different sliders:

SHARPEN EYES

To sharpen the eyes (or other facial features) without over-sharpening the rest of the face, use a soft-edged brush set to + *Sharpness*.

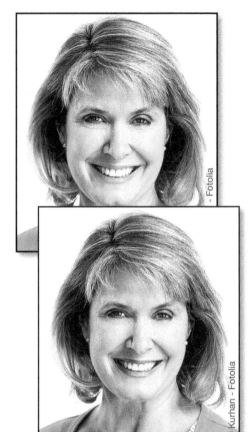

FIX RED EYE

Red eye—or green eye in dogs—is caused by the flash being too close to the lens. To fix it, use a small, relatively hard edged brush set to roughly -4 *Exposure* and - *Saturation* and paint over the highlight on the pupil.

REDUCE BLOOD SHOT EYES

If the subject's eyes are blood shot, the redness can be reduced using a small brush set to + *Exposure*, + *Shadows* and - *Saturation*.

Exposure and -60 *Saturation*. You may need to increase or decrease the *Exposure* slider to suit the photo.

ENHANCE THE IRIS COLOR

To brighten the iris of the eyes (the colored bit!), paint a selection using a small brush and try settings like +0.35 *Exposure*, +10 *Clarity* and +40 *Saturation*. You might also want to adjust the *Temp* or *Tint* sliders to change the color slightly.

SOFTEN THE SKIN

To soften skin over the face, use a soft edged brush set to around -100 *Clarity* and +25 *Sharpness*, but be careful to avoid the eyes, eyebrows, nose, mouth, hair and clothing.

WHITEN TEETH

To whiten yellowing teeth, try around +0.20

On page 242, we'll also discuss how to remove blemishes and bags under eyes using the Healing Brush, and then we'll do a start-to-finish edit on page 270.

FIXING DISTORTION

19

Distortions caused by lens imperfections and the angle of the camera are really quick and easy to fix, and can make a big difference to the quality of your photos.

IN THIS SECTION, WE'LL CONSIDER:

• How to remove chromatic aberration fringes.

• How to use lens profiles to remove vignetting and barrel/pincushion distortion.

• How to automatically correct geometric distortions.

• How to draw lines on the photo to correct geometric distortions.

• How to manually warp the photo.

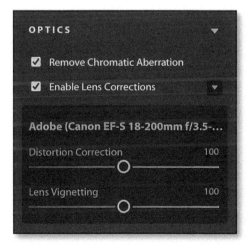

FIXING OPTICAL DISTORTIONS

The physical limitations of lenses can create distortion in your images. Lightroom corrects three types of optical distortions— vignetting (darkening around the edges of the photo), barrel and pincushion distortion (curved lines that should be straight) and chromatic aberration (colored halos). JPEGs are usually fixed by the camera, so these corrections mainly apply to raw files.

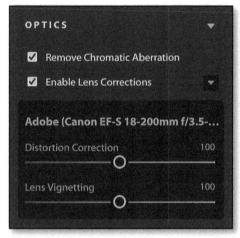

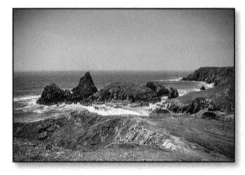

This photo has vignetting in the corner and barrel distortion

The Optics controls are currently more limited on iOS (below) than on Android or on the desktop (above)

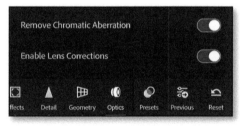

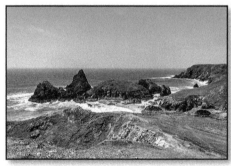

These distortions can be removed using Lightroom's Optics panel

REMOVE CHROMATIC ABERRATION

Lateral chromatic aberration, or CA, causes two different colored fringes to appear on opposite sides of your image details around the edges of the photo, most frequently as magenta and green halos.

This type of chromatic aberration is fixed

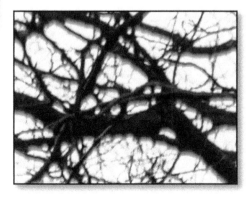

Chromatic aberration creates colored fringes

using the **Remove Chromatic Aberration** checkbox in the Optics panel, or as part of a lens profile.

It's disabled by default as it can slow Lightroom down slightly, and in rare cases may introduce new fringing, but if you find any chromatic aberration in the corners of your photo, simply check the box.

BUILT-IN LENS CORRECTIONS FOR MIRRORLESS CAMERAS

Most compact and mirrorless cameras have lens profile information embedded in the raw file by the manufacturer and applied by Lightroom. To check which corrections are being automatically corrected, click on **Built-in Lens Profile Applied** at the bottom of the Optics panel on a desktop computer. (The information isn't visible on mobile, but the built-in lens profiles are still applied).

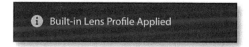

The built-in profile can apply corrections for distortion, chromatic aberration and/or vignetting. For example, the Sony RX100 applies corrections for distortion and chromatic aberration behind the scenes, but you might still want to apply a lens profile to remove vignetting.

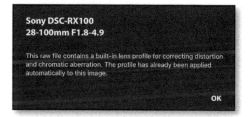

LENS CORRECTIONS FOR DSLR'S

If you're shooting with a DSLR or another camera that doesn't embed lens data, you can apply a lens profile by checking the **Enable Lens Corrections** checkbox.

Lightroom checks the EXIF metadata to try to identify the lens. If it finds a matching profile, it automatically selects the right profile, and fixes the distortions.

Lens metadata standards are quite new, so Lightroom may need some help to identify the right lens. If so, the desktop app says **Manually select a profile....** (This option isn't currently available on iOS.)

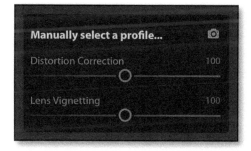

Click on that text to show the Select Lens Profile dialog, then select the correct lens profile in the **Make, Model** and **Profile** pop-ups.

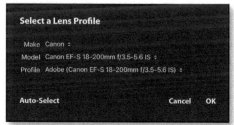

NO PROFILE AVAILABLE

To create a profile, Adobe must have access to the lens, or the manufacturer can create the profile and send it to Adobe. This means that profiles are available for many current lenses, but older lenses may not have profiles.

If your lens doesn't appear in the Lens

Profile pop-up menus and isn't built into the image file, you have a couple of different options:

• Wait for Adobe to create a profile for that lens. Lens profiles are being added gradually in each dot release.

• (Advanced users) Switch to the Geometry panel's *Manual Transforms* and adjust the sliders manually (page 232).

Many of the lens profiles are built for raw files only. If a profile is usually available for your lens, check the format of your selected photo in the Info panel (page 81), as it may be a JPEG or TIFF/PSD.

REDUCING THE EFFECT

In some cases, you might want to use some of the profiled correction, but not all of it. For example, if you're using a fisheye lens, you might want to remove the vignetting automatically, but keep the fisheye distortion. The **Distortion Correction** and **Lens Vignetting** sliders (not currently available on iOS) act as a volume control, increasing or decreasing the amount of profiled correction that's being applied. 0 doesn't apply the correction at all, 100 applies the profile as it was designed, and higher values increase the effect of the correction.

FIXING PERSPECTIVE USING UPRIGHT

If you've ever shot a photo of a building, you've probably noticed it seems to be leaning backwards. This is called keystoning.

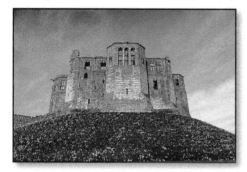

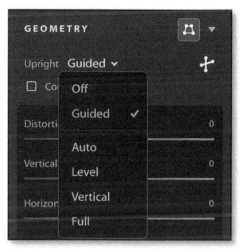

To avoid it, you'd have to keep the camera sensor perfectly aligned with the subject, but unless you like to go around climbing trees or you carry an expensive tilt-shift lens, that's probably not realistic. Instead, Lightroom helps you fix the distortion, using a tool called *Upright* in the Geometry panel.

UPRIGHT OPTIONS

In the **Upright** pop-up, there's a series of automatic adjustments:

Off is simple—*Upright* is disabled, so no adjustments are made.

Guided allows you to draw lines directly on the image to show Lightroom which lines

should be horizontal or vertical. We'll come back to this option shortly.

Auto is the most artificially intelligent option. It not only tries to level the photo and correct converging horizontal and vertical lines, but it also takes into account the amount of distortion that's created by the correction. It aims to get the best visual result, even if that's not perfectly straight.

Level only tries to level the photo, fixing tilted horizons or vertical lines. It's similar to straightening the photo when cropping. It doesn't try to adjust for converging lines.

Vertical not only levels the horizon, but also

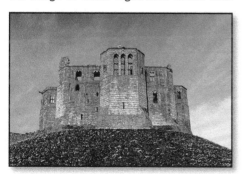

Auto Upright Correction

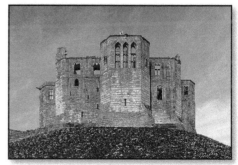

Full Upright Correction

fixes converging verticals.

Full is the most extreme option. It levels the photos and fixes converging horizontal and vertical lines, even if that means using very strong 3D corrections which distort image features.

More often than not, the *Auto* button gives the best fully automated result.

USING THE GUIDED UPRIGHT TOOL

Upright's Guided mode allows you to draw lines on the image, so you can decide which lines should be vertical or horizontal. The resulting correction is usually better than automatic Upright corrections.

Windows/Mac

1. First, enable the lens profile in the Optics panel (page 226). This results in a more accurate correction.

2. In the Geometry panel, click the **Guided Upright Tool** button, which looks like a hand-drawn + symbol.

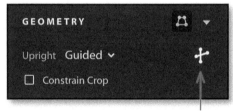

Guided Upright tool

3. To **draw a line**, click at the beginning of your vertical or horizontal line (for example, the wall of a building) and drag to the end of the line.

As you float over the photo, the floating Loupe tool displays a zoomed section to help you make an accurate selection.

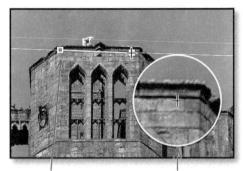

Click and drag   Zoomed section helps
to draw a line   you draw accurately

Hold down Alt (Windows) / Opt (Mac) to slow down the Upright cursor for greater accuracy.

4. Repeat to add additional lines—a maximum of two horizontal and two vertical. As you add the second and any subsequent lines, Lightroom updates the perspective of the image so you can preview the effect.

5. When you're finished, click on the *Guided Upright Tool* button again to hide the tool.

To **adjust an existing line**, click on the square at the end of the line and move it to a new position.

To **delete a line**, click on it to select it and press the Delete key on the keyboard. To remove all of the lines, right-click on the photo and select *Reset Upright Guides*.

iOS/Android

The principles are the same on mobile, but the interface is slightly different.

1. First, enable the lens profile in the Optics panel (page 226). This results in a more accurate correction.

2. In the Geometry panel, click the **Guided Upright Tool** button, which looks like a hand-drawn + symbol.

Guided Upright tool

3. Drag your finger across the photo to **draw the line**. It's easiest if you zoom in so you can see the line. The two-finger pinch/ spread gestures work while the Guided Upright tool is active, or you can turn the *Add Line* button off to move around the photo without drawing accidental lines.

4. Repeat to add additional lines—a maximum of two horizontal and two vertical. As you add the second and any subsequent lines, Lightroom updates the perspective of the image so you can preview the effect.

5. When you're finished, tap the *Done* button.

To **adjust an existing line**, tap on the line to reselect it, then drag the circles at the end of the line and move them to a new position.

To **delete a line**, tap on it to select it and press the Delete (trashcan) icon.

REDUCE THE EFFECT

We're used to seeing converging verticals in everyday life, so full correction can look unnatural. Using the *Manual Transform* sliders, you can adjust individual axes of rotation, reducing their effect. For example, setting the *Vertical* slider to +10 reintroduces some converging verticals, giving a more natural appearance. We'll discuss these sliders in the next lesson (page 232).

CONSTRAIN CROP

When you pull the pixels around to fix the geometry of a photo, white areas appear. You can crop these white areas away manually using the Crop tool (page 129), but the **Constrain Crop** checkbox does it for you automatically. Unchecking the *Constrain Crop* checkbox doesn't remove the crop, but if you don't like the result of the automatic crop, you can adjust it using the Crop tool.

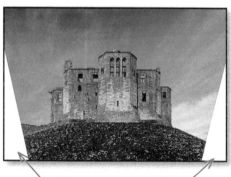

White space caused by distortion correction

Click and drag to draw a line

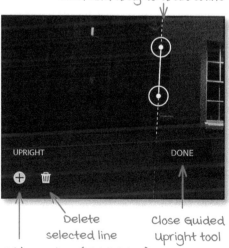

Delete selected line

Close Guided Upright tool

Add new line (highlighted) or view only (+ sign only)

FIXING LENS DISTORTION MANUALLY

The *Manual Transform* sliders are not often needed, however they can be useful for slimming people and recovering pixels pushed out of the frame by other lens and perspective corrections.

To **show or hide the sliders** on the desktop, click the button at the top of the Geometry panel. They're not hidden in the mobile apps.

The **Distortion** slider corrects for barrel or pincushion distortion, which can be useful if you don't have a lens profile. It can also be used to create a fisheye type effect.

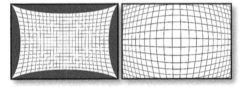

The **Vertical** and **Horizontal** sliders adjust for perspective. They're most useful for reducing the effect of Upright corrections, to make it look more natural.

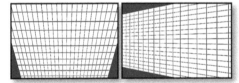

Click to show the manual Transform sliders

GEOMETRY

Upright Off ⌄

☐ Constrain Crop

Distortion   0

Vertical   0

Horizontal   0

Rotate   0

Aspect   0

Scale   100

X Offset   0

Y Offset   0

The **Rotate** slider adjusts for camera tilt. It's applied at a much earlier stage in the processing than the crop, with a different result. *Rotate* pivots on the center of the uncropped photo instead of the center of the crop.

If you're using these *Manual* sliders to correct perspective and your camera wasn't level, it's better to use *Upright* or the *Rotate* slider to level the camera rather than *Straighten* in the Crop tool. If you're not using the other *Manual* sliders, don't worry about this slider!

The **Aspect** slider squashes or stretches the photo to improve the appearance. Strong keystone corrections (such as the *Upright* tool) can make a photo look unnatural, especially when they include people. The slider direction depends on the image rotation, but in most cases, dragging the slider to the left makes things look wider, and dragging the slider to the right makes them look taller and thinner.

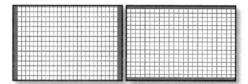

Even if you haven't used the other perspective corrections, moving the *Aspect* slider slightly (usually to the right) slims down the subject, reversing "the camera adds 10lbs!"

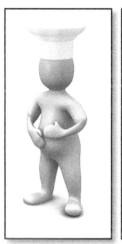 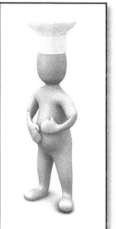

The **Scale** slider shrinks the image within the frame to recover pixels which have been pushed out of the frame by geometric corrections.

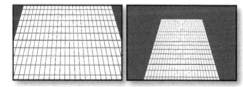

Lightroom has to interpolate the data (create new pixels based on surrounding pixels) to resize the image within the frame, which can reduce image quality, so it's best avoided where possible.

Scale can also "zoom in" to remove blank areas of the photo caused by the lens and perspective corrections, however using the Crop tool (page 129) to remove these blank areas maintains the quality, and is

therefore a better choice.

The **X Offset** and **Y Offset** sliders shift the photo left/right/up/down. This is useful when a geometric adjustment has pushed the important section of the photo out of the frame. The *Offset* sliders move the important section of the photo back into the frame without interpolation, retaining the best image quality possible.

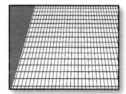

RETOUCHING DISTRACTIONS

20

Retouching has long been the domain of pixel-based photo editors such as Photoshop, but Lightroom has advanced healing tools that can remove many distractions without a round trip to Photoshop.

The Healing Brush can remove sensor dust spots in the sky, litter on the ground, rain drops on the lens, acne on faces, or even more complex distractions. If there's something more complicated to retouch, Lightroom can send the photo to Photoshop.

PROS AND CONS

There are pros and cons to retouching in Lightroom. Being able to edit the raw file in Lightroom means you don't need another

large TIFF file taking up space in the cloud or on your hard drive, and it's non-destructive, so you can go back and change your edits again later.

On the down side, Lightroom is a parametric editor, which means it has to constantly re-run text instructions, so it gets slower with the more local adjustments (spots, brushes) that you apply.

The point where a pixel editor becomes more efficient than Lightroom depends on your computer hardware, as well as the retouching you're trying to do. As a rule of thumb, when it gets frustrating, stop and switch to Photoshop!

IN THIS SECTION, WE'LL CONSIDER:

• How to retouch spots as well as larger distractions using Lightroom.

• How to send a photo to Photoshop for more extensive editing.

HEALING BRUSH

Mode **Heal** ⌄

Size   75

Feather   0

Opacity   100

☑ Visualize Spots

Threshold   64

RETOUCHING SPOTS

The Healing Brush is ideal for removing distractions against plain backgrounds, such as sensor dust in the sky. We'll look at more complex retouching in the next lesson, but first, let's get an overview of how the Healing Brush works.

HEALING SPOTS

To **open the Healing Brush tool** and show the Healing Brush panel on the desktop, click the icon in the right panel bar or press the H key.

On mobile, select the Healing tool from the Edit view toolbar.

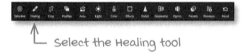

Select the Healing tool

Lightroom can do two different kinds of repair, selected using the **Mode** pop-up on the desktop, or using the buttons on mobile.

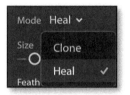

Heal

Clone

Clone simply picks up the pixels and drops them in another location.

Heal attempts to intelligently match the texture, lighting and shading to blend the repaired pixels seamlessly into the surrounding area.

For most spots, the *Heal* option works best, particularly in clean areas such as sky. If you're trying to retouch a spot along an edge in the photo, for example, a roof line against the sky, the *Heal* tool can smudge, in which case the *Clone* option may work better.

HEALING BRUSH (WINDOWS/MAC)

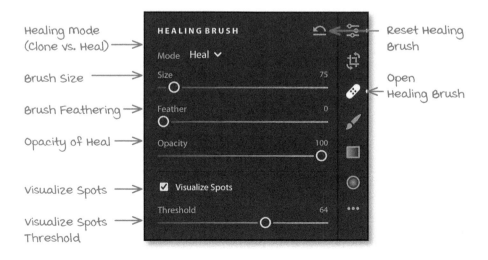

Healing mode (Clone vs. Heal) →

Brush Size →

Brush Feathering →

Opacity of Heal →

Visualize Spots →

Visualize Spots Threshold

Reset Healing Brush

Open Healing Brush

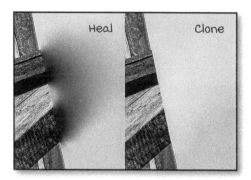

Against hard edges, Heal mode can smudge, so Clone is a better choice

CHOOSING THE RIGHT BRUSH

Before you start retouching, you need to decide on the size and feathering of the brush you'll use.

On the desktop, these are controlled using sliders in the Healing Brush panel, and the size and feathering are previewed on the cursor, with two lines close together for minimal feathering, and further apart for greater feathering.

On mobile, hold your finger on the *Size*, *Feather* or *Opacity* icon and drag up or down to increase or decrease the slider value. The numeric value displays at the top of the screen, and a red preview displays in the center of the screen, so you can see how big or hard the brush will be.

Size runs from 0, which is a tiny brush, to a maximum size of 100. On the desktop, you can also use the [and] keyboard shortcuts or your mouse scroll wheel to adjust the size.

Feather runs from 1, which is a hard edged brush, to 100 which is soft. On the desktop, the Shift-[and Shift-] keys also adjust the feathering.

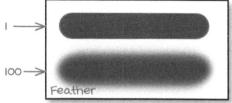

A *Clone* spot stands out if it has hard edges, so select a higher feathering value, such as 90-100. The *Heal* mode works best with *Feather* set to 0 as it automatically attempts to blend the edges into the surroundings. If you feather a *Heal* spot, you may end up with unhealed patches in the center of the healed area.

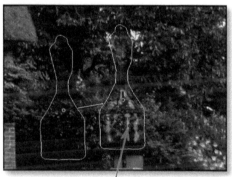

To prevent gaps in the middle of repaired areas, set feathering to 0 when using Heal mode

The **Opacity** slider allows you to fade the retouching, for example, you may not want to completely remove the lines on a person's face, but just fade them slightly. If you want to remove a blemish completely, leave it set to 100.

DRAWING SPOTS

There are two kinds of spot repair that you can apply to your photo, depending on whether the distraction is circular or not.

HEALING BRUSH (IOS/ANDROID)

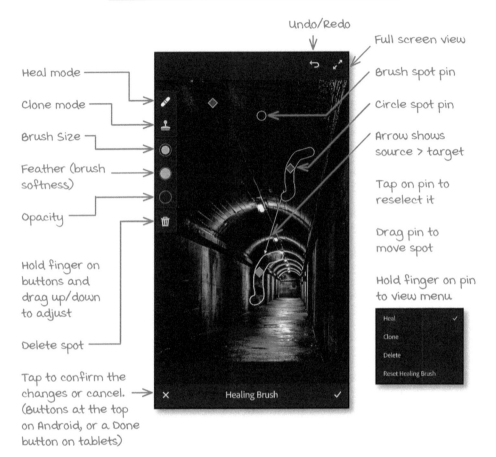

Undo/Redo

Full screen view

Heal mode

Clone mode

Brush Size

Feather (brush softness)

Opacity

Hold finger on buttons and drag up/down to adjust

Delete spot

Tap to confirm the changes or cancel. (Buttons at the top on Android, or a Done button on tablets)

Brush spot pin

Circle spot pin

Arrow shows source > target

Tap on pin to reselect it

Drag pin to move spot

Hold finger on pin to view menu

Heal ✓
Clone
Delete
Reset Healing Brush

Healing Brush

To **create a circle spot**, for example, to remove sensor dust, simply click/tap on the distraction. Circle spots display as single round spots and they can be moved and resized later.

To **create a brush spot** (non-circular healing), click/tap and drag over the distraction. A brush stroke appears, and it's then replaced by two white outlines showing the source and target. Brush spots can have an arbitrary shape, and you can change the feathering after creation, but the brush stroke can't be resized later.

To create straight lines on the desktop, click

at the beginning of the line to create a circle spot, and then hold down the Shift key and click at the end of the line. Lightroom joins the spots using a straight brush spot. It's a handy trick for power or telephone lines.

When you create a circle or brush spot, Lightroom intelligently searches for the most suitable **source of replacement pixels**, even if that's outside of the current crop boundary. If the suggested replacement pixels are not a great match, press the / key to make Lightroom try again (desktop only), or click and drag the source spot to a better source.

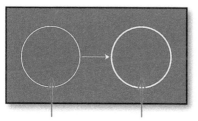

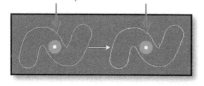

Source of new pixels   Retouched area

It's easiest to zoom in before creating the brush spot, so you can see the photo in detail. On the desktop, hold down the Spacebar while clicking and dragging, to move around the photo without accidentally creating extra spots. On mobile, pinch, spread and drag the photo around using two fingers.

STEP-BY-STEP

We'll look at more complex retouching in the next lesson, but for now, let's focus on sensor dust and other distractions against plain backgrounds, such as this one:

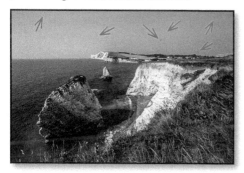

1. Select the Healing Brush tool.

2. Using the options in the Healing Brush panel, set the brush options to:

Mode: Heal

Size: to suit the size of the distraction

Feather: 0 (because we're using Heal)

Opacity: 100 (because we want the distraction completely gone)

3. Click/tap on the spot in the photo.

4. The spot overlay appears on the screen, showing the outline of the retouched area and the source of the new pixels. Lightroom automatically tries to find a good source, but you can drag the overlays to fine tune the correction.

5. For non-circular distractions, click/tap and drag over the distraction to display the overlay, then drag the overlays to find a good source.

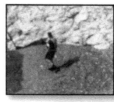
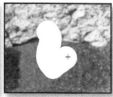
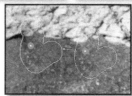

EDITING EXISTING SPOTS

Because Lightroom is a non-destructive editor, you can come back and change your retouching later.

To **find existing retouched spots**, you'll

need to see the overlay. If it isn't showing on the desktop, press the O key and float the cursor over the photo.

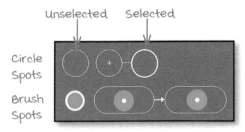

The pins and overlays look slightly different on mobile.

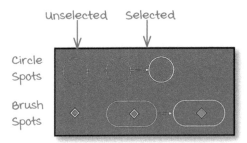

To **resize a circle spot** on the desktop, hover over the edge of the outline, so the cursor changes to a double-headed arrow, and then drag the edge to adjust the size.

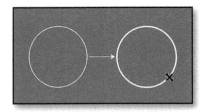

On mobile, select the circle spot and then drag up/down on the brush size icon. (Remember you can't resize non-circular brush strokes.)

To **move a spot**, drag the center of a spot or its source to a new location.

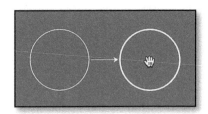

To **delete a spot** on the desktop, click on the spot to make it active, and then press the Delete key on your keyboard, or right-click on the spot to delete using the menu. On mobile, select the pin and then tap the trashcan icon.

To **delete multiple spots** on the desktop, hold down the Alt key (Windows) / Opt key (Mac) so the cursor changes to a pair of scissors, then drag a rectangular shape around the spots to delete them.

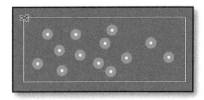

To **delete all spots**, press the *Reset* button in the Healing Brush panel on the desktop, or hold your finger on a pin and select *Reset Healing Brush* from the menu.

DON'T MISS A SPOT

On the desktop, there's a handy trick to view the entire photo at 1:1 zoom without missing any spots. Zoom into 1:1 and view the top left corner and then press the Page Down key (Windows) / Fn down arrow key (Mac). Lightroom divides the photo up into an imaginary grid, so when you reach the bottom of the first column, it automatically returns to the top of the photo and starts on the next column. By the time you reach the bottom right corner, you'll have checked the entire photo without missing any spots.

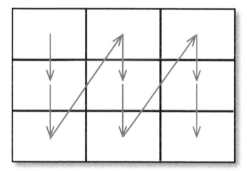

VISUALIZE SPOTS

By checking the **Visualize Spots** checkbox in the Healing Brush panel (desktop only), Lightroom displays a black and white edge mask of your photo, which makes it easier to spot any dust spots. You can adjust the **Threshold** slider to increase or decrease the amount of white borders displayed.

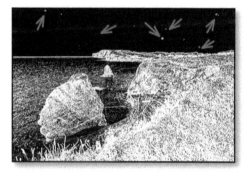

ADVANCED RETOUCHING USING LIGHTROOM

In the previous lesson, we learned how to remove simple distractions using the Healing Brush tool, but it gets more complicated when the distraction isn't on a plain background or borders against something else.

REMOVING LARGE DISTRACTIONS AND EDGES

Complicated distractions are quicker and easier to retouch using a pixel-based editing tool such as Photoshop, but with a bit of patience, it is possible to do it in Lightroom. The trick is to chop the distraction up into bite-size pieces, and handle each section individually.

The duck photo-bombed this photo of a pelican, so let's remove him...

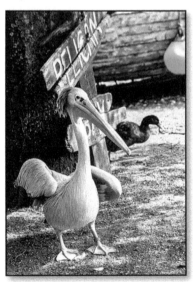

If we just brush up to the edge of the beak and sign in *Heal* mode, it leaves a dark smudge, but using *Clone* mode doesn't match the texture and leaves harsh edges.

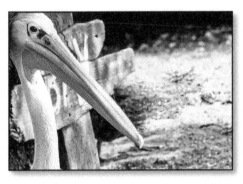

Retouching against an edge using Heal mode leaves a dark smudge

What we need is the best of both worlds. To remove the duck, we'll use both the *Clone* and *Heal* modes.

1. Use two thin *Clone* lines along the edge of the beak and sign. When you then paint a large *Heal* stroke over the duck's head and body, and slightly overlap the these *Clone* strokes, you'll get a much cleaner result, as there won't be any adjacent dark pixels to smudge.

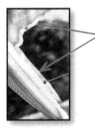

Retouch the edge using Clone lines to create a clean boundary

2. In this case, there's only one suitable small clone source to the right of the duck's head, which isn't big enough to clone over his whole head and body. To solve this, we'll divide him up using additional *Clone* strokes.

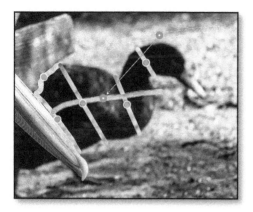

Add additional Clone lines to divide the area into smaller chunks if it's too big

3. Brush over the individual duck sections one at a time using a *Heal* brush, slightly overlapping the clone dividers. This step is tricky, because Lightroom tries to select the existing brush strokes when you get close to them. Start the brush stroke from the center of the section and brush toward the *Clone* strokes, and zoom in closer if necessary.

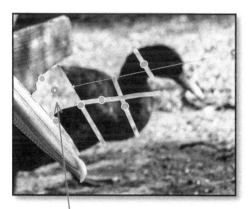

use Heal brush strokes to fill each individual section, overlapping the clone strokes

4. Additional strokes can be used to heal any leftover artifacts. Repeat the same process for the duck's body and legs to remove him completely.

RETOUCHING FACES

Faces also need slightly more advanced retouching. For softening skin, brightening eyes, whitening teeth and similar retouching, you'll need to use the Selective Editing tools (page 224). Spot removal, however, can be useful for reducing wrinkles and bags under eyes and removing pimples and scars.

If you remove bags and wrinkles completely, it looks unnatural, so try a brush set to *Clone* mode, and reduce the *Opacity* to around 20-25. Select a source that's similar in tone and texture, such as the skin immediately underneath.

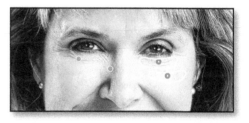

For blemishes, use a *Heal* brush slightly larger than the pimple, set to full *Opacity*. (Severe acne may still need the power of Photoshop.)

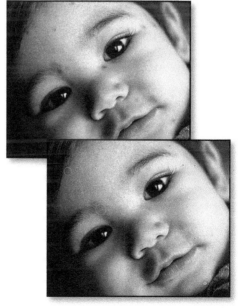

SENDING PHOTOS TO PHOTOSHOP ON THE DESKTOP

Lightroom offers a wide range of tools to cater for most of your editing needs, but sometimes you'll need a pixel-based photo editor such as Photoshop. For example:

• Swapping heads, changing backgrounds and merging photos are jobs for Photoshop.

• Some distractions, such as flare on glasses, can be reduced in Lightroom, but can be removed more effectively in Photoshop.

• Removing some distractions, particularly when they're on a complex or detailed background, is much faster and easier in Photoshop.

• Doing lots of retouching on a single photo is faster in Photoshop, as Lightroom slows

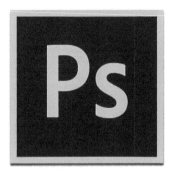

down with lots of edits.

Lightroom and Photoshop handle the color and file management, so you only need to worry about editing skills. Since this is not a Photoshop book, we won't go into detail, but we'll learn how to hand the files off to Photoshop...

LIGHTROOM EDITS FIRST

Lightroom's editing tools work best on raw files, because they have the largest amount of data available. For this reason, it's usually best to do most (if not all) of your Lightroom adjustments before moving to Photoshop or other editing software.

There are a couple of exceptions:

• You may prefer to leave cropping until after your external edits, leaving you the flexibility to non-destructively crop to different ratios without having to repeat your retouching and other edits.

• If the photo is going to be in both B&W and color, you may want to retouch the color version and then convert the retouched TIFF to B&W so that you only have to do the retouching once.

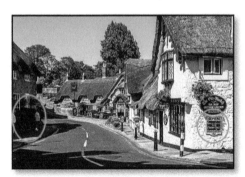

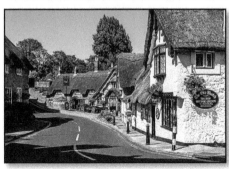

The signs, van and people couldn't have been easily removed using Lightroom alone

• If your photo was shot in JPEG, or it's a scan, the workflow order isn't as important. For example, you may decide to retouch dust on negative scans in Photoshop before adding them to Lightroom.

SENDING PHOTOS TO PHOTOSHOP

To open a photo in Photoshop (CS6 or CC), right-click and select **Edit in Photoshop** or use the shortcut Ctrl-E (Windows) / Cmd-E (Mac). You'll also find it in the *File* menu. The photo opens in Photoshop with your Lightroom edits applied. Leave Lightroom open in the background so it can keep track of the file and automatically add it to your library.

REDUCING FILE SIZE

By default, Lightroom opens the photo in Photoshop as a 16-bit ProPhoto RGB file, which it then saves a TIFF.

16-bit ProPhoto RGB TIFFs are the best choice for quality, retaining the largest amount of data and smooth color gradations (e.g. in the sky). However, they're large files, especially when you add layers, so they'll take up a lot of space in the cloud.

If it's your favorite photo, and you've spent hours working on it in Photoshop, keep the full 16-bit TIFFs, because it leaves your options open for the future. However, if you only flipped into Photoshop to quickly remove a distraction, and you're just going to post it on social media, you may decide to reduce the file size before saving the photo. To do so, follow these steps in Photoshop:

1. Go to *Image menu > Convert to Profile > Adobe RGB* (because ProPhotoRGB is too wide a color space for an 8-bit file).

2. Go to *Image menu > Mode > 8-Bits/Channel* to reduce the bit depth.

3. If you no longer need the layers, go to *Layers menu > Flatten Image* to flatten the layers.

RETURNING TO LIGHTROOM

To return to Lightroom after editing in Photoshop, go to *File menu > Save*. This saves the file back to Lightroom with *-Edit* on the end of the file name. You can use *Save As* to change the file name if you prefer, but don't change the file type or Lightroom will lose track of it.

Close the file in Photoshop and switch back to Lightroom. The edited photo is automatically stacked on top of the original in the selected album and *All Photos*, but not in other albums.

RETAINING LAYERS

If you open a layered TIFF/PSD into Photoshop again later, the behavior depends on whether you've done further editing in Lightroom:

If you haven't edited the TIFF/PSD in Lightroom, it opens in Photoshop with its layers intact.

If you've applied edits to the TIFF/PSD in Lightroom, the layers are flattened when you open it in Photoshop.

SENDING PHOTOS TO OTHER EDITING APPS ON MOBILE

Like the desktop version, there are occasions when you might want to switch to a pixel-based editing app. For example, some of the features in other Adobe apps that may be useful include:

Photoshop Fix specializes in editing facial features, fixing red eye, and warping the image using Liquify.

Photoshop Mix allows you to cut out and combine elements from different images, blending the layers.

Photoshop Express creates collages, adds text and borders, and applies graphical watermarks.

EDIT IN PHOTOSHOP FIX ON IOS

There's a direct link from Lightroom CC to Photoshop Fix on iOS.

1. From Detail view, tap on the Share menu.

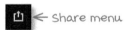 ← Share menu

2. Select **Edit In** and choose *Maximum Available* for the image size.

3. Select *Healing in Photoshop Fix* to use the Spot Healing tool, Patch tool, Clone Stamp or to fix Red Eye, or select *Liquify in Photoshop Fix* to push the pixels around, for example, to enlarge the eyes.

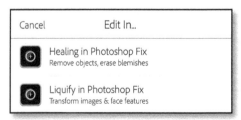

4. When you've finished editing in

Photoshop Fix, tap the *Save and return to Lightroom* button at the top.

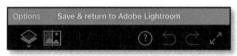

OPEN DIRECTLY FROM PHOTOSHOP FIX OR MIX

On both operating systems, Photoshop Fix and Mix can access albums and photos in your Lightroom CC cloud, and automatically add the edited photo back to your photo library in the cloud.

OPEN IN OTHER PHOTO EDITING APPS

On Android, and for other photo editing apps on iOS, you'll need to copy the photo to the app via the Share sheet. To do so:

1. Turn off the watermark if you have it enabled (page 281).

1. From Detail view, tap on the Share menu.

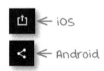

2. On iOS, select **Open In** to show available apps, then choose *Maximum Available* for the image size. (This step isn't required on Android.)

3. Select the app of your choice, for example, Photoshop Express. The options will depend on which photo editing apps are installed on your device.

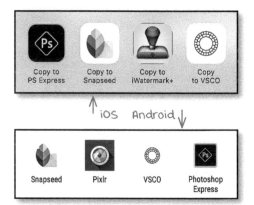

4. When you've finished editing save the result back to the camera roll (iOS) / gallery (Android) and add it to Lightroom.

START-TO-FINISH EDITS

21

So far, we've learned how to use the sliders individually and how they interact within their panels.

Now it's time to start putting it all together and edit a series of photos from start to finish, using a whole range of different tools.

We'll start each lesson with an image analysis, and then briefly cover the thought process behind each slider adjustment.

You can download most of these images from the Members Area, so you can follow along on your own computer.

You might prefer a different end result, and that's fine, because editing is subjective and we're all continually learning and changing.

IN THIS SECTION, WE'LL CONSIDER:

• How to edit a whole range of photos using different Lightroom tools.

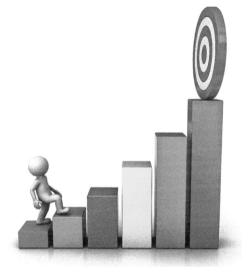

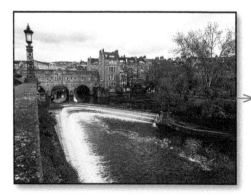 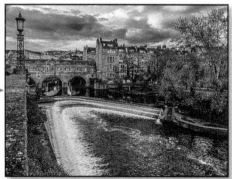

EARLY MORNING COUNTRYSIDE

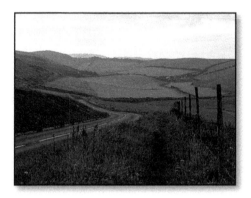

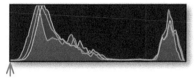

No true black, but
otherwise good range

ARTISTIC INTENT

Purpose

I liked the empty winding road
leading off into the rolling
hills in the background.

Story

Early morning solitude.

Mood/Emotion

Peaceful, soft.

Simplify the Scene & Draw the Eye

Couple of road signs are
distracting and need removing.

Draw the eye along the road and
the fence towards the rolling hills.

TECHNICAL

Exposure

Underexposed, very
flat, no true black.

Color

Needs warming, and more vibrant.

Detail

Shot at low ISO, so no notable noise,
and using fast shutter speed.

Optical & Geometric Distortion

Micro four thirds, so lens
corrections automatically applied.

Sensor Dust

None noted.

Output

Lounge wall, 20"x 16".

1. Change the profile to **Adobe Landscape** to enhance colors and detail in the greenery.

   Steps 1-5 brightness/contrast adjustments

2. **Highlights -80** to pull back the cloud detail.

3. **Shadows +45** to bring out verge detail.

4. **Whites +23** & **Blacks -50** to bring back global contrast.

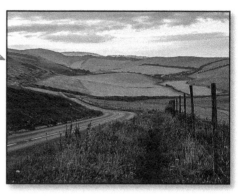

5. **Clarity +70** to add more local contrast to highlight the textures.

   Steps 6-7 color adjustments

6. **Temp 6100** to warm it up.

7. **Vibrance +50** to make the colors more punchy.

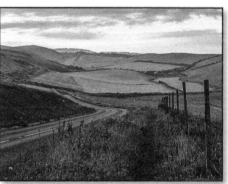

8. **Linear Gradient** from top to half way down, with central line on horizon, set to *Temp -10, Exposure -0.20, Clarity 100* to enhance the cloud detail and reduce the yellow in the sky.

   Step 8 Linear Gradient (red mask shown)

9. **Sharpen 50, Radius 0.8, Masking 77** to sharpen the foreground without over-sharpening the sky.

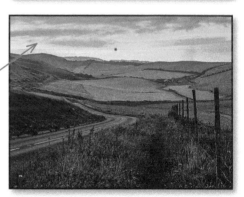

10. **Healing Brush** to remove distracting road signs and debris on the road.

11. **Crop** to 4x5 ratio for 16"x20" print.

   Steps 9-11 Sharpen, retouch & crop

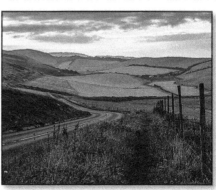

KANIKA THE LEOPARD CUB

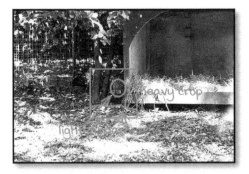

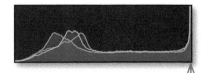

Highlights are clipped

ARTISTIC INTENT

Purpose

Create ongoing series of photos of Kanika growing up.

Story

This was Kanika's first trip out of her den, so she was shy but also inquisitive and playful.

Mood/Emotion

Excitement of first outing, so use plenty of contrast and punchy colors.

Simplify the Scene & Draw the Eye

Needs a heavy crop to remove excess background and zoom in on leopard cub.

Reduce brightness of foreground to reduce distraction.

Lighten cub's face to draw the eye toward her.

TECHNICAL

Exposure

Cub is too dark as in the shadows, but foreground is too bright. Some detail in the leaves is clipped.

Color

Needs increase of saturation and warmth to enhance cub's coat.

Detail

Sharpen to highlight whiskers. High ISO and heavy crop will make noise more noticeable.

Optical & Geometric Distortion

Not needed.

Sensor Dust

None found.

Output

Square crop to match set.

1. **Crop** first to zoom in on subject.

2. **Exposure +0.80** to brighten overall.

Steps 1-5 → incl. Crop & tonal adjustments

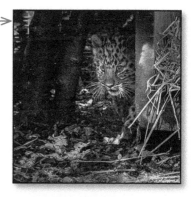

3. **Highlights -100** to reduce glare of light falling through the tress.

4. **Shadows +80** to bring up the shadow detail.

5. **Blacks -60** to bring back the contrast lost by *Highlights/Shadows* adjustments.

6. **Clarity +54** to add punch and bring out the detail in the cub's coat.

Steps 6-9 incl. Clarity & color → adjustments

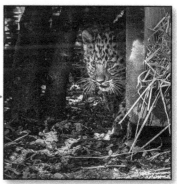

7. **Contrast +8** to add midtone contrast.

8. **Temp 4577** and **Tint +31** to warm it up, as auto white balance left the photo too cool.

9. **Vibrance +48** and **Saturation +9** to bring out the color in her coat.

Steps 10-12 Selective → edits

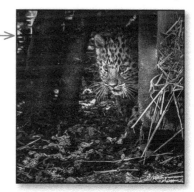

10. **Radial Gradient** set to -1.84 *Exposure*, -73 *Contrast*, -100 *Highlights*, -52 *Clarity* to create an off-center vignette, drawing the eye to the cub.

11. **Brush** set to *Temp +10, Contrast +20* and *Saturation +32*, brushed over the cub's face and legs to warm her up further.

12. **Healing Brush** used to patch the light patch on her den to reduce the distraction.

Step 13 Noise → Reduction

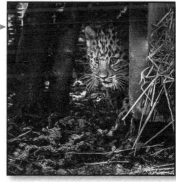

13. **Noise Reduction +25** to minimize noise.

14. **Send to Photoshop**. The leaves at the front were completely clipped, and trying to recover them has just turned them gray, but these could be retouched using Photoshop.

SUNSET AT STEEPHILL COVE

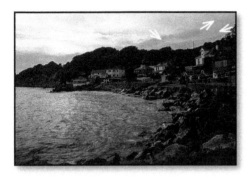

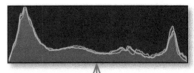

Full range of tones, but not
a lot in the midtones

ARTISTIC INTENT

Purpose

Capture this pretty hidden
cove at sunset.

Story

This perfect little cove can't be
reached by road, so at the end
of the day, when everyone's gone
home, it's a beautiful little spot.

Mood/Emotion

Relaxed and peaceful, but wonder
at the power of the waves
and beauty of the sunset.

Simplify the Scene & Draw the Eye

Start with the eye on the setting
sun (warmth, brightness), then go
to the warm reflection, then the
buildings (bright) then run round
the curve of the rocks (lines,
contrast, reflected warmth).

TECHNICAL

Exposure

Shadows need brightening, while
retaining highlight detail.

Color

The sun had already set, so
light was cool, but clouds in the
sky would look great warmer.

Detail

Slight noise on the rocks,
but it just adds texture.

Optical & Geometric Distortion

Some barrel distortion. Chromatic
aberration visible along tree line.

Sensor Dust

Spots in the sky on the right.

Output

Framed print on the lounge wall.

1. Change the profile to **Adobe Vivid**, as we want to enhance the sunset.

2. **Straighten 0.80**, using *Straighten* tool to draw line down central building.

3. **Healing Brush** (*Heal, size 46, feather 0, opacity 100*) to remove spots in sky.

4. **Enable Profile Corrections** (Canon 18-200) to remove barrel distortion and check **Remove Chromatic Aberration**.

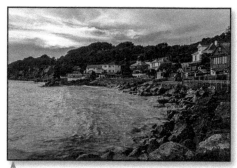

⌐ Steps 1–6 incl. Highlights & Shadows

5. **Highlights -100** to recover and enhance the detail in the sky and **Shadows -80** to bring out detail in rocks and houses.

6. **Whites +14** so the sun is just short of clipping and **Blacks -26** blocks the darkest shadows in the rocks, where I'm willing to sacrifice the detail to increase the overall contrast.

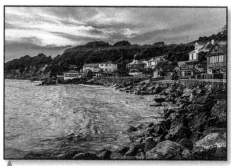

⌐ Steps 7–8 Clarity & Saturation

7. **Clarity +100** is an extreme adjustment, but it's just flat and boring, and using too much *Contrast* would lose sky/rocks detail. The local contrast created strong halos along the tree line, so I reduce it with a soft **-Highlights -Whites brush**.

8. **Saturation +70** to make it much more colorful. *Vibrance* would have enhanced the blues on the building and protected the yellows, whereas I want to pump up the yellow tones. Doing this before white balance will help me set *Temp & Tint* to taste.

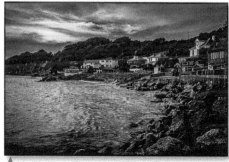

⌐ Steps 9–10 White Balance & Vignette

9. **Temp 5450** and **Tint +18** to warm it up.

10. **Vignette -30** with **Feather 70** to bring down the brightness of the corners, especially on the left.

11. It's still a little flat and dark, so **Contrast +20** and **Exposure +0.20** to finish.

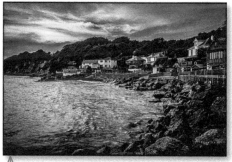

⌐ Step 11 Contrast & Exposure

UNDERGROUND HOSPITAL

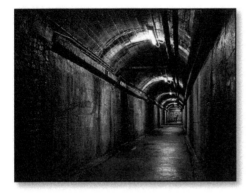

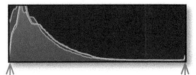

Slight spike of white strip light, and some blocked blacks

TECHNICAL

Exposure

Exposure's not bad, but enhance the shadow detail in the walls. Light is clipped, but that's expected.

Color

Adjust white balance to cool blues.

Detail

It was shot at ISO 800 on a small sensor, so it is noisy, but that adds to the gritty dramatic feel.

Optical & Geometric Distortion

micro four thirds, so no profile needed.

Sensor Dust

None found.

Output

Portfolio?

ARTISTIC INTENT

Purpose

Capture the eerie feeling and interesting lines.

Story

This was an underground hospital in Guernsey used to care for German soldiers during World War 2.

Mood/Emotion

It was cold, damp and eerie. I'd have hated to be a patient there! Enhance that feeling using cool blues.

Simplify the Scene & Draw the Eye

The lines of the tunnel lead the eye towards the person at the end, but could do with enhancing.

There's a fire exit sign which wouldn't have been there in the 1940's.

1. **Exposure -0.25** because it's a little bright.

Step 1 Exposure →

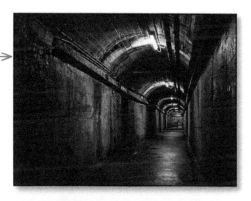

2. **Temp 2400** and **Tint +22** to make it a really cool blue.

3. **Clarity +40** to bring out the detail in the brickwork and increase the "wet" look.

4. **Healing Brush** used to remove the fire exit sign.

5. **Send to Photoshop**. The man at the end of the tunnel was pulling up his sock, so I'd also take the photo to Photoshop to move his leg too.

Step 2 White Balance →

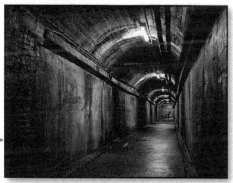

Step 3 Clarity →

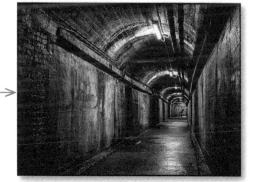

Step 4 Healing Brush →

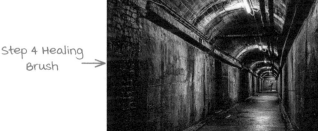

NIGHTTIME COBBLES

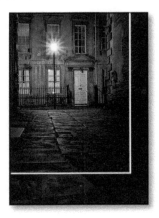

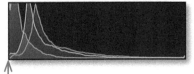

Blue channel clipping in the shadows

TECHNICAL

Exposure

Overall exposure is ok but enhance shadow detail.

Color

Yellow street lighting doesn't add anything. B&W would enhance lines of cobbles and texture of brickwork.

Detail

No notable noise, but sharpen to enhance local contrast.

Optical & Geometric Distortion

Micro four thirds, so already applied.

Sensor Dust

None found.

Output

Wall with other B&W photos.

ARTISTIC INTENT

Purpose

To illustrate the timeless beauty of the historic English town of Bath, with its detailed architecture and cobbled streets.

Story

Welcome home!

Mood/Emotion

A quiet street in the middle of town, but still felt quite safe.

Simplify the Scene & Draw the Eye

Enhance the diagonal lines of the wet cobbles, leading toward the light and doorway.

Crop to remove some of the blank wall on the right to draw the eye to light at the end of the alleyway and the doorway.

Darken the light slab on the left.

1. **Highlights -34** to reduce the glare of the light.

2. **Shadows +100** to bring out the detail in the cobbles & brickwork.

   Steps 1-5 Brightness/ contrast adjustments →

3. **Whites +56** and **Blacks -3** to bring back the contrast lost by *Highlights* and *Shadows*.

4. **Clarity +100** to enhance the local contrast further.

5. **Contrast +22** to add a little more global contrast.

   Step 6 Fix white → balance

6. **Temp 2500** and **Tint +34** to remove the worst of the strong yellow color cast.

7. **Upright Auto** to straighten it.

8. **Crop** to remove the brickwork on the right.

9. Switch to **B&W** mode. I like the default **Adobe Monochrome** conversion, and playing with the B&W mix doesn't improve it due to the lack of different colors in the original capture.

   Steps 7-9 Geometric corrections, crop and B&W conversion →

10. **Dehaze +13** to add a little more local contrast.

    Steps 10-13 Selective Edits →

11. **Vignette -21** to darken the corners and draw the eye into the photo.

12. **Healing Brush** to remove alarm on wall.

13. **Brush** (*Highlights -100 Whites -100*) to darken slab on left that now stands out.

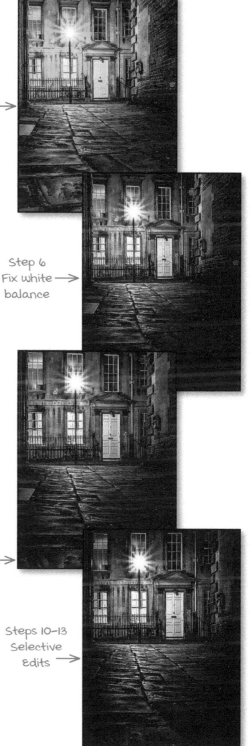

THE HUNGRY CATERPILLAR

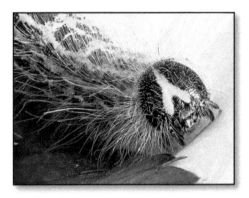

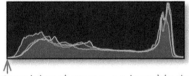

↑
Great tonal range, no true black

TECHNICAL

Exposure

Whites are a little bright, but otherwise pretty good.

Color

White balance is good, but increase vibrancy of yellows.

Detail

Sharpen carefully to enhance fine hairs.

Optical & Geometric Distortion

Micro four thirds, so automatically applied.

Sensor Dust

None found.

Output

Nothing specific.

ARTISTIC INTENT

Purpose

Capture the incredible detail of this scary little beast.

Story

I had a new camera and wanted to try the automatic focus stacking, and this little guy was busy eating all the leaves on my birch tree.

Mood/Emotion

Awe at the amount of detail on this tiny little creature.

Simplify the Scene & Draw the Eye

Reduce the brightness of the white background. Focus attention on the tiny hairs.

1. ***Exposure -0.20*** to reduce brightness slightly.

2. ***Highlights -25*** and ***Shadows +15*** to bring back a little more detail.

Steps 1–4 Brightness & Contrast →

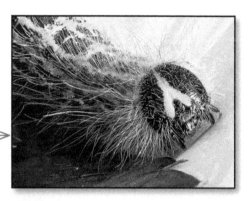

3. Since this is a JPEG, there's no detail to recover in the clipped highlights, so ***Whites -15*** just brings down their brightness slightly.

4. ***Blacks -20*** to make some pixels truly black.

5. ***Temp +3*** to warm it up very slightly and ***Vibrance +15*** to strengthen the yellow.

Step 5 Color Adjustments →

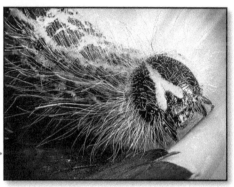

6. ***Clarity +30*** to add more definition, especially to the fine hairs.

7. ***Radial Filter*** on the caterpillar, set to *Exposure +0.50, Clarity +48, Sharpness +20* and *Saturation +25*.

Steps 6–8 Clarity & Selective Edits →

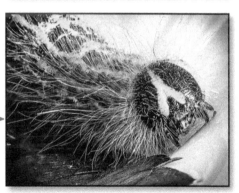

8. Second ***Radial Filter inverted*** to affect the background, set to *Exposure -0.80, Clarity -84, Saturation -57*.

9. ***Vignette -28, Midpoint +60, Roundness -46*** to reduce the edge distractions.

10. ***Healing Brush*** to remove the tiny brown spots on the leaf.

Steps 9–10 Vignette & Healing brush →

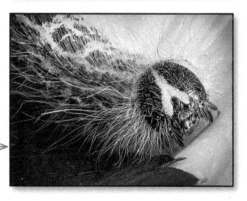

SUNNY COAST

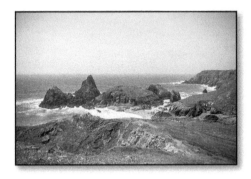

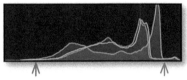

Low dynamic range

ARTISTIC INTENT

Purpose

Capture the lovely cove where we stopped for lunch. Loved the turquoise blue sea against the green grass.

Story

A peaceful walk along the coast on a summer's day.

Mood/Emotion

Warm, happy, majestic.

Simplify the Scene & Draw the Eye

Too much sky, crop some out.

Focus on the island outcrop between the two coves.

Highlight the movement in the sea.

TECHNICAL

Exposure

A little too bright, very hazy and lacking contrast.

Color

White balance is about right, but I'd like a little more depth to the color.

Detail

Sharpen to bring out the detail in the stones.

Optical & Geometric Distortion

Some vignetting visible, apply lens profile.

Sensor Dust

None found.

Output

Framed print on the wall.

1. Apply **Camera Landscape** profile, because the stones are too red in *Adobe Landscape*.

2. **Enable Lens Corrections** to remove vignetting and distortion.

3. **Dehaze +40** to reduce the atmospheric haze.

4. **Highlights -100** to bring detail back into the waves on the shoreline.

5. **Shadows +40** to increase detail in the rock face.

6. **Auto Whites +17** and **Blacks -56** to expand the tonal range, compressing the deepest shadows.

7. **Brush** over breaking waves and rocks with *+100 Clarity* for impact.

8. **Crop** to 16x9 ratio for panoramic effect.

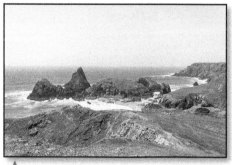

Steps 1-2 Profile & Lens Profile

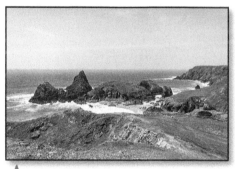

Step 3 Dehaze

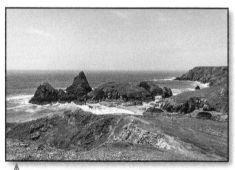

Steps 4-6 Tonal Adjustments

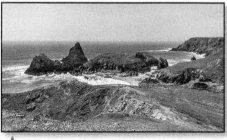

Step 7-8 Selective Edits & Crop

KIDS LOVE BOXES!

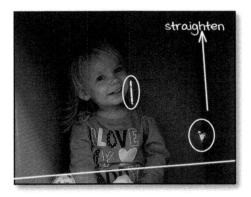

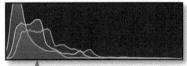

Data to left of histogram
= photo is dark

ARTISTIC INTENT

Purpose

Capture the little girl having fun.

TECHNICAL

Exposure

It's underexposed and
lacking contrast.

Color

White balance isn't great, and
the color doesn't really add
to the photo, so try in B&W.

Detail

Very high ISO (6400 on a micro
four thirds sensor) so lots of
noise reduction needed.

Optical & Geometric Distortion

Profile applied automatically
but needs straightening.

Sensor Dust

None found.

Output

Framed shelf portrait.

Story

Every child loves a cardboard box!

Mood/Emotion

Cute, mischievous.

Simplify the Scene & Draw the Eye

Remove distraction of tear and
slot so eye goes to her face
instead of the bright spots.

1. **Exposure +0.50** as underexposed.

2. **Auto Whites +15** and **Auto Blacks -22** to expand to fill tonal range.

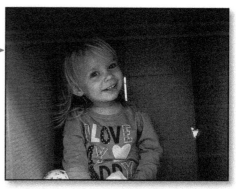

Steps 1-4 — Brightness & color

3. **Clarity +20** to add contrast. No wrinkles to worry about here, and it'll enhance the lines in the box.

4. **Temp 3050** and **Tint -1** to improve white balance to give a cleaner starting point for the B&W conversion.

5. Convert to **B&W** by selecting the **B&W Orange Filter** profile, because red/orange filters traditionally lightened skin tones.

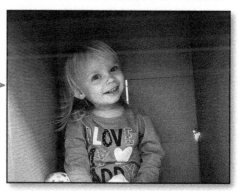

Step 5 B&W

6. **Linear Gradient** diagonally from bottom left corner, set to *Exposure -1.27* and *Clarity +88* to even up the lighting. **Brush** to lighten and define eyes slightly, set to *Exposure +0.3* and *Clarity +10*.

7. **Healing Brush** set to *Clone* mode to retouch the top and bottom of bright line, as *Heal* mode would smudge where it meets other image detail. Then use *Heal* mode for the rest of the bright line and tear in the box. (Due to the noise levels, Photoshop would work better.)

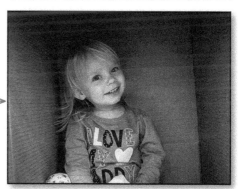

Step 6-7 — Selective edits & retouching

8. **Noise Reduction 35** to reduce high ISO noise. (*Color Noise Reduction* is fine at the default of 25.)

9. **Crop** to straighten lines and remove bright knees.

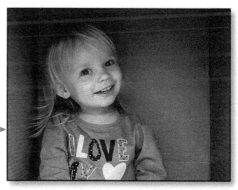

Steps 8-9 — Noise Reduction & Crop

ORANGE WINDOWS

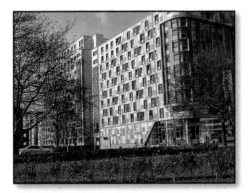

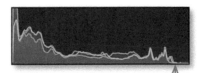

Lacking pure white. After crop,
may not have pure black either

TECHNICAL

Exposure

Needs a little more contrast.

Color

White balance is good, but
shift orange tones toward red
to fit in with office decor.

Detail

Light noise reduction
as small sensor.

Optical & Geometric Distortion

Major geometric distortions.

Sensor Dust

None found.

Output

Abstract square print for office wall.

ARTISTIC INTENT

Purpose

I was waiting for a bus and noticed
these odd orange windows. No
time to compose properly, but I
thought they could be interesting.

Story

Unusual abstract pattern to these
windows. Architect with imagination!

Mood/Emotion

Hard, clean, repetitive pattern.

Simplify the Scene & Draw the Eye

Needs a heavy crop to
emphasize the repetition.

1. Draw four **Guided Upright** lines using the windows for guides to correct the geometric distortion.

2. **Crop** to 1:1 ratio.

3. **Whites +34** and **Blacks -41** to extend the tonal range.

4. **Clarity +35** and **Contrast +15** to highlight the clean lines.

5. **Color Mix** to change orange to a deeper red to find in with office decor.
    Hue: Red -20, Orange -60
    Saturation: Red +20, Orange +14
    Luminance: Red +22, Orange -50

6. **Sharpening 45, Radius 2, Detail 11, Masking 50** to emphasize the strong edges without sharpening the panels.

7. **Noise Reduction 10**.

8. **Healing Brush** to remove tiny spot in bottom window.

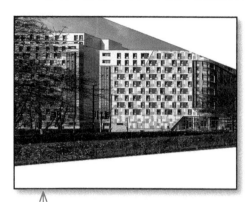

Step 1
Guided
Upright

Step 2 →
Crop

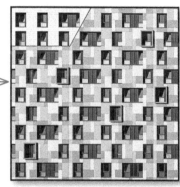

Steps 3-4 →
Brightness
& contrast
adjustments

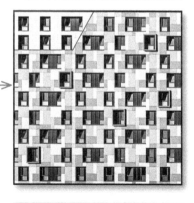

Steps 5-8 →
HSL and
Detail
adjustments

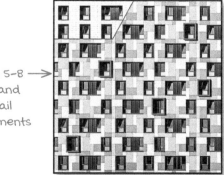

THE GUY ON THE STEPS

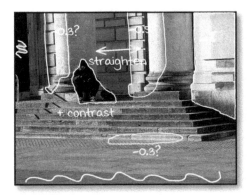

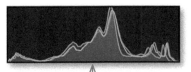

Good dynamic range, no
notable clipping

ARTISTIC INTENT

Purpose

The guy looked small and
insignificant against the huge
pillars of the government building.

Story

Is he homeless? Or just
waiting for a friend?

Mood/Emotion

Very cold day (hat). Feeling lonely?
High contrast B&W with lots of local
contrast for a gritty urban look?

Simplify the Scene & Draw the Eye

Notes scribbled on photo.

Crop to remove the door
and sign on the left.

Even up lighting on the pillars, front
step and bricks in the background
to reduce background contrast.

Increase contrast on face/
clothing of man to draw the eye
in that direction even more.

TECHNICAL

Exposure

Needs a little more detail
in his clothes. No pure white
expected in the photo.

Color

Color doesn't add to the photo.
The strong lines and stone
texture would work well in B&W.

Detail

Shot at low ISO in good light, so no
notable noise. Texture of stone can
take some crunchy sharpening.

Optical & Geometric Distortion

Horizon needs straightening
(use bricks in background).

Sensor Dust

None found.

Output

Nothing specific planned.

1. **Crop** to remove dark door at side and excessive foreground.

2. **Exposure 0.71** to lighten photo overall.

3. **Highlights -80** to reduce brightness of pillars.

4. **Shadows +60** to show more detail in his clothes.

5. **Whites +7** and **Blacks -23** to compensate for loss of contrast.

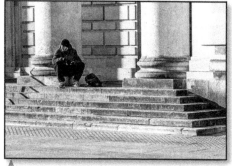
Steps 1–5 Crop & tonal adjustments

6. Convert to B&W using the **Adobe Monochrome** profile. There are no contrasting colors in the photo, so manually mixing the channels won't help much.

7. **Clarity +100** and **Contrast +70** to give a gritty feel.

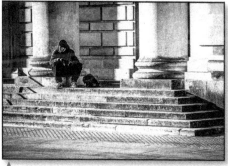
Steps 6–10 Gritty B&W effect

8. **Vignette -23, Feather 63** to darken the bright edges and draw the eye into the photo.

9. **Exposure** increased to **1.04** as it looked too dark in B&W.

10. **Grain 57** to add to gritty urban look.

11. **Linear Gradient** from right side of photo to darken, set to *Exposure -0.80* and *Highlights -36*.

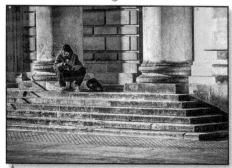
Step 11 multiple brush selections

12. **Brush** used with multiple different strokes, mainly set to varying Exposure values to lighten and darken different areas of the photo.

13. **Noise Reduction 20** as many areas have been significantly lightened and therefore show more noise.

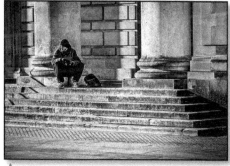
Steps 11–13 Selective edits applied

FAMILY DAY OUT

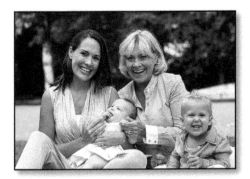

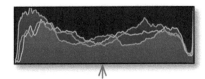

Good dynamic range, slight
highlight clipping

ARTISTIC INTENT

Purpose

Capture the family together
while the children are still
small (and clean!)

Story

This is a family day out
with the grandchildren.

Mood/Emotion

Happy, relaxed.

Simplify the Scene & Draw the Eye

There are some light areas in the
background that are distracting.

Some facial wrinkles to
reduce but not remove.

Draw the viewer's eye to
the people's eyes.

Don't make it look retouched!

TECHNICAL

Exposure

The exposure is fine and
this is a JPEG so we're not
going to mess with it.

Color

The color's fine as it is.

Detail

Child bottom right is slightly out
of focus, but otherwise good.

Optical & Geometric Distortion

None as it's a JPEG, so
corrected in-camera.

Sensor Dust

None noted.

Output

Small print on the fireplace.

1. Using **Brush** set to *Exposure -1.95* and *Highlights -87*, brush over the light areas in the background to stop them competing for the viewer's attention.

2. Using **Healing Brush** set to *Clone* mode, *Feather 100*, *Opacity 25*, retouch the bags/lines under the eyes, selecting nearby skin as the source to avoid changing the texture. We don't want to remove the lines, but just lighten them slightly.

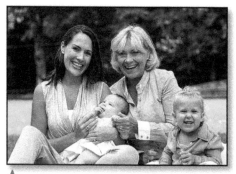
⌐Step 1 Brush distractions at back

3. Using the **Brush** tool set to *Exposure +0.33* and *Sharpening 25*, brush over the eyes to brighten and sharpen them slightly to draw the eye.

4. Using another **Brush**, paint over the skin with *Clarity -42*. This softens the skin a little bit, reducing some of the contrast, but still looks natural. The red mask overlay helps you see where you're painting, as you don't want to soften the eyes or other facial features.

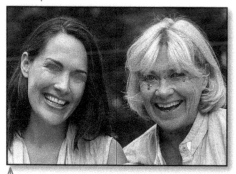
⌐Steps 2-3 Brush & Healing Brush around eyes

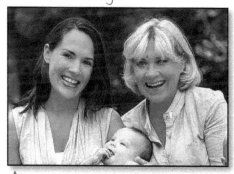
⌐Step 4 Brush over skin to soften

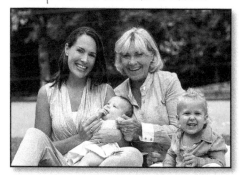

PULTENEY BRIDGE

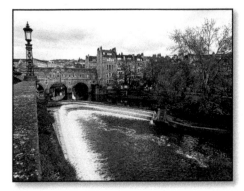

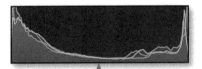

High dynamic range

TECHNICAL

Exposure

There is highlight and shadow detail but the contrast is far too high.

Color

The cool white balance doesn't show off the warm Bath stone.

Detail

No noticeable noise, but the textures would benefit from sharpening.

Optical & Geometric Distortion

The lamp on the left leans out of the frame due to perspective.

Sensor Dust

None found.

Output

Hang in the dining room.

ARTISTIC INTENT

Purpose

Capture the beautiful Georgian architecture in soft evening light, when most of the tourists have gone home.

Story

This is an early evening stroll after a relaxing dinner, enjoying the sunset.

Mood/Emotion

Calm, relaxed, peaceful.

Simplify the Scene & Draw the Eye

There's a little yellow flower bottom left that is slightly distracting.

1. Select **Adobe Landscape** profile, as we want the extended dynamic range.

2. **Highlights -100** to bring back the detail in the clouds.

   Steps 1-5 Brightness and Clarity →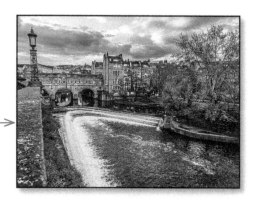

3. **Shadows +100** to bring back detail in the buildings.

4. **Exposure -0.45** to darken the photo overall.

5. **Clarity +80** for extreme local contrast, to give it that crunchy HDR feel.

   Steps 6-7 Color adjustments →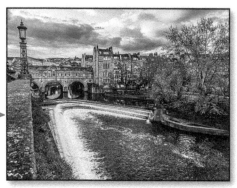

6. **Temp 9650** and **Tint +30** to warm it up to show off the reflected sunset in the clouds and the warm Bath stone.

7. **Vibrance +68** to enhance the colors.

   Step 8 Tone curve →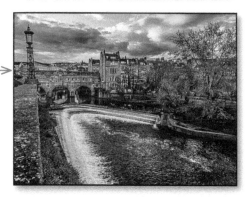

8. **Tone Curve** (Parametric) set to **Highlights +43, Darks -45, Shadows -7**. This increases the contrast in the buildings and brightest clouds, while sacrificing contrast in the deepest shadows.

9. Use **Upright** to correct the perspective, drawing a line up the center of the light stand and another up the central building.

10. **Crop** to remove the flower in the bottom left corner.

    Steps 9 & 10 Upright & Crop →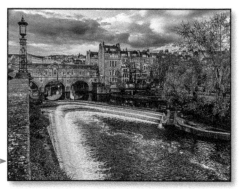

BACK TO THE OLD DAYS

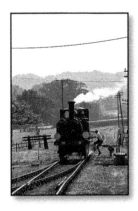

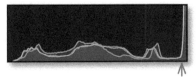

Clipped whites

TECHNICAL

Exposure

There's a large expanse of white sky, but the train is lacking shadow detail.

Color

The white balance is fine, but I want a sepia tone to suit the old-fashioned feel.

Detail

Low ISO, so there's no notable noise to worry about.

Optical & Geometric Distortion

Shot on a DSLR, so will need a lens profile.

Sensor Dust

No visible dust.

Output

Vacation album, only a small print.

ARTISTIC INTENT

Purpose

Visiting a steam railway, seeing how things were done in the past.

Story

The guy had just hopped out to change the points to go along a different track. No modern technology here!

Mood/Emotion

Historical scene, so go for a sepia toned monochrome with plenty with grain, to imitate photographs of that time period.

Simplify the Scene & Draw the Eye

Remove all the plain white sky at the top.

might be worth removing the wires in the background.

Draw the eye to the train driver, and retain detail in the train itself.

Highlight the steam.

Leading lines of train tracks.

1. **Enable Lens Profile** to correct the distortion. It's automatically selected the right profile.

   Steps 1–3 Lens profile, Crop and Toned B&W →

2. **Crop** the photo to remove the sky, cable and left hand side.

3. Convert to B&W using **Adobe Monochrome** profile, then use Split Toning to add a sepia tone to the shadows (**Shadow Hue 40**, **Saturation 30**).

4. Use **Dehaze +20** to remove some of the atmospheric haze.

   Steps 4–5 Tonal →
   Adjustments

5. Bring back highlight and shadow detail using **Highlights -90** and **Shadows +80**.

6. In the B&W Mix, set to **Orange +11** and **Yellow +25** to lighten the grass, creating a greater contrast with the train driver.

   Steps 6–7 B&W mix →
   and Tone Curve

7. Adjust the parametric Tone Curve to **Highlights -43**, **Lights -17**, **Darks +4** and **Shadows -20** to increase the contrast in the steam, at the expense of the midtones (which is mainly the background trees).

8. Add a **Vignette -30** to darken the edges, with **Highlights 80** so the sky doesn't get too dark.

9. Add **Grain 38**, **Size 48** and **Roughness 78**, for a really rough grain.

   Steps 8–9 Vignette →
   and Grain

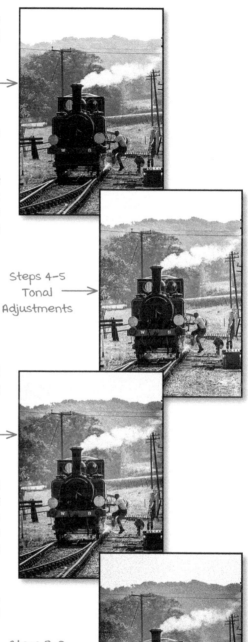

SAVING &
SHARING PHOTOS 22

Having selected all of your best photos and edited them until you're proud of the result, don't keep them to yourself. Share them with the world!

Lightroom offers a number of different ways of sharing your photos. At the time of writing, you can't print directly from Lightroom on the desktop, but you can save the photo as a JPEG to send to an online lab or open into another program to print. You can also save a smaller file to email to a friend or share on Facebook, Instagram or other social media apps.

If you have a whole selection of photos to share, you can share the entire album as a web gallery, and even add additional text to describe the photos and tell the story.

IN THIS SECTION, WE'LL CONSIDER:

• How to save edited photos to your hard drive.

• How to share photos to social media.

• How to share entire albums of photos using Lightroom Web.

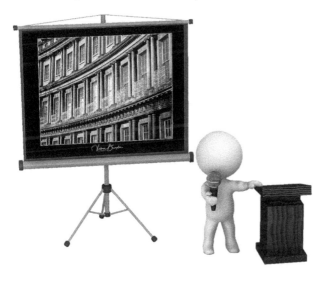

SAVING PHOTOS

You might want to save edited copies of your photos for different purposes, including:

- Send to other people.

- Upload to photo sharing websites.

- Upload to online labs or take to local photo labs to be printed as photographic prints.

- Upload to online printers to create books, calendars and other products.

- Print using other software.

- Open in other software for further editing, such as Nik, On1, Topaz, etc.

There's no need to keep these edited copies once they've served their purpose, as you can save a new copy at any time.

SAVING A PHOTO ON THE DESKTOP

To **save a photo to the hard drive**, go to *File menu* > *Save To* or click the Share icon.

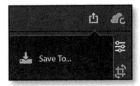

In the Save dialog, you have a number of choices:

File Type only offers two choices:

○ **Original + Settings** creates a copy of the photos with updated metadata (stars, keywords, Info panel contents) but doesn't apply any edits to the photo image data. This is useful for editing in other software that can handle raw files.

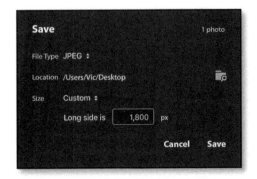

○ **JPEG** creates a copy of the photo with both updated metadata and with your edits applied to the image. This is the best choice for sharing with other people or opening in other photo editing apps for pixel-based retouching and special effects. It uses JPEG quality 80, with some gentle output sharpening to make the photos look great.

Location controls where the file is saved. By default, it saves to *Pictures/Lightroom Saved Photos*, but if you click on the *Browse* button or file path, you can use the operating system dialog to select another folder or another hard drive.

Size offers three choices, but only if you're saving as a JPEG:

○ **Full Size** uses the pixels created by the camera, without creating new ones or throwing any away (other than those you've cropped). This is also known as "full resolution" or "native resolution."

○ **Small** is 1024px along the long edge. It's a small file, ideal for emailing or posting on the web.

○ **Custom** asks for the length of the long edge in pixels. We'll learn how to calculate the file size in the next lesson on page 280.

SAVING A PHOTO ON MOBILE

To **save a single photo to the phone/ tablet's camera roll**:

1. From the Detail view, tap on the Share menu (iOS) / ... menu (Android).

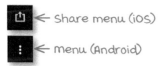

← Share menu (iOS)

← menu (Android)

2. Select **Save to Camera Roll** (iOS) / **Save to Device** (Android) to save to the normal photos app, or **Save to Files** (iOS) to save to a folder or other cloud storage. (To save to Google Drive or other cloud storage on Android, see the instructions on page 284.)

3. Choose the image size: either *2048px* or the *Maximum Available* (iOS) / *Highest Quality Available* (Android).

To **save multiple photos** in one go:

1. From the Grid view, hold your finger on a photo to enter selection mode, then tap on the photos you want to save, or drag your finger across multiple photos.

2. On iOS, tap on the Share button and select **Save to Camera Roll**. Or on Android, tap on the ... menu and select **Save to Device**.

3. Choose the image size: either *2048px* or *Maximum Available* (iOS) / *Highest Quality Available* (Android).

UNDERSTANDING FILE RESOLUTION

When it comes to saving files, you need to work out the size you need, and this depends on how the file will be used. For example, you'll need a big file to print a poster, but there's no point sending a file that big if it's only going to be displayed on a computer monitor or mobile device.

WHAT IS RESOLUTION?

When digital photographers speak of image size, they're usually referring to the pixel dimensions—the number of pixels along a photo's width and height.

Pixels don't have a fixed physical size. They expand or contract to fill the space available. If you expand them too far, the photo appears blurry and pixelated (you can see the squares), so the aim is to keep the pixels smaller than or equal to the monitor pixels or printer dots.

For example, this smiley face looks sharp when it's printed small, but the individual pixels are visible when it's enlarged too far.

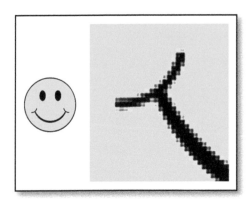

When you set a size in the Save dialog, Lightroom creates new pixels or selectively throws away spare pixels to fit your chosen size. This process is called resampling (but the original file isn't touched!)

CALCULATING THE SIZE YOU NEED FOR PRINT

To work out how many pixels you need for a specific print size, it's a simple calculation. Let's use a 8" x 10" print:

$$10" \times 300ppi = 3000px$$

$$8" \times 300ppi = 2400px$$

Inches—The length/width of the print size in inches.

PPI (pixels per inch)—300ppi is traditionally the resolution used for printing. For very large prints, you can get away with a lower value as you view them from a distance, but even then, aim for no less than 200ppi.

Result—The minimum number of pixels you need along that edge, to get a high quality print.

You can reverse the calculation, dividing the number of pixels by 300ppi to get an idea of how large a print you can make.

SIZES FOR SCREEN IMAGES

For displaying on computer screens, the files can be much smaller. Relatively few screens display more than 2048px along the longest edge, so there's no point sending someone a larger photo unless they're likely to print it.

Likewise, Facebook recommends uploading photos that are 720px, 960px or 2048px along the long edge. Instagram suggests up to 1080px wide and up to 1350px high. Other photo sharing websites make similar recommendations.

ADDING A WATERMARK

Some photographers use a subtle watermark to 'sign' their artwork. Others use it as part of their branding, promoting their website. Many believe a watermark helps to discourage people from stealing photographs, however remember that if the watermark is large enough to be difficult to remove, it can also be a significant distraction for the people viewing your photo. Other people feel that a watermark is tacky and should never be used.

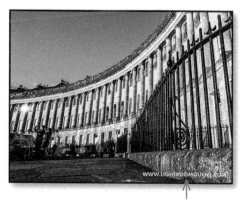

Watermark

Whether you should watermark is the subject of many flame wars online, so I'll leave you to make your own decision!

DESIGNING YOUR WATERMARK

Lightroom CC has a simple text watermark tool on mobile, but not yet on the desktop. Plain text watermarks aren't the most visually pleasing, but you do have some control over how the watermark looks.

To **create your watermark** on iOS/Android, go to *Preferences > Sharing Options*, toggle the *Include* switch, enter your watermark text and then tap *Customize* to design your watermark, including:

Text—Depending on your reason for watermarking, you may decide to use your name, your business name, your website, your social media handle, or any combination. Your text may be less distracting in all capital letters, rather than a mix of upper and lower case.

Font—You can select a font from a limited range (you can't load custom fonts) as well as making the text bold or italic.

Color—Neutral tones are less distracting than color, so Lightroom only offers black or white. These can be toned down to shades of gray using the *Opacity* slider. The choice of black or white will often depend on the content of the individual photo.

Opacity—Reducing the opacity can help to make a watermark less obtrusive.

Size—Some watermarks are so small they're illegible, which defeats the purpose. On the other hand, you don't want the watermark to distract the viewer, so set your size carefully for its intended purpose. For example, if you're putting the photo on Instagram, it will probably be viewed on a smaller screen than on your website.

Position & Offset—Even if your watermark is small, you're adding a focal point to your photo, so think about the placement carefully. Traditionally, artists have signed their work in the lower left or right corner, inset slightly from the edges the frame.

Rotation—On page 112, we learned that text has significant visual mass. By rotating the watermark by 90°, you may find it's less distracting, as your viewers will be less inclined to stop and read it.

APPLYING WATERMARKS WHEN SHARING PHOTOS

The watermark applies to any photos you share from Lightroom mobile (page 278) or open in other apps, but it's not applied to shared web galleries (page 285) or your original photos. If you're sending a photo to another app for further editing (page 246), you'll want to first disable the watermark, otherwise it will be embedded in the image data.

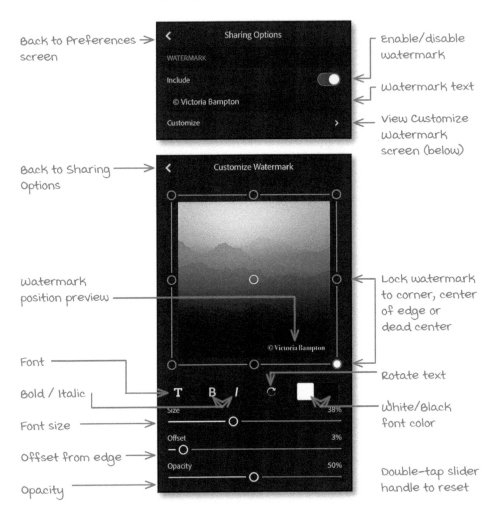

WATERMARK (IOS/ANDROID)

Back to Preferences screen

Enable/disable watermark

Watermark text

View Customize Watermark screen (below)

Back to Sharing Options

Watermark position preview

Lock watermark to corner, center of edge or dead center

Font

Bold / Italic

Rotate text

White/Black font color

Font size

Offset from edge

Opacity

Double-tap slider handle to reset

SHARING SLIDESHOWS ON MOBILE

If you hand your phone or tablet over to someone to show them your photos, you may be worried that they'll change your flags or star ratings with an accidental swipe. The best way to avoid this is to put Lightroom into Slideshow mode.

To **access the Slideshow view**, go to ... *menu > Slideshow*.

On iOS, a Grid view shows initially, then when you tap the triangular play button, it starts playing the slideshow. On Android, it immediately starts playing the slideshow.

If you tap the ... icon at the top, you can **change the slide transition** effect and the slide duration.

If you **pause the slideshow** using the Play/ Pause button, the viewer can swipe through the photos without worrying that they'll accidentally change your ratings.

It's not a completely failsafe way of protecting your photos, as tapping the X in the top left corner returns to the normal Lightroom interface, but it's a handy protection against accidents.

SLIDESHOW VIEW (iOS/ANDROID)

Close Slideshow view   Play / Pause   Back to Slideshow Grid (iOS only)

... menu

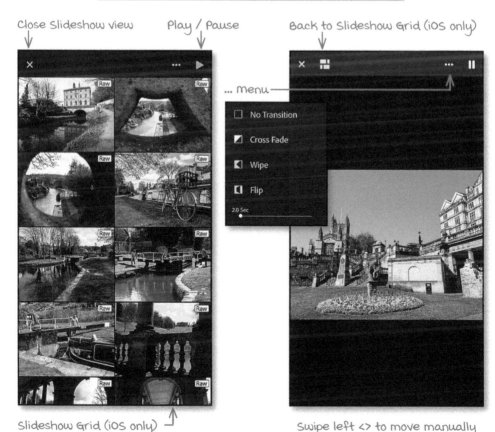

Slideshow Grid (iOS only)   Swipe left <> to move manually

SHARING PHOTOS ON SOCIAL MEDIA

You can save photos to the hard drive and upload to a variety of social media websites from the desktop, but it's far easier to post using the mobile apps.

1. To share multiple photos from Grid view, hold your finger on a photo to enter selection mode, then tap on the photos you want to share. Alternatively, open a single photo in Detail view.

2. Tap on the Share menu icon.

3. Choose the image size: either *2048px* (that's usually plenty!) or the *Maximum Available*.

4. Select the social media app from the Share sheet. (If the app you need isn't showing, make sure it's installed and can accept more than one photo at a time.)

5. Add your comment and click *Share*, *Post* or similar.

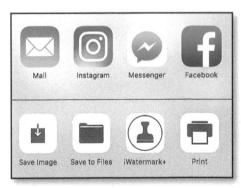

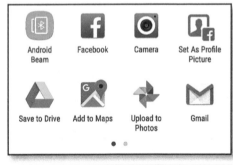

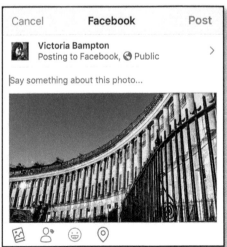

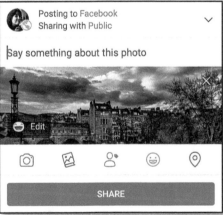

Share Sheets and Facebook on iOS (left) and Android (right)

SHARING WEB GALLERIES

Entire albums of photos can be shared with others by sending a link to a web gallery. On that web gallery, they can:

- View the photos in a Grid or Detail view.

- View the photos as a slideshow.

- Like or comment on the photos.

SHARING FROM THE DESKTOP

To **share an album** on the desktop:

1. Right-click on the album in the Albums panel and choose **Share Album**.

2. Set the Sharing Preferences.

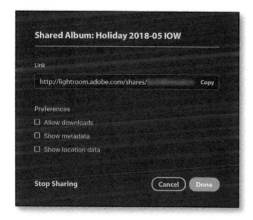

3. Copy the link to the clipboard and send it by email, text message, Facebook, etc.

4. Click *Done*.

To **stop sharing an album**, right-click on it again and choose *Stop Sharing*.

To **access these options** again later, right-click on the album again and select the *Share Settings*, *View on Web* or *Copy Link* menu commands.

SHARING FROM MOBILE

To **share an album** from your phone/tablet:

1. From the Organize view, tap on the album's ... menu, or from the Grid view, tap on the Share menu (iOS) / ... menu (Android).

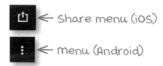

2. Select **Share Web Gallery** (iOS) / **Share Album** (Android).

3. Toggle **Enable Sharing**.

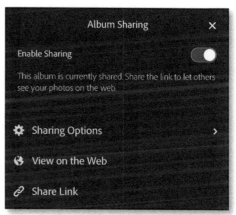

4. (Optional) Adjust the **Sharing Options**.

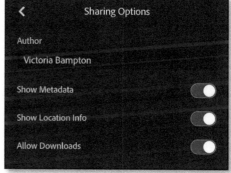

5. Tap **Share Link** to access normal sharing options, such as Messages or Mail, or copy the link to the clipboard.

iOS Share
Options

Android Share
Options

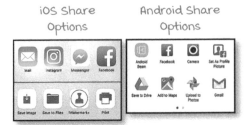

To **stop sharing an album**, follow steps 1 and 2 and then toggle *Enable Sharing* off.

WEB SHARING OPTIONS

There are currently three web sharing preferences available through the desktop and mobile apps:

Allow Downloads displays a download button in the viewer's web gallery, allowing them to download full resolution JPEGs of the images.

Show Metadata and ***Show Location Data*** limit the amount of metadata your viewers can see in the Info panel of the web gallery.

To access additional share preferences, go to https://lightroom.adobe.com and sign in to your account. Select the album in the left panel and click the *Sharing* button at the top of the Grid view. As well as the standard sharing preferences/options, you can choose to show only some photos based on their flag status.

EMBEDDING A GALLERY

If you have your own website or blog, you can embed a slideshow of a web gallery into an existing web page.

Copy the *Embed Code* from the Sharing Preferences to the clipboard, then paste

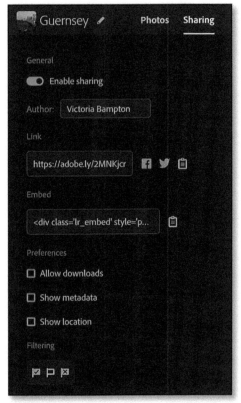

into your webpage's HTML code.

If you're familiar with basic coding, you can tweak the default embed code, for example, you might change *background_color=%23191919&color=%23cccdcd* to *background_color=white* to change the slideshow background to match the background color of your page.

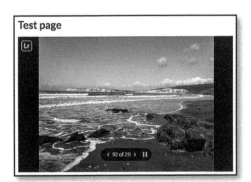

THE LIGHTROOM WORKSPACE (WEB)

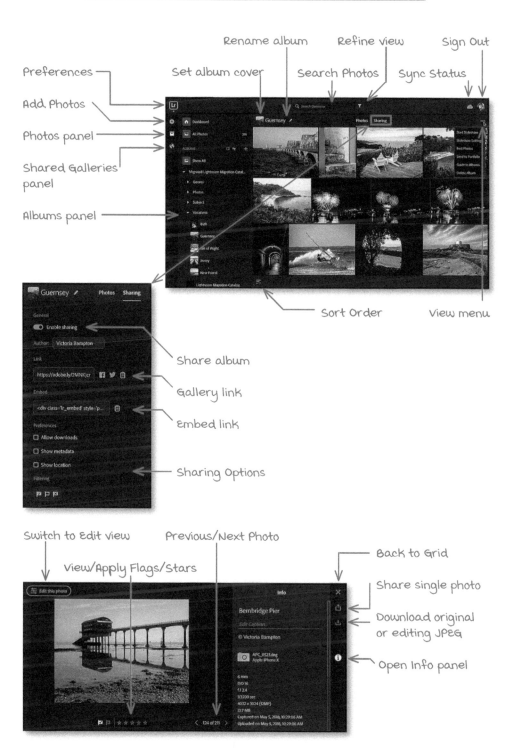

SHARING WITH CUSTOM TEXT & LAYOUT

You can create a more interesting web gallery by splitting the grid of photos and inserting descriptive text.

In the Web interface, click the checkboxes on any thumbnails you want to include in your Custom Share. Click *Share* above the grid, then select **Create a New Share**.

Under *Settings (cog icon) > Display*, there are alternative layout options, shown to the right. Using the various controls marked in the diagram below, you can design your custom gallery.

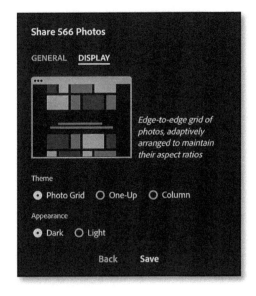

CUSTOM SHARE (WEB)

Share link

Settings dialog

Preview slideshow & set options

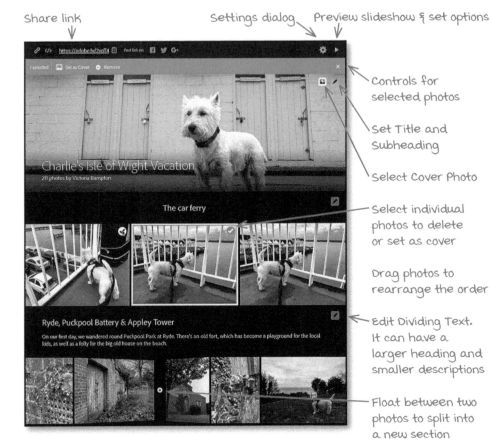

Controls for selected photos

Set Title and Subheading

Select Cover Photo

Select individual photos to delete or set as cover

Drag photos to rearrange the order

Edit Dividing Text. It can have a larger heading and smaller descriptions

Float between two photos to split into a new section

CREATING A GALLERY INDEX PAGE

You can also create an index page of chosen shared galleries, perhaps to use as your portfolio.

To do so, click the globe icon in the left toolbar to show the Shared Galleries panel. Click *Gallery* at the top, enable the index and add the albums of your choice.

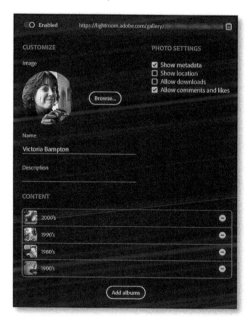

SENDING TO ADOBE PORTFOLIO

To build a more advanced portfolio website,

you can send up to 200 images from Lightroom CC to Adobe Portfolio from the Share Options dialog, or from the Adobe Portfolio website you can access your Lightroom albums. It's not part of Lightroom CC itself, so we won't go into further detail in this book, but you can learn about Adobe Portfolio at https://www.myportfolio.com

VIEWING VISITOR'S ACTIVITY

When your friends, family or clients visit the web gallery link, they can view the photos in a Grid or Detail view, or watch a slideshow of your photos.

If they sign in using an Adobe ID, or a Facebook/Google account, they can like and comment on your photos too.

You can view the likes and comments in the web interface, but at the time of writing, there isn't an easy way to find them.

The iOS app has an Activity view, which can be selected in the Detail view pop-up on the iPhone or using the buttons in the right toolbar of the Detail view on the iPad. It allows you to view the comments and likes directly from the app. By two-finger tapping

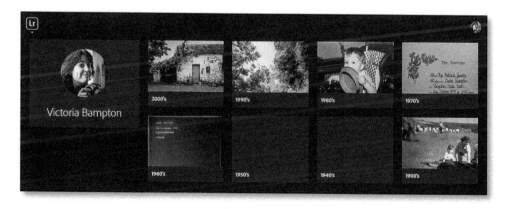

PUBLIC VIEW (WEB)

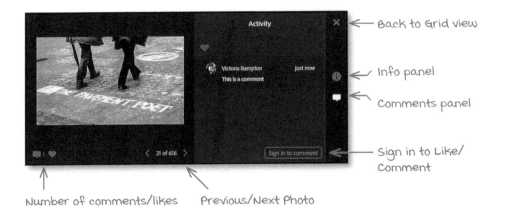

← Back to Grid view

← Info panel

← Comments panel

— Sign in to Like/ Comment

Number of comments/likes   Previous/Next Photo

on the Grid view, you can display icons on the thumbnails to show which photos have comments and likes, and the app may also request permissions to send you notifications of new likes/comments. There isn't an equivalent feature on the Windows/ Mac/Android apps at this time.

VIEWING PHOTOS ON APPLE TV

Lightroom CC for Apple TV allows you to view your photos and videos on your big TV screen, so you can view them with your friends, family or clients.

INSTALLING LIGHTROOM

To run the Apple TV app, you'll need an Apple TV 4th generation or newer, running on tvOS 11.0 or later.

To get started, search the App Store for *Lightroom* and click *Install*, then click *Open*.

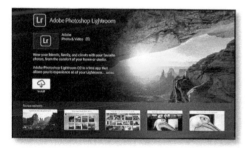

To sign in, the app asks you to use a web browser on another device to visit https://lightroom.adobe.com/tv, sign in, and type in the number shown on your TV screen. No fiddling with entering passwords on your remote!

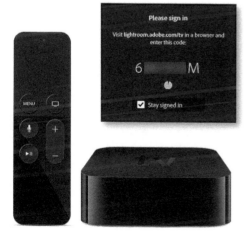

ORGANIZE VIEW

The first screen displays folders and below that, any root-level albums (that's albums that aren't inside folders).

Navigate around the screen using the touch surface on your remote, then click the touch surface to open the selected folder or album. To go back up a level, press the Menu button.

GRID VIEW

In Grid view, you can scroll up and down the thumbnails of the photos to view them in context. When viewing a large album, swipe along the right edge of the remote's touch surface to quickly scroll.

Click the Sort icon on the left to sort by capture date (*Newest First* or *Oldest First*) or by a *Custom* order set using the iOS app, or click the Refine icon to filter by flags or star rating, and click again to clear the filters.

To return to the Organize view, press the Menu button, or click on a photo to open it in Detail view.

DETAIL VIEW

Detail view displays the photo in full screen. Clicking the remote again zooms in so you can see all of the detail, and you can pan around using the touch surface.

If you swipe down from the top of the touch surface of the remote, Lightroom displays a Filmstrip view at the top the screen. Swipe left or right on the touch surface to quickly navigate through the photos and videos, and swipe up to hide it again.

APPLE TV

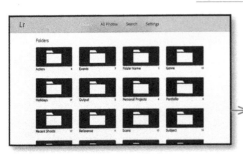

In Organize view, click on a folder to show the albums inside.

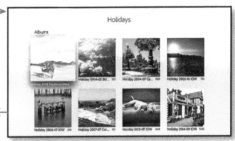

Click on an album to show its photos in Grid view.

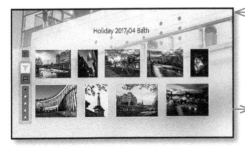

Click on a thumbnail to enlarge it in Detail view.

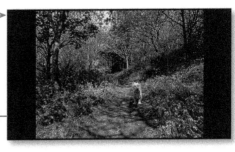

Click again to zoom in and out again, or long-press to start a slideshow.

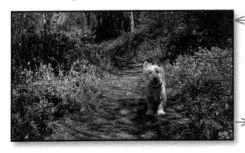

Swipe down from the top to view the filmstrip.

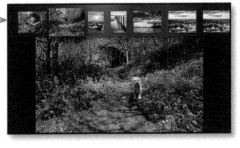

When you're done, press the Menu button to return to Grid view.

SLIDESHOW

In Grid or Detail view, click the Play/Pause button on the remote or long-press the touch surface to start a slideshow of photos or play the selected video, and again to pause it. Swiping left <> right manually switches photos.

You can change the Slideshow Speed in Lightroom's Settings, accessed through the menu at the top of the Organize or Grid view.

You can't add music to your slideshow in Lightroom, however, you can keep playing the background music from another app. To do so, start the music playing, switch back to Lightroom and start or pause the slideshow by long pressing on the remote's touch surface, rather than using the Play/Pause button.

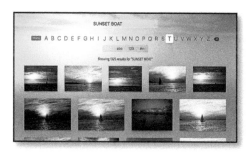

ALL PHOTOS VIEW

The **All Photos** view is divided by month, and like the album grid view, you can change the sort order or filtering, and swipe along the right edge of the remote to quickly scroll.

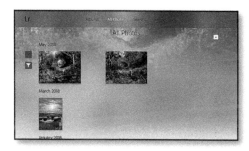

SEARCHING PHOTOS

To search for photos, select **Search** from the menu at the top of the Albums/All Photos view and then use the on-screen keyboard to search for words such as *dog*, *cat* or combinations like *sunset boat*. To dictate the search words, highlight the on-screen keyboard and hold down the Siri button while speaking.

RANKING & EDITING PHOTOS

The Apple TV app is designed for viewing photos, rather than editing them, but if you're working on a photo on another device, it should also update on the tv screen. If they don't update correctly, go to *Settings > Reload Albums*.

If you need the full Lightroom iOS interface on your Apple TV, perhaps to flag the photos while you're viewing them, you could enable Screen Mirroring instead of using the Apple TV app. To do so, swipe up from the bottom of the phone/tablet to reveal Control Centre, then should tap *Screen Mirroring* (iOS 11) / *AirPlay* (iOS 10) and select *Apple TV*.

REFERENCE INFORMATION

23

We'll finish the book with some reference information you may need in the future.

There aren't too many preferences in version 1, but it's handy to know what they do.

Computers don't always behave the way they're designed to work, so we'll also discuss how to handle the most frequent problems.

IN THIS SECTION, WE'LL CONSIDER:

• What the different preference settings do.

• How to solve the most likely problems.

• How to move to a new computer.

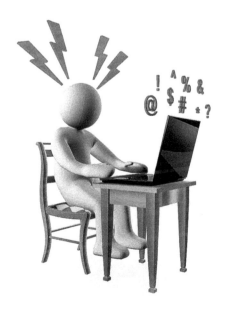

SETTING PREFERENCES

There aren't too many preferences to worry about, and the default settings are good, but here's what all of the sliders, buttons and checkboxes do:

ACCOUNT PREFERENCES (WINDOWS/MAC)

Subscription Status —

Opens the — Adobe website to manage your account

Check how much cloud storage space is available. If you run out of space, you can buy more

Restart Lightroom

Diagnostic Log buttons only show when you hold down Alt (windows) / Opt (mac). They help Adobe staff figure out sync issues

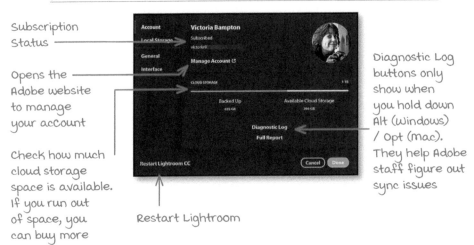

LOCAL STORAGE PREFERENCES (WINDOWS/MAC)

Click to show your local cache folder (page 45)

Limit the amount of space Lightroom uses to store photos on your hard drive (page 45) —

keep a copy of the smart previews and/or originals on your hard drive, in case your internet connection goes offline (page 45)

View additional information about storing your originals

Decide where to store the local cache of original image files (page 46)

Reset moves the original photos back to the default library location (page 46)

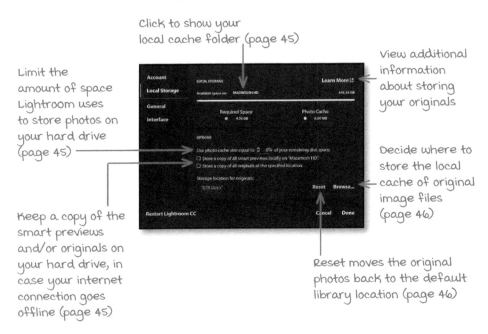

GENERAL PREFERENCES (WINDOWS/MAC)

Prevent system sleep during sync keeps the computer awake so the photos can be safely uploaded

System Info lists your system specs to help Adobe staff troubleshoot

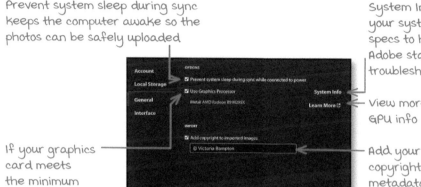

View more GPU info

If your graphics card meets the minimum specifications, Lightroom can use it to accelerate preview rendering on high resolution screens (e.g., Retina, 4K and 5K displays). If you're using a standard resolution screen, you may find Lightroom runs faster with the checkbox unchecked

Add your copyright metadata to new photos, as long as they don't have existing copyright metadata (page 80)

INTERFACE PREFERENCES (WINDOWS/MAC)

By default, Lightroom uses the operating system language. The language setting also determines the text search language (page 88)

Change the size of slider labels etc.

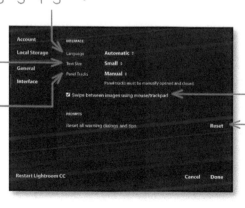

Use simple gestures to flick through the photos

By default, when you open a panel on one side, the other side closes. Changing to manual keeps the side panels open until you choose to close them (page 18)

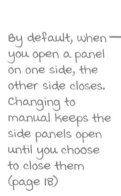

Reset all warning dialogs and tips brings back any dialogs that you've hidden using "Don't Show Again"

PREFERENCES/SETTINGS (IOS)

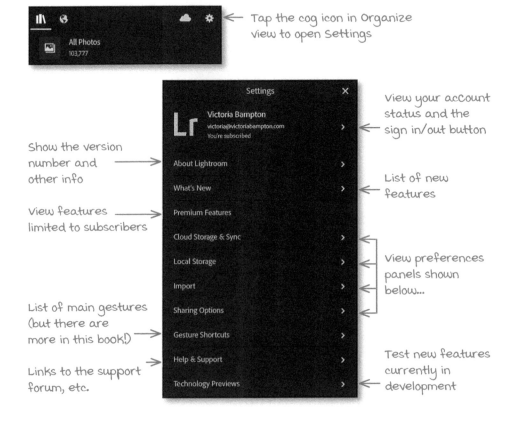

Tap the cog icon in Organize view to open Settings

View your account status and the sign in/out button

Show the version number and other info

List of new features

View features limited to subscribers

View preferences panels shown below...

List of main gestures (but there are more in this book!)

Links to the support forum, etc.

Test new features currently in development

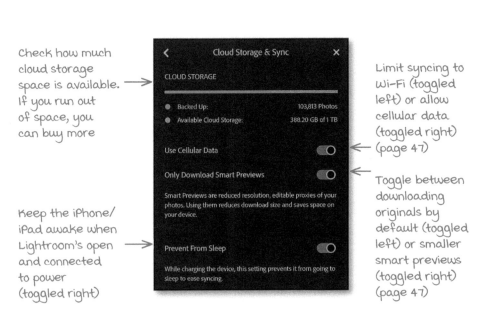

Check how much cloud storage space is available. If you run out of space, you can buy more

Limit syncing to Wi-Fi (toggled left) or allow cellular data (toggled right) (page 47)

Toggle between downloading originals by default (toggled left) or smaller smart previews (toggled right) (page 47)

Keep the iPhone/ iPad awake when Lightroom's open and connected to power (toggled right)

Local Storage shows how much space is available on your device ⟶

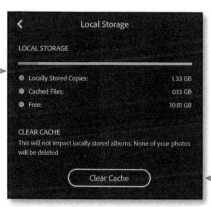

Clear Cache clears space on your device, as long as the photos are safely stored in the cloud. It doesn't clear any albums you've marked for offline use (page 47)

Automatically add new photos and videos shot with other camera apps (page 29) ⟶

Show Touches is used for demonstrating Lightroom on another screen, such as during a video tutorial or presentation ⟶

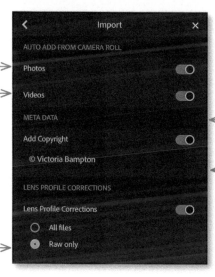

Automatically add your copyright to new photos as they're added (page 80)

Automatically apply the default lens profile to new photos as they're added (page 232)

Include metadata when saving/ sharing your photos. Copyright is always included, but you can choose whether to include the Caption, Camera & Camera Raw (edits) information and Location

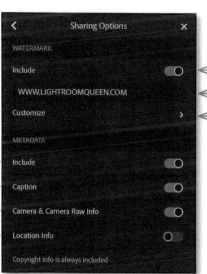

Add text watermark when saving/sharing photos (page 278)

Watermark text

Customize watermark font, position and size

PREFERENCES/SETTINGS (ANDROID)

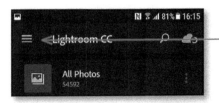

Tap the menu icon in Organize view to open Settings

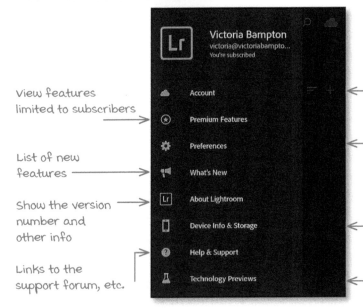

View your account status, amount of cloud storage space available, and the sign in/out button

View features limited to subscribers

View Preferences screen shown below...

List of new features

Show the version number and other info

View Device Info & Storage preferences screen shown overleaf...

Links to the support forum, etc.

Test new features currently in development

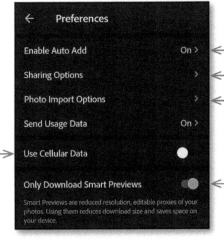

View preferences screens shown on following page...

Toggle between downloading originals by default (toggled left) or smaller smart previews (toggled right) (page 47)

Limit syncing to Wi-Fi (toggled left) or allow cellular data (toggled right) (page 47)

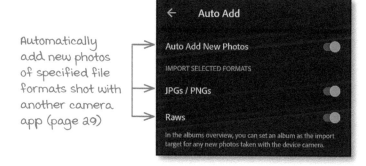

Automatically
add new photos
of specified file
formats shot with
another camera
app (page 29)

Include metadata
when saving/
sharing your
photos. Copyright
is always included,
but you can
choose whether
to include the
Caption, Camera
& Camera Raw
(edits) information
and Location

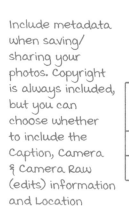

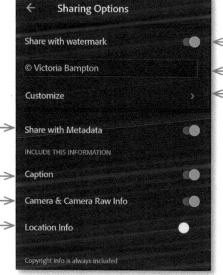

Add text
watermark when
saving/sharing
photos (page 278)

Watermark text

Customize
watermark font,
position and size

Automatically
apply the default
lens profile to
new photos as
they're added
(page 232)

Automatically add
your copyright
to new photos as
they're added
(page 80)

Device Storage
shows how much
space is available
on your device ───────→

Clear Cache clears
space on your
device, as long as
the photos are
safely stored in ───────→
the cloud. It doesn't
clear any albums
you've marked
for offline use
(page 47)

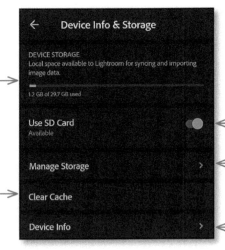

move Lightroom
data to expansion
storage (SD card)
where available
(page 47)

View manage
Storage screen
← shown below...

System
specifications,
← and information
including whether
your device can
capture raw
or HDR files

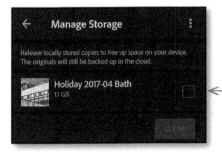

Clear cache for
albums marked
for offline use
← (page 47)

Import issues are fairly rare, but there are a couple of things you may run into on the desktop version of Lightroom.

CAN'T FIND DEVICE

If the camera or card reader doesn't show up in the Add Photos dialog, check that it's visible in Explorer (Windows) / Finder (Mac). Lightroom relies on the operating system to show the mobile device or memory card. Card readers are usually more reliable than camera cables.

FADED THUMBNAILS

If you can see thumbnails in the Add Photos dialog, but they're faded, then Lightroom knows that they're duplicates of existing photos. When you float the cursor over the photo, it reminds you that the photo is already in Lightroom.

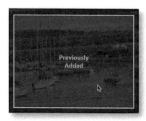

Lightroom errs on the side of caution, calculating a checksum (hash) of the file to be sure that it's an exact duplicate. It won't identify duplicates that are edited versions of an existing photo, or if another program has changed the metadata in the file. If you believe a photo has been falsely identified as a duplicate, rename it in Explorer (Windows) / Finder (Mac) to force Lightroom to import it.

PREVIEW UNAVAILABLE

If you can't see thumbnails of your photos, but you can just see gray rectangles, go ahead and try to add them. Lightroom then provides additional information in an error message, or builds the previews from the full resolution file.

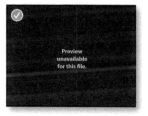

ERROR MESSAGES

If Lightroom is unable to add all of the selected images, it displays an error message at the end of the import. These are the most frequent error messages, their causes and solutions:

The file appears to be unsupported or damaged has a few possible causes:

• The raw file format isn't supported by your Lightroom version. To fix it, check for updates (page 17). If the camera is very new, you may need to wait for an update that supports your camera. You can check whether your camera is currently supported at https://www.Lrq.me/camerasupport

• The file is corrupted. There's usually nothing you can do to fix a corrupted file, other than adding the same file from an uncorrupted backup.

• The file format isn't on the list of supported file types (https://www.Lrq.me/file-formats), for example, it uses an unsupported color mode (e.g. duotone), it's too big, or it's a

PSD file that was saved without *Maximize Compatibility* enabled.

Error duplicate image within session means some of the thumbnails you checked in the Add Photos dialog are exact duplicates of other checked photos in the same import. This error message is for information only.

LOW DISK SPACE

When you add photos, Lightroom copies the selected photos to its own folder on your computer's hard drive and then uploads them to the cloud. Once they're uploaded, it can free up space on your hard drive again, but if you're doing a big import (such as all of your existing photos), you may run out of space.

If so, you can add the photos in smaller chunks and wait for these to finish uploading before adding more, or better still, change the location of the originals to another drive that has more space available (page 46).

SOLVING SYNC PROBLEMS

Syncing between multiple devices is complex, and although it usually "just works," there are a few hiccups that can arise. The most frequent issues have simple solutions, which we'll cover in this lesson, and I've included Adobe's contact details for more complex issues.

FREQUENT SYNC PROBLEMS

If Lightroom says it's syncing but nothing seems to be downloading, or edits made on other devices aren't showing up, check the other devices have finished uploading.

If edits made in the current version of Lightroom aren't uploading to other devices, check that sync isn't paused.

If you're not sure which device has the sync issue, check the web interface at https://lightroom.adobe.com to see whether the photos have safely uploaded to the cloud.

UNABLE TO DOWNLOAD ORIGINAL

If Lightroom says it's unable to download the original photo, there are three likely causes:

• You're offline (no internet connection) or sync is paused.

• The photo was added on another device and hasn't uploaded to the cloud yet.

• The photo was added on another device but you've run out of cloud storage space.

OUT OF SPACE

If Lightroom says you've run out of cloud space, click the cloud sync icon and then select the *Upgrade* button on the desktop to pay for additional cloud storage space, or log into your account on Adobe's website. Alternatively, you could delete photos you no longer want (e.g., the rejects or 1 star photos you kept "just in case") to clear space.

If it says you've run out of local hard drive space, you can move the originals to another drive (page 46). If you still don't have enough space, you'll need to clean up your boot drive using Windows/macOS tools or upgrade the size of your boot drive.

TROUBLESHOOTING WITH ADOBE

More unusual sync issues may require a little help from Adobe. This also allows them to investigate and figure out the cause of the problem, so they can avoid it in future releases.

To **request support from Adobe**, it's best to post at https://feedback.photoshop.com/ as the engineers themselves watch this forum. There are separate sections for the desktop apps (marked as Lightroom CC) and the mobile apps (marked as Lightroom for mobile).

When posting, don't forget to include your Lightroom version and operating system. The easiest way to find the information on the desktop is to go to *Help menu > System Info* and just copy the first block of text. On a mobile device, you'll find this information in Lightroom CC's *Preferences > About Lightroom*. And of course, don't forget to include a detailed description of what's wrong!

Adobe support staff may ask you to create a *Diagnostic Log* or **Full Report**.

To do so on the desktop, go to *Edit menu* (Windows) / *Lightroom menu* (Mac) > *Preferences > Account section* and hold down the Alt key (Windows) / Opt key (Mac) to display the buttons. Lightroom generates the log and offers to open it in your web browser or show it in Explorer (Windows) / Finder (Mac) ready to email to the support staff.

On mobile, go to *Settings > Help & Support* and hold your finger on the *Access our Support Forum* button. The diagnostic log is automatically attached to a draft email, ready to send.

RESETTING THE LOCAL CACHE

If you're having significant sync problems that Adobe can't solve, sometimes the "nuclear" option is the simplest solution. Obviously you'll need to ensure that all photos have finished syncing to the cloud or back them up before deleting the local cache.

Local Files (Desktop)—To reset the local cache, delete the following files from the problem computer:

Windows—C: \ Users \ [your username] \ AppData \ Local \ Adobe \ Lightroom CC \ Data \

Mac—Macintosh HD / Users / [username] / Pictures / Lightroom Library.lrlibrary

When you next open Lightroom, it will create a new local cache from the cloud.

Local Files (Mobile)—To clear the local cache on your iOS or Android device, simply delete the app and re-download from the App Store (iOS) / Play Store (Android), then sign in and allow it to sync the photos again.

DELETING EVERYTHING

If you want to wipe absolutely everything from the cloud and all devices, go to https://lightroom.adobe.com, sign in, click the LR icon in the top left corner, select *Account Info* and then press the *Delete Lightroom Catalog* button. But **make sure you have a copy of all of your photos and settings** on another disconnected hard drive because it really will delete them from everywhere that Lightroom CC controls.

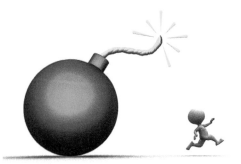

STANDARD TROUBLESHOOTING STEPS

If your issue isn't covered by the previous sections, or in the specific topic area of the book, there are some general troubleshooting steps you can try, whether you're using a desktop computer or a mobile device.

DESKTOP

1. Restart Lightroom

Many issues fix themselves by simply quitting and reopening Lightroom.

2. Reboot the Computer

If you're having odd problems with any computer program, the age-old wisdom "turn it off and turn it on again" still works wonders.

3. Check for Updates

Make sure you're running the latest updates, both for Lightroom (by going to *Help menu > Check for Updates*) and also for your operating system, as the issue you're running into could be a bug that's been fixed in a later release. Also update drivers on your machine, particularly the graphics card drivers and any mouse or tablet drivers

4. Turn off the GPU

Buggy graphics card drivers can cause no end of trouble. Go to *Preferences > General tab* and uncheck *Use Graphics Processor*. If that helps, check the graphics card manufacturer's website for an updated driver (Windows) / Software Update for an operating system update (Mac) .

5. Reset Preferences

If you're still having problems, resetting Lightroom's Preferences file can solve all sorts of 'weirdness,' so it's a good early step in troubleshooting. If you reset your Preferences file, the main settings that you lose are those in the Preferences dialog. Your photos, metadata, edits, presets and other important settings are unaffected by deleting the Preferences file.

There's a simple automated way of resetting preferences. Just hold down Alt and Shift (Windows) / Opt and Shift (Mac) while opening Lightroom and it will ask whether to reset the preferences. The timing is crucial—hold them down while clicking/double-clicking on the app/shortcut.

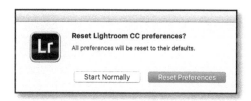

If you need to delete preferences manually, the preferences files are stored in hidden folders at:

Windows—C:\ Users \ [your username] \ AppData \ Roaming \ Adobe \ Lightroom CC \ Preferences \ Lightroom CC Preferences. agprefs

Mac—Macintosh HD / Users / [your username] / Library / com.adobe. lightroomCC.plist and com.adobe. lightroomCC.mcat-daemon.plist. (Reboot the computer before reopening Lightroom, as the old preferences will be still cached if deleted manually.)

6. Uninstall/Reinstall Lightroom

Some problems can be caused by a corrupted installation. To rule this out, uninstall Lightroom CC by opening the CC app (page 16) in the system tray (Windows) / menu bar (Mac) and clicking the arrow to the right of Lightroom CC and selecting *Uninstall*. Restart your computer to clear out any gremlins, and then return to the CC app to reinstall Lightroom CC.

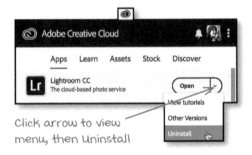

Click arrow to view
menu, then Uninstall

7. Ask for Help

If you're still stuck, post a description of your problem at https://feedback.photoshop.com/ tagged as Lightroom CC. Don't forget to include a full description of the problem, as well as your exact Lightroom version and operating system. You'll find this information under *Help menu > System Info* on the desktop.

MOBILE

1. Force Quit the App

If an app is misbehaving, one of the first things to try is quitting and reopening the app.

On most iOS devices, double-click the Home button to show your most recently used apps, swipe right or left to find the app that you want to close, then swipe up on the app's preview to close the app.

On Android, go to *Settings app > Apps > Lightroom CC* and tap *Force Stop*.

2. Reboot the Mobile Device

Like a desktop computer, rebooting a mobile device can often solve odd issues.

On iOS, a hard reset or force restart clears out RAM, which a standard restart doesn't. On older devices, hold down the Home button on the front and the power button, and keep them held down until the Apple logo appears, then let go of the buttons and wait for it to finish restarting. For newer devices without a Home button, hold the power button and volume down key until you see the Apple logo, then let go and wait for it to finish restarting.

On Android, hold down the power button and then press the *Restart* button on the screen.

3. Check for Updates

Check the App Store (iOS) / Play Store (Android) for an updated version of Lightroom, as you may be running into a bug that's already been fixed.

4. Ask for Help

If you're still stuck, post a description of your problem at https://feedback.photoshop.com/ tagged as Lightroom for mobile. Don't forget to include a full description of the problem, as well as your exact Lightroom version and operating system. You'll find this information under *Settings > About Lightroom*.

MOVING TO A NEW COMPUTER OR DEVICE

Since the cloud is the main repository for your photos, moving to a new computer/device is simple, but if you've been managing files in folders on your local hard drive for years, it's a new thought process.

DECOMMISSIONING THE OLD COMPUTER

You can have Lightroom CC activated on two computers at a time. To deactivate on an old computer, go to *Help menu > Sign Out* or uninstall the software.

Mobile devices don't have the same limitations, but if you're passing your old device onto someone else, you'll want to wipe your data by resetting your device back to factory defaults.

To avoid losing any photos or edits, ensure that your old computer or device has finished syncing with the cloud before you decommission it.

INSTALLING ON THE NEW COMPUTER

On the new computer or mobile device, install Lightroom CC and sign in (page 16), and allow Lightroom to download the photos and metadata from the cloud.

If you've cloned your whole boot drive (desktop) or restored from a backup (desktop or mobile), follow the instructions on page 306 to reset Lightroom CC's local cache, so that it syncs as a new device. This prevents sync problems that can result from working off a clone.

MINIMIZING BANDWIDTH

If you have many GB's of photos stored in the cloud and you had *Store a copy of all originals at the specified location* checked in *Preferences > Local Storage* on the old desktop computer, you can minimize the bandwidth by moving the originals to the new computer and telling Lightroom where to find them.

To do so, sign in on the new computer and then go to *Preferences > Local Storage*, check the same checkbox and navigate to the location of the originals. Lightroom will still need to sync the latest metadata from the cloud, but it won't need to download another copy of the originals.

MIGRATING TO LIGHTROOM CLASSIC

If you find that Lightroom CC is missing some features that you can't live without, or your internet connection is too slow to upload all of your photos, it is possible to migrate to Lightroom Classic. (That's the traditional desktop-based version of Lightroom.)

It's not as simple as migrating from Lightroom Classic (discussed on page 39), as it's not a direction Adobe intended people to take. There are two main options:

SAVING SETTINGS TO FILES

Saving settings to the files works well if you've added keywords to your photos and want to retain them when moving to Lightroom Classic (or any other photo cataloging software, for that matter).

1. Filter the photos to show the flagged photos and assign a star rating or a keyword (e.g., flagged) to help identify them later, as flags aren't written to the files metadata. Repeat for rejected photos.

2. Select all of the photos in an album and add a keyword to identify the album (e.g., album-vacation 2018), as album membership isn't written to the file metadata. Repeat for each album.

3. Select all of the photos and go to *File menu > Save To* (page 278). Select *Original & Settings* format and save the photos to a folder.

4. Open Lightroom Classic to a new catalog and go to *File menu > Import Photos*, then select *Move* at the top of the Import dialog. This will move the photos out of the large single folder into a more orderly folder structure that you select in the Destination panel.

SYNCING TO LIGHTROOM CLASSIC

Syncing photos from the cloud works well if you migrated from Lightroom Classic, or you haven't added keywords in Lightroom.

1. If you originally migrated from Lightroom Classic, open that migrated catalog. Otherwise, open Lightroom Classic to an empty catalog.

2. In *Edit menu* (Windows) / *Lightroom menu* (Mac) > *Preferences > Lightroom Sync*, set a custom location for mobile downloads.

3. Click on the Identity Plate and click the *Start* button next to *Lightroom Sync* to begin syncing. This downloads the original photos and metadata from the Lightroom CC cloud, storing them on your local hard drive. It doesn't sync keywords, or album folders, but it does sync the albums themselves.

Lightroom Classic is discussed in great detail in my book, *Adobe Photoshop Lightroom Classic CC - The Missing FAQ*. If you're going to continue syncing Lightroom Classic with the Lightroom CC cloud, I'd strongly recommend reading the Cloud Sync chapter of that book. Lightroom Classic is only a distant cousin of the Lightroom CC ecosystem, and therefore there are some things that don't sync, and some other unexpected behaviors to look out for.

GLOSSARY

Album—a set of photos grouped for a specific purpose.

AI (Artificial Intelligence)—a computer imitating intelligent human behavior.

All Photos—all of the photos and videos stored by Lightroom CC, found at the top of the Photos panel.

Aspect Ratio—the proportional relationship between the width and height of the photo, otherwise known as the shape.

Black Point—small area of the photo that is pure black.

Bounding Box—the edge of the crop.

Brightness—radiated or reflected perception of luminance of a subject.

Cache—a temporary storage location on your computer.

Chromatic Aberration—when a lens is unable to bring all wavelengths of color to the same focal plane point, causing fringes of color along high contrast edges.

Clipping—the loss of either highlight or shadow details when tonal information is driven to pure white or black.

Cloud—the server on the internet where your images are processed and stored.

Cloud-Native—photos are stored in the cloud and available on all connected devices.

Color Cast—an unwanted color shift in the photo.

Color Temperature—the color of the light source.

Contrast—the difference in brightness between light and dark areas of a photo.

Crop—to trim a portion of the photo.

Curve—a line graph that illustrates or controls the brightness and contrast of different image tones.

Deconvolution—type of sharpening which attempts to calculate and reverse the cause of blurring.

Distortion—a warping or transformation of an object and its surrounding area.

DNG Format—open-source raw file format.

Dynamic Range—the difference between the brightest and darkest tones in a photo.

ETTR—stands for "expose to the right" and means setting the exposure to be as bright as possible without clipping the highlights to pure white.

Exposure—a measure of the amount of

light in which a photo was taken, or the adjustment made in photo editing software.

GPS data—the location co-ordinates captured using the Global Positioning System navigational satellites.

HDR (High Dynamic Range)—process that combines multiple exposure variations of an image to achieve a dynamic range exceeding that of a single exposure.

Highlights—the light tones in the photo.

Histogram—a bar graph showing the relative population of pixels at each level.

Hue—the shade of a color.

JPEG—stands for Joint Photographic Experts Group, is a lossy compression technique for color photos (so photo data is compressed, resulting in smaller files with variable loss of data).

Keepers—photos you decide are worth keeping.

Kelvin Scale—unit of measure for temperature relating to color temperature of light sources.

Keystoning—where a building seems to lean backwards in a photo.

Lightroom CC—the new cloud-native version of Lightroom.

Lightroom Classic—the traditional folder-based version of Lightroom.

LUT (Look Up Tables)—used by profile developers for advanced color adjustments.

Members Area—password-protected area on the Lightroom Queen website at https://www.lightroomqueen.com/members

Metadata—data describing the photo, such as how the photo was taken (camera, shutter speed, aperture, lens, etc.), who took the photo (copyright), descriptive data about the content of the photo (keywords, caption), and edits made using Lightroom.

Midtones—range of tones that lie between highlights and shadow.

Noise—common term to describe visual distortion, equivalent of grain in film cameras.

Panorama—wide format (usually a landscape) made by overlapping individual shots and merging them into a long thin image.

Pixel—a photo is made up of a number of pixels, each of them representing an individual dot of information.

Posterization— A visual defect (also called banding) in an image created by insufficient amounts of data to maintain the appearance of continuous tone.

Preset—a set of edit settings that can be applied to other photos.

Preview—a small copy of the edited photo for display within Lightroom.

Profile—a starting point for editing your raw photo, like choosing a film stock. Also used for special effects.

Raw File—the unprocessed sensor data from the camera.

Rendered File—the processed image data in a standard image file format.

Resample—changing the pixel dimensions of a photo.

Resolution—the number of pixels in an image.

Saturation—the intensity or purity of a color.

Shadows—darker tones in a photo.

Smart Preview—a small copy of the raw data for use within Lightroom.

Specular Highlights—areas of a photo that are meant to be pure white without detail, such as reflections on shiny objects.

Stack—a group of photos that appears as a single photo in the Grid view.

Sync—to synchronize data between the cloud server and other devices.

TIFF—stands for Tagged Image File Format, a computer file format with lossless compression (so no detail lost).

Tone-mapping—redistributing tonal information to correspond more closely to the way our eyes see light.

USM (unsharp mask)—a type of sharpening that creates halos either side of an edge.

Vignette—a reduction or increase of brightness or saturation in the corners of a photo, which may be a lens defect or added for effect.

White Balance—removing unrealistic color casts so that objects the eye expects to be white appear so, for example, a white wedding dress.

White Point—pixels that are pure white.

Workflow—a series of steps undertaken in the same order each time.

Zoom—magnify or reduce the view of a photo.

THE LIGHTROOM CC MEMBERS AREA

With your book purchase, you also get a year's access* to my Lightroom CC Members Area.

YOUR LIGHTROOM CC MEMBERS AREA ACCESS INCLUDES:

• **Multiple eBook formats** of this book.

• **New Lessons** in the Members Area, as Adobe adds new features to Lightroom CC.

• **Email Support** from the author, in case you get stuck.*

• **Blank Image Analysis Worksheet** to help you analyze your own photos.

• **Sample Images** so you can follow along with key editing examples.

• **Keyboard Shortcuts** to speed up your workflow.

• **Discounts** on future purchases on the Lightroom Queen website.

* Members Area access is valid for 365 days from date of book purchase. Email support is valid for 90 days from date of book purchase. When your Members Area access expires, you're welcome to extend it at a low cost, so you always have the most up to date information about Lightroom CC.

ACCESS TO THE MEMBERS AREA & BONUS DOWNLOADS

If you purchased this book direct from https://www.lightroomqueen.com, your book is already registered, and you should have received your Members Area login details by email shortly after ordering. If you haven't received your login details, just send me an email.

If you purchased from a third-party retailer, such as Amazon or Book Depository, you'll need to register your book.

To register your book, I need both:

☐ Proof of Purchase, for example, your confirmation email, shipping confirmation, a scan/photograph of the packing slip, a screenshot of the order confirmation on Amazon's website, etc.

☐ The book reference code:
  CC12018LS278

Send me the details using either:

• The book registration form:
https://www.lightroomqueen.com/register

• Email: registration@lightroomqueen.com

What happens next?

We'll create your Members Area account and send you the login details. This can take up to 48 hours, as it requires a real human (usually me!) to press the buttons.

You can then log into the Members Area at https://www.lightroomqueen.com/members to access the bonus downloads and support contact form.

INDEX

Lightning Source UK Ltd.
Milton Keynes UK
UKHW021813211218
334317UK00002B/37/P